That Time I Got Reìncarnated as a SLIME

The Ways of the Monster Nation

7

Sho Okagiri   Original Story: **FUSE**   Character Design: **Mitz Vah**

The Story So Far

Framea, a young rabbitfolk girl, attracted the attention of the demon lord Rimuru after going around Tempest and giving star ratings to all its food stalls. Now she's busy writing Tempest's first guidebook for him—but one day, her father shows up and tries to drag her back home. But after she introduces her new boss to him...the demon lord himself ends up accompanying her back to the rabbitfolk village!

Contents

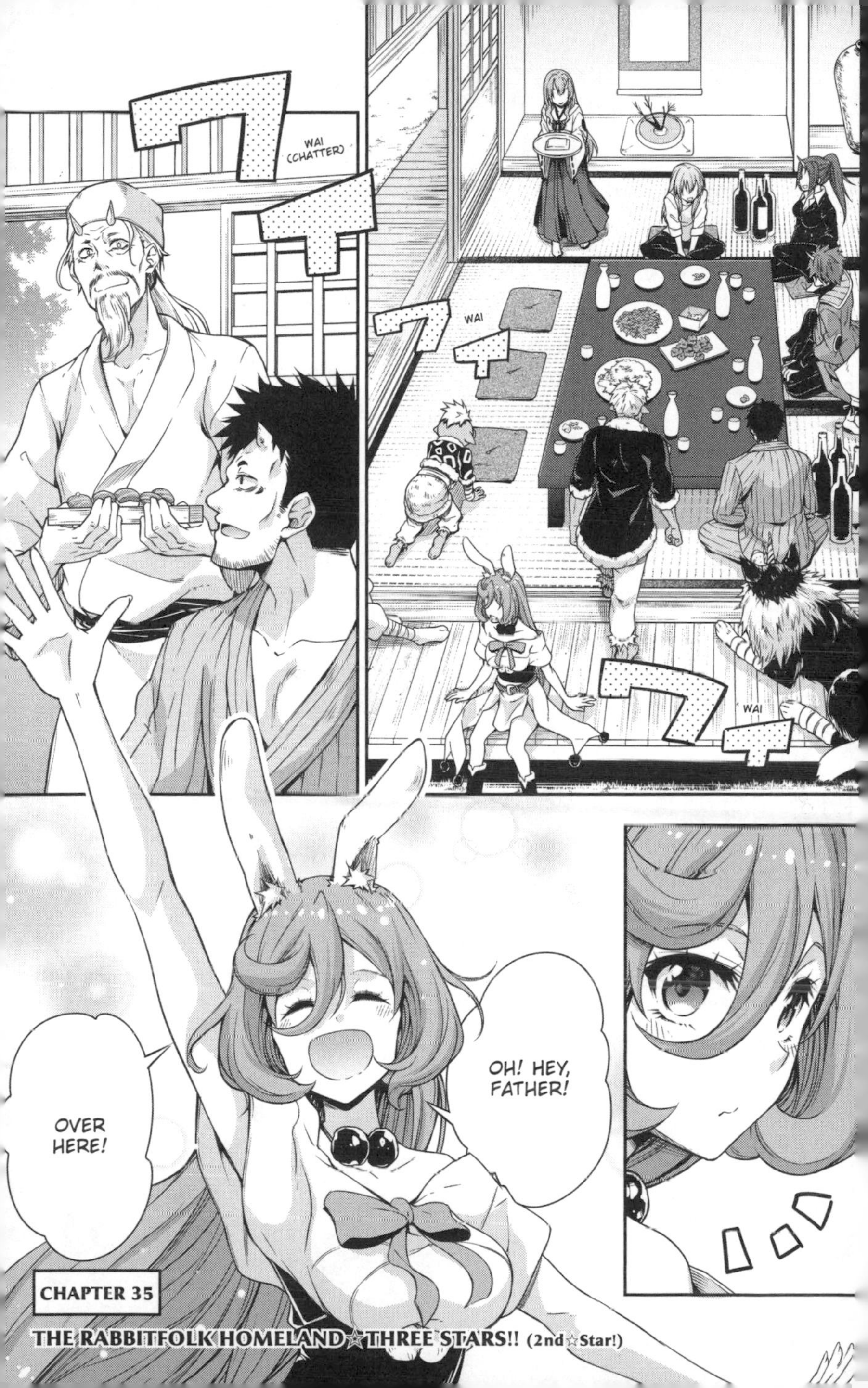
WAI
WAI
WAI (CHATTER)
OH! HEY, FATHER!
OVER HERE!

CHAPTER 35

THE RABBITFOLK HOMELAND☆THREE STARS!! (2nd☆Star!)

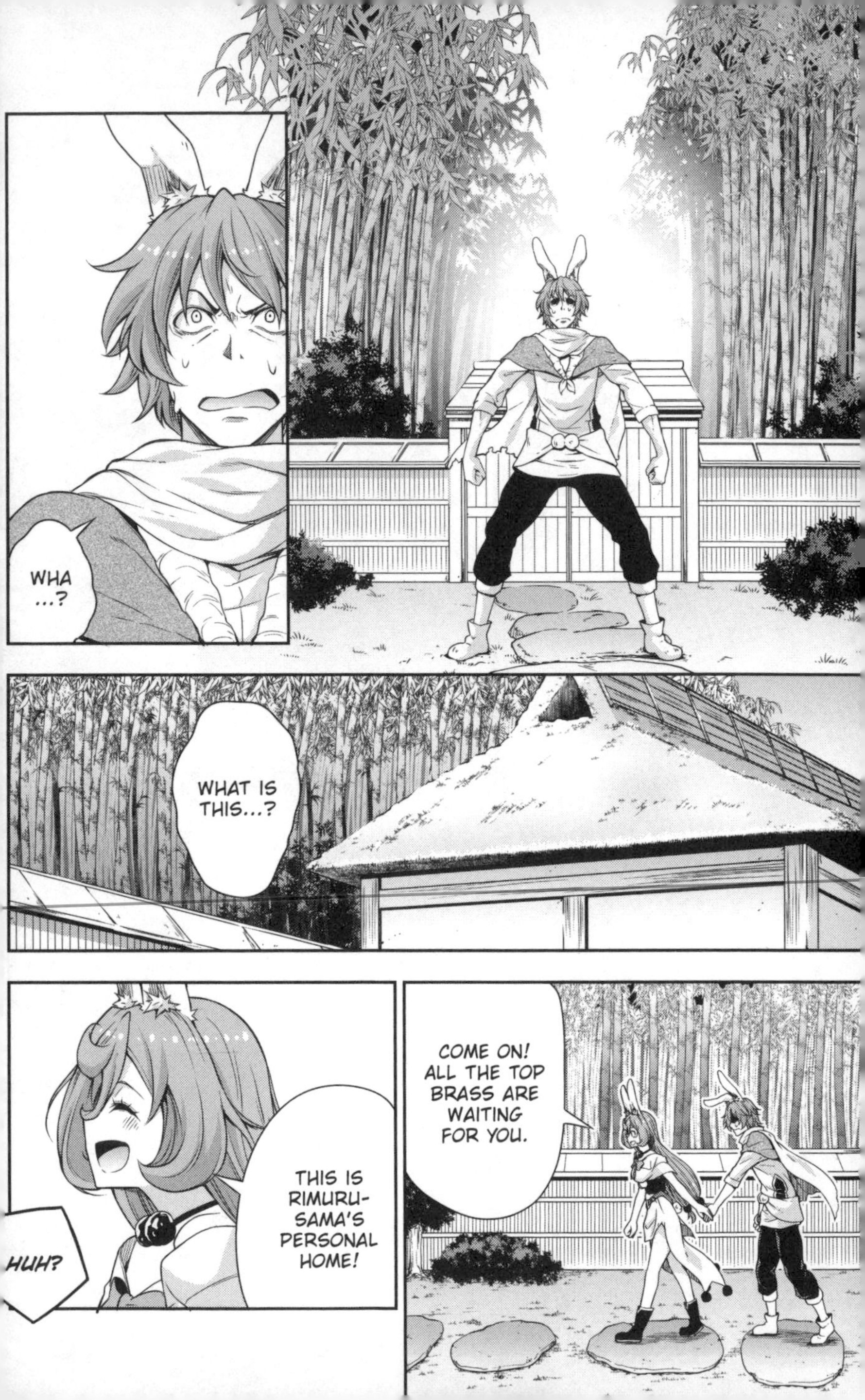
WHA ...?
WHAT IS THIS...?
COME ON! ALL THE TOP BRASS ARE WAITING FOR YOU.
THIS IS RIMURU-SAMA'S PERSONAL HOME!
HUH?

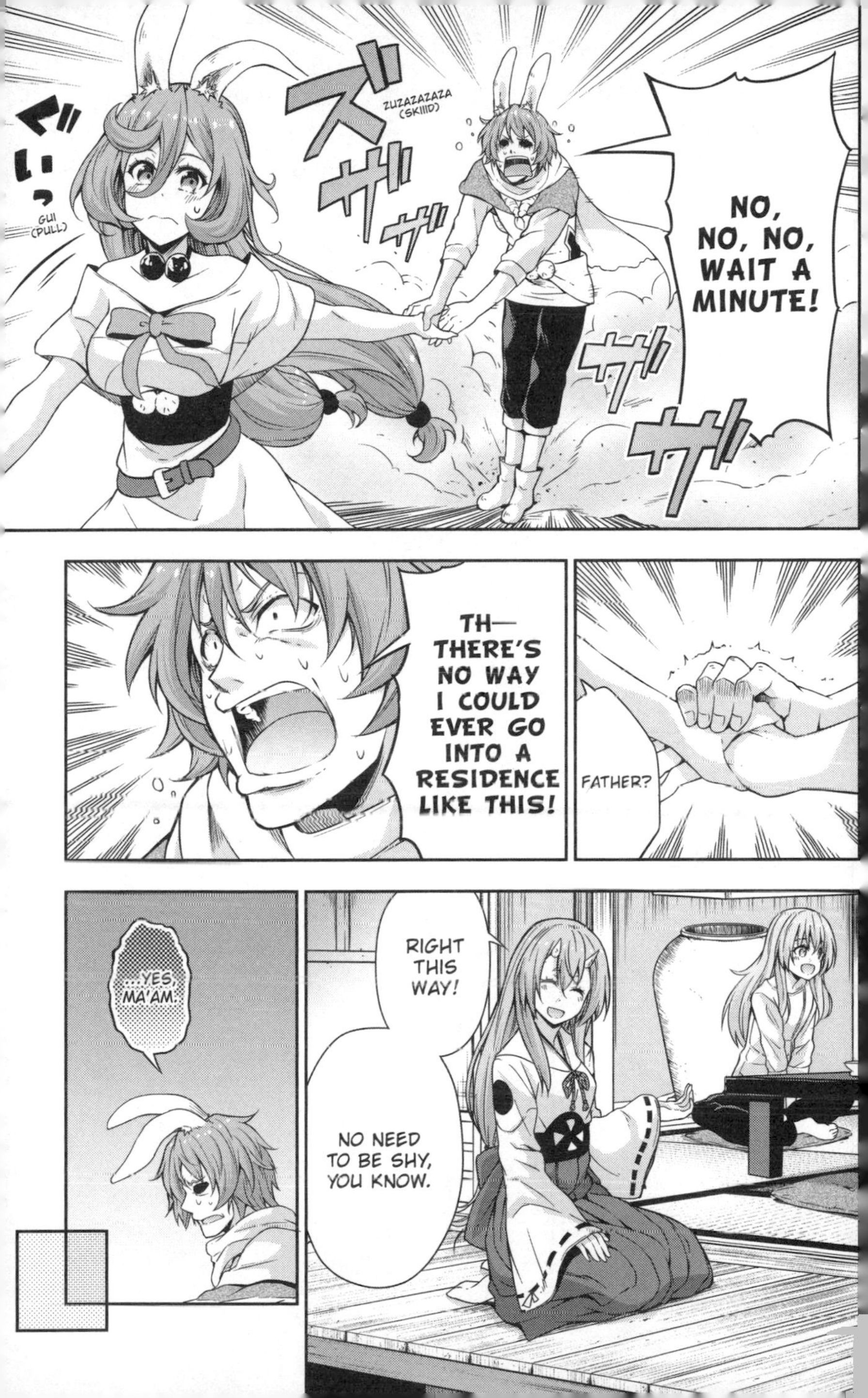
NO, NO, NO, WAIT A MINUTE!
ZUZAZAZAZA (SKIIID)
GUI (PULL)
FATHER?
TH— THERE'S NO WAY I COULD EVER GO INTO A RESIDENCE LIKE THIS!
RIGHT THIS WAY!
NO NEED TO BE SHY, YOU KNOW.
...YES, MA'AM.

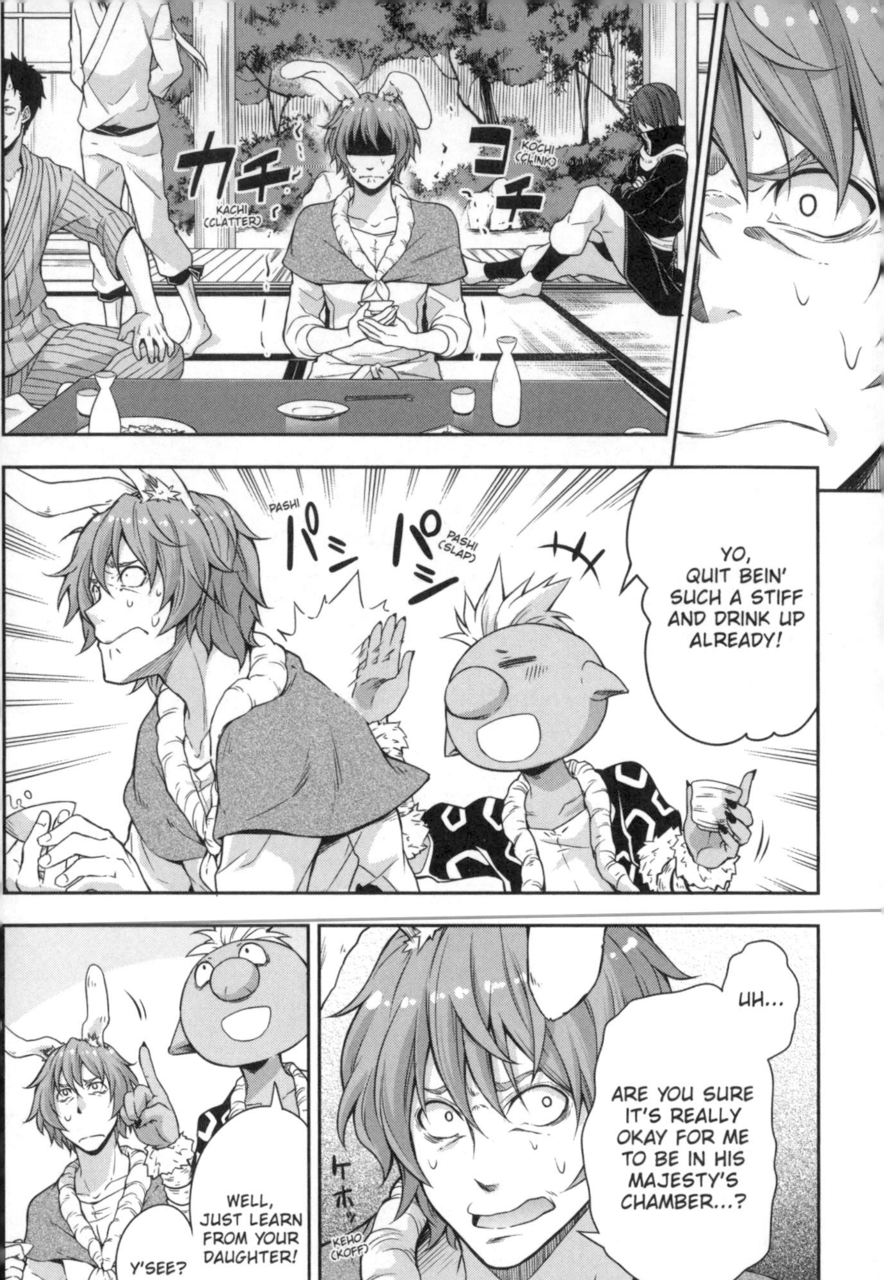
カチ
KACHI (CLATTER)
コチ
KOCHI (CLINK)
パシ
PASHI
パシ
PASHI (SLAP)
YO, QUIT BEIN' SUCH A STIFF AND DRINK UP ALREADY!
UH...
ARE YOU SURE IT'S REALLY OKAY FOR ME TO BE IN HIS MAJESTY'S CHAMBER...?
ケホッ
KEHO (KOFF)
WELL, JUST LEARN FROM YOUR DAUGHTER!
Y'SEE?

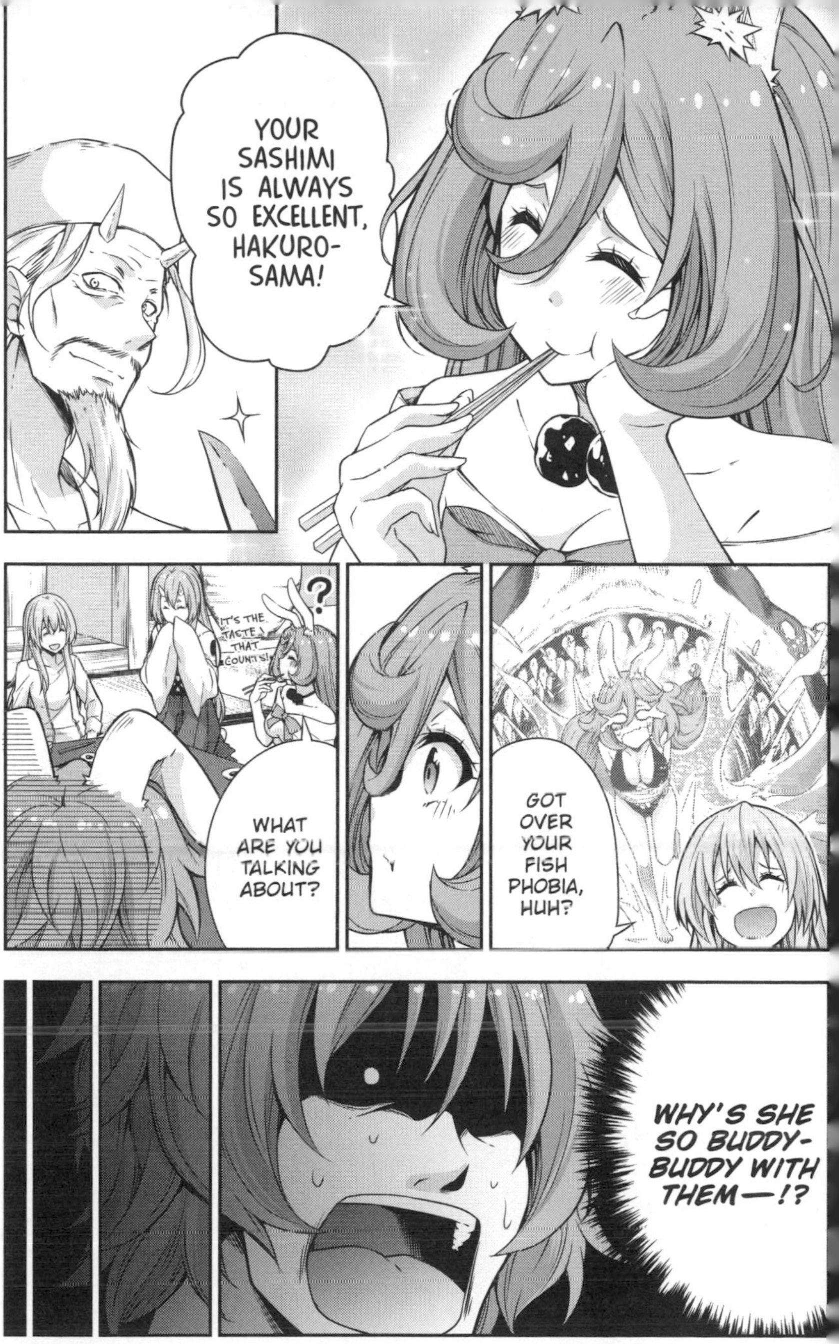
YOUR SASHIMI IS ALWAYS SO EXCELLENT, HAKURO-SAMA!
GOT OVER YOUR FISH PHOBIA, HUH?
?
IT'S THE TASTE THAT COUNTS!
WHAT ARE YOU TALKING ABOUT?
WHY'S SHE SO BUDDY-BUDDY WITH THEM—!?

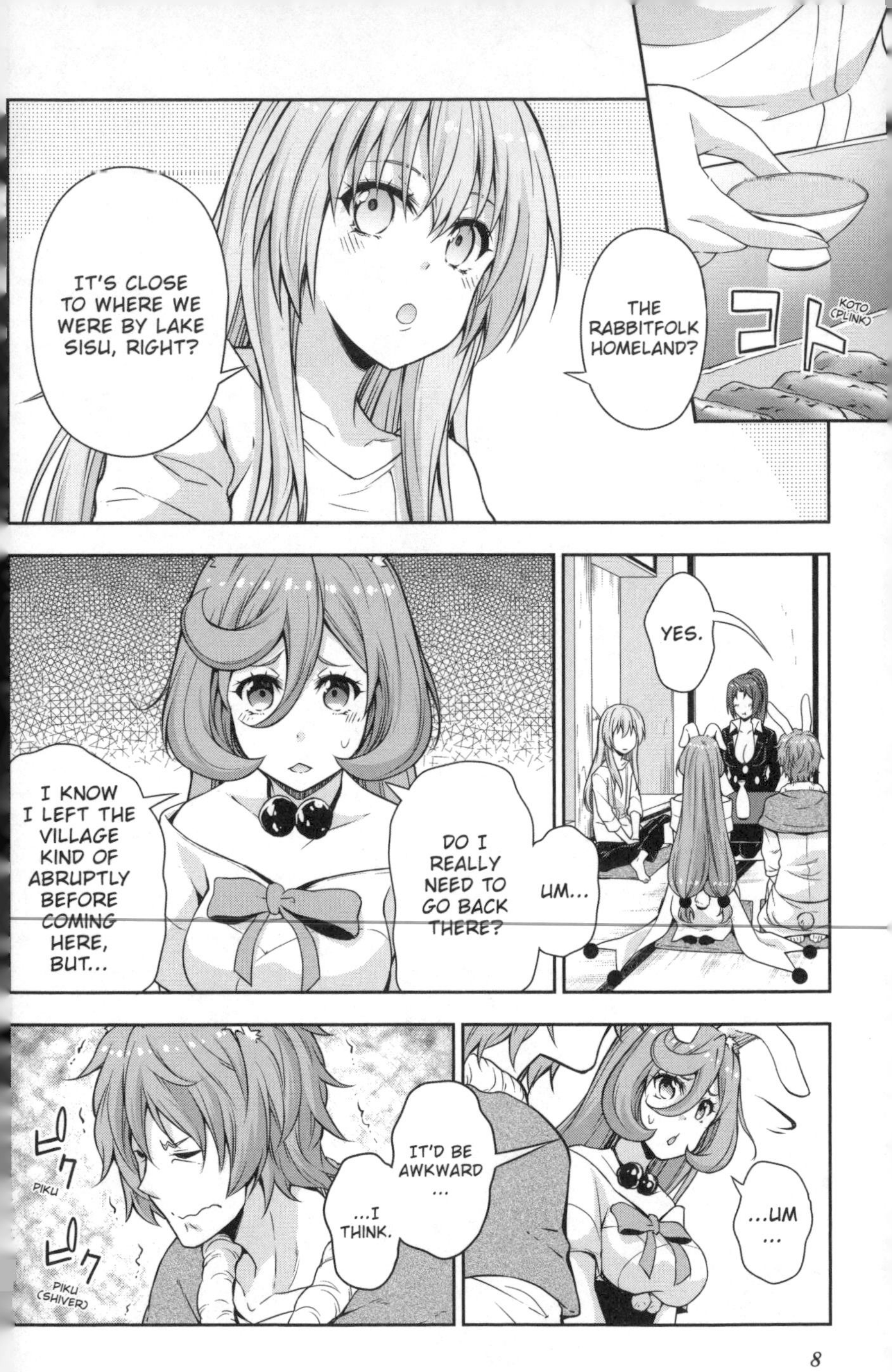
コト
KOTO (PLINK)
THE RABBITFOLK HOMELAND?
IT'S CLOSE TO WHERE WE WERE BY LAKE SISU, RIGHT?
YES.
UM...
DO I REALLY NEED TO GO BACK THERE?
I KNOW I LEFT THE VILLAGE KIND OF ABRUPTLY BEFORE COMING HERE, BUT...
...UM ...
IT'D BE AWKWARD ...
...I THINK.
ピク
PIKU
ピク
PIKU (SHIVER)

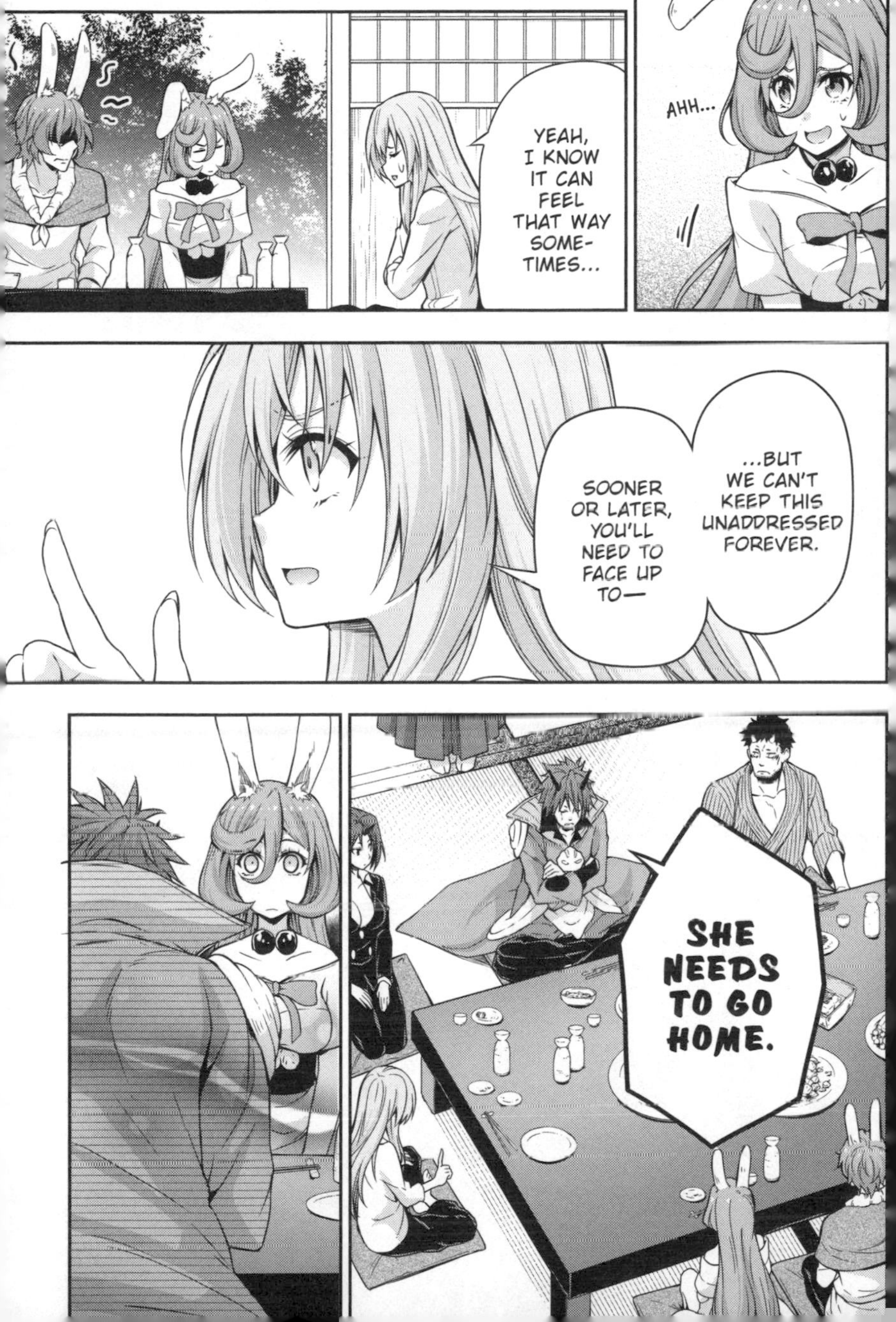
AHH...
YEAH, I KNOW IT CAN FEEL THAT WAY SOME-TIMES...
...BUT WE CAN'T KEEP THIS UNADDRESSED FOREVER.
SOONER OR LATER, YOU'LL NEED TO FACE UP TO—
SHE NEEDS TO GO HOME.

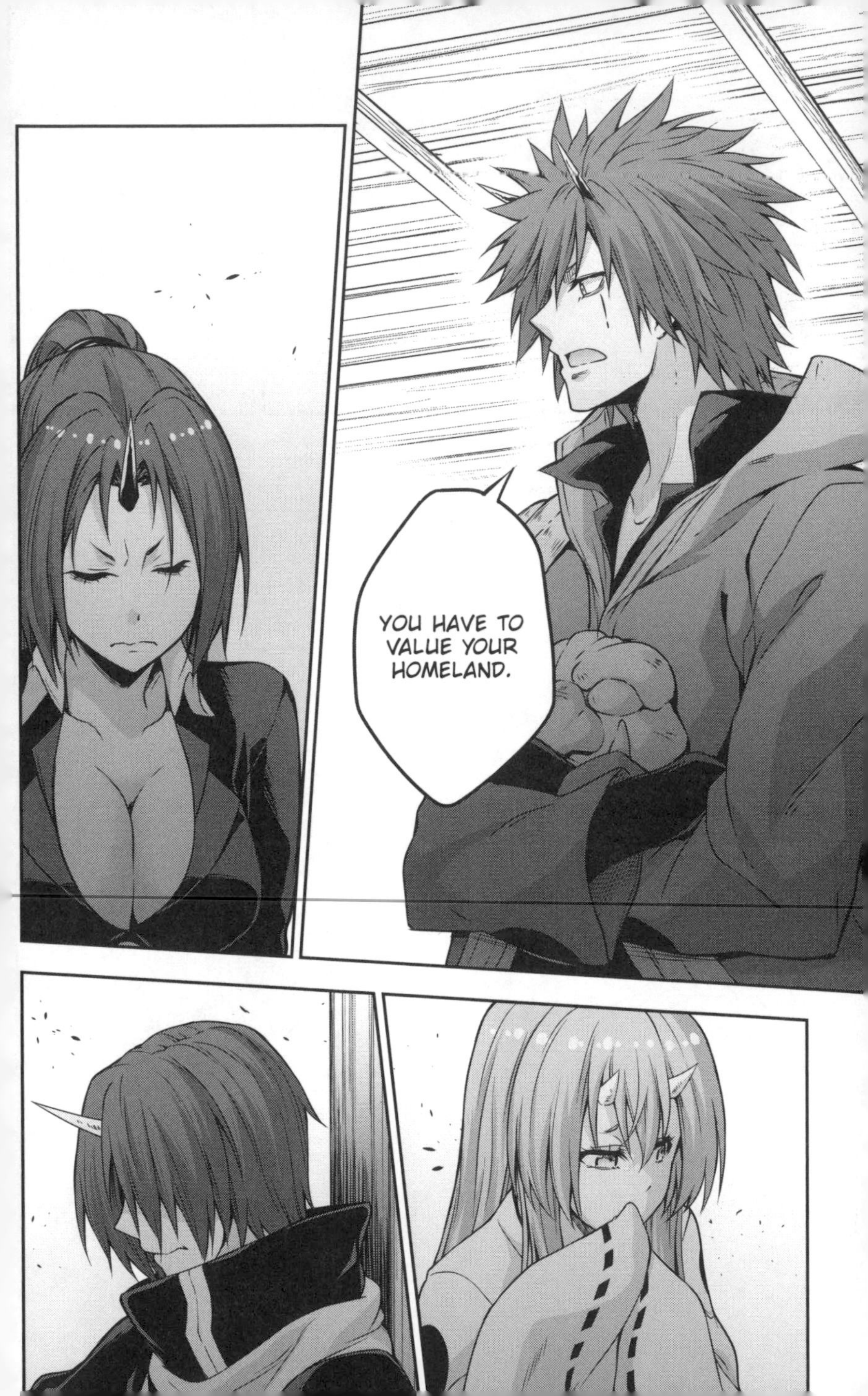
YOU HAVE TO VALUE YOUR HOMELAND.

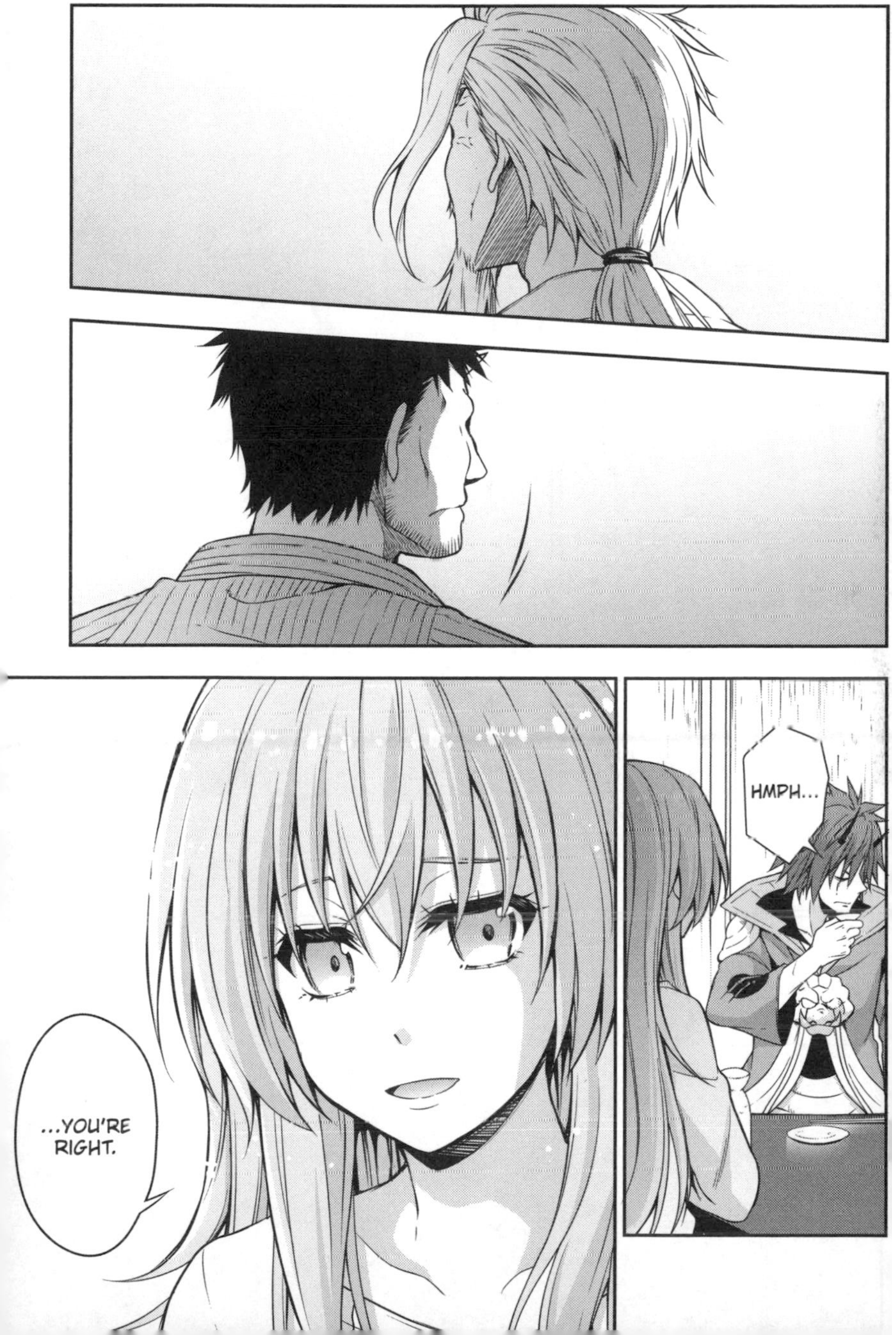
HMPH...
...YOU'RE RIGHT.

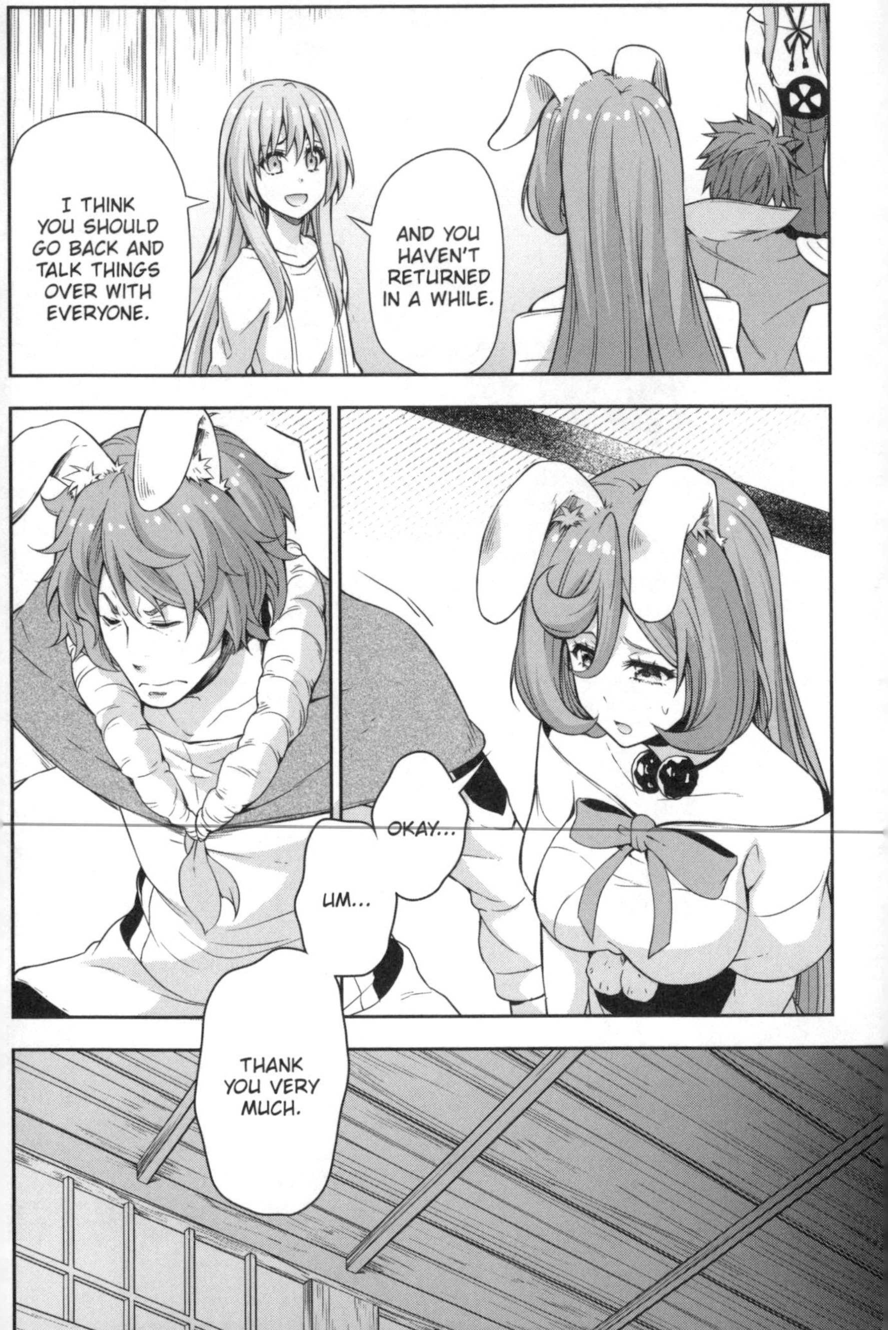
I THINK YOU SHOULD GO BACK AND TALK THINGS OVER WITH EVERYONE.
AND YOU HAVEN'T RETURNED IN A WHILE.
OKAY...
UM...
THANK YOU VERY MUCH.

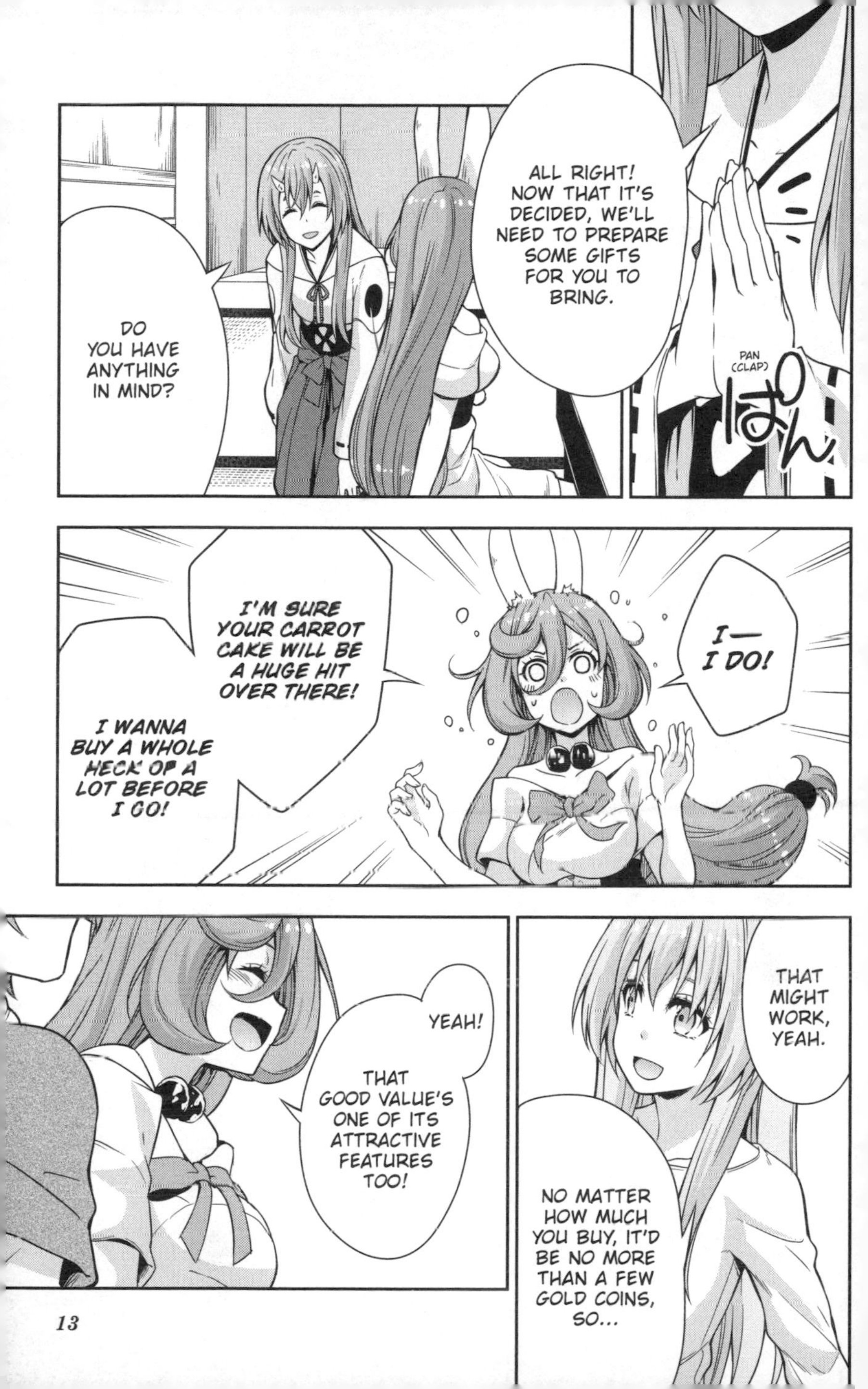
ALL RIGHT! NOW THAT IT'S DECIDED, WE'LL NEED TO PREPARE SOME GIFTS FOR YOU TO BRING.
PAN (CLAP)
ぱん
DO YOU HAVE ANYTHING IN MIND?
I— I DO!
I'M SURE YOUR CARROT CAKE WILL BE A HUGE HIT OVER THERE!
I WANNA BUY A WHOLE HECK OF A LOT BEFORE I GO!
THAT MIGHT WORK, YEAH.
NO MATTER HOW MUCH YOU BUY, IT'D BE NO MORE THAN A FEW GOLD COINS, SO...
YEAH!
THAT GOOD VALUE'S ONE OF ITS ATTRACTIVE FEATURES TOO!

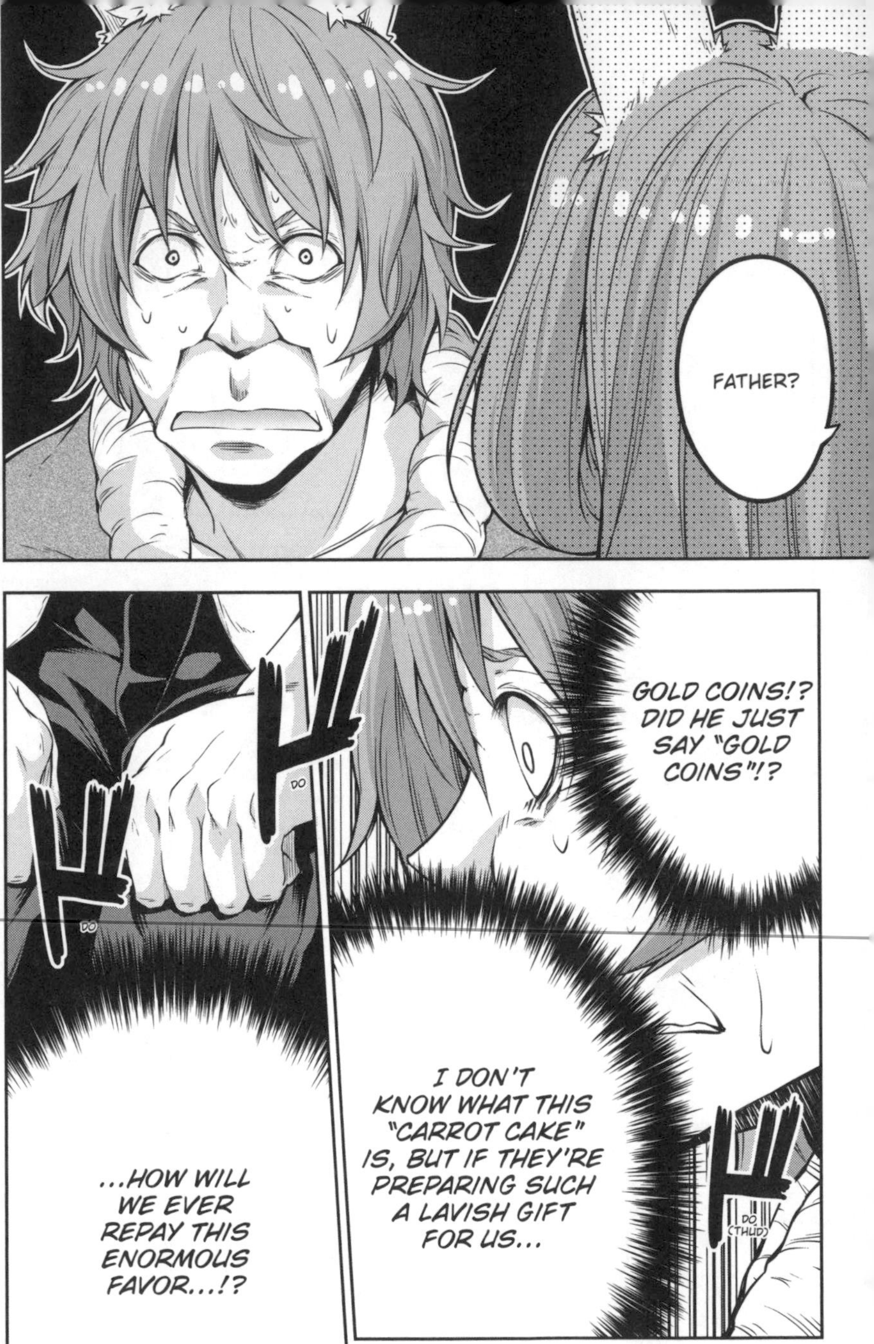
FATHER?
GOLD COINS!? DID HE JUST SAY "GOLD COINS"!?
I DON'T KNOW WHAT THIS "CARROT CAKE" IS, BUT IF THEY'RE PREPARING SUCH A LAVISH GIFT FOR US...
DO (THUD)
DO
DO
...HOW WILL WE EVER REPAY THIS ENORMOUS FAVOR...!?

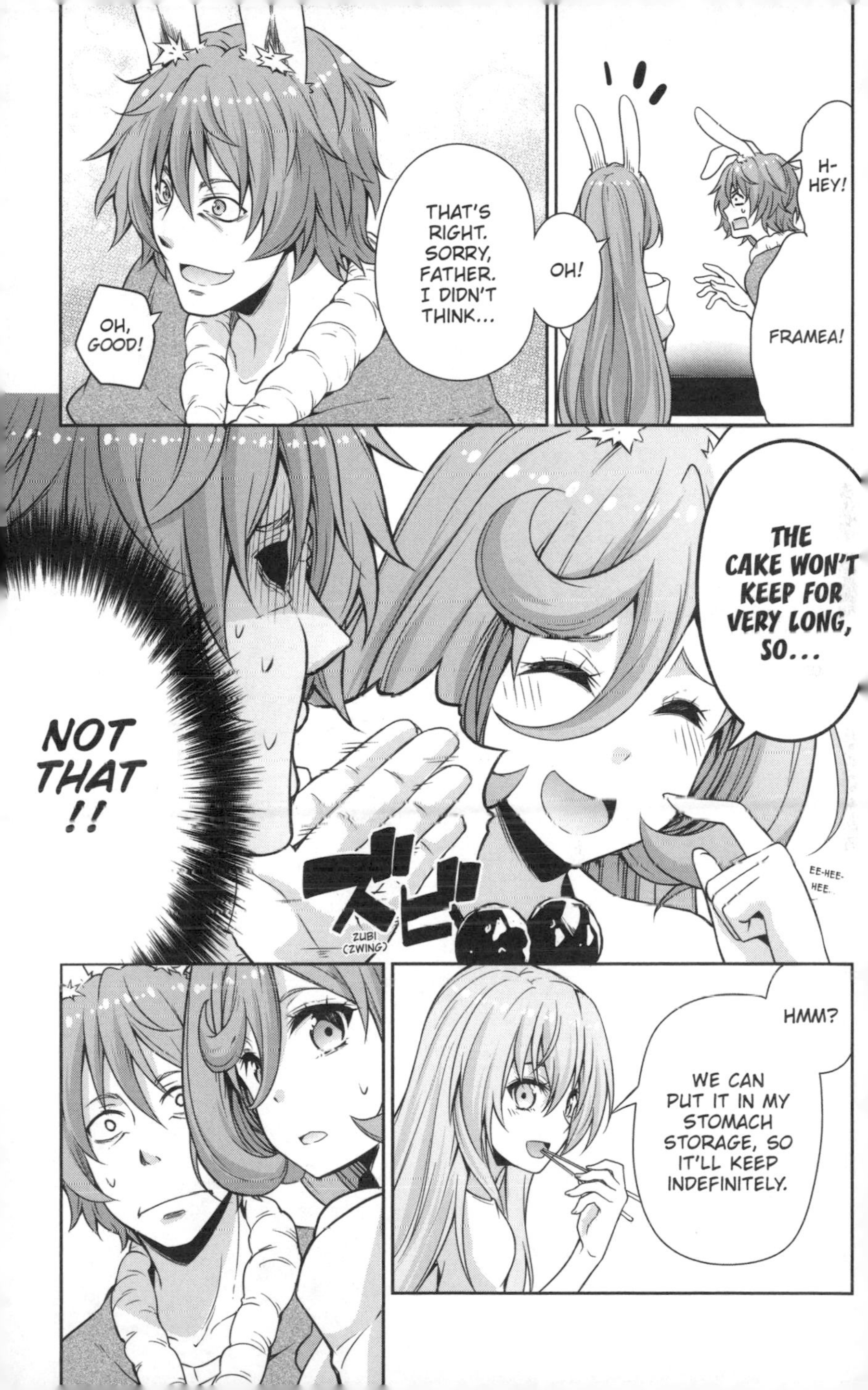
H-HEY!
FRAMEA!
OH!
THAT'S RIGHT. SORRY, FATHER. I DIDN'T THINK...
OH, GOOD!
THE CAKE WON'T KEEP FOR VERY LONG, SO...
EE-HEE-HEE..
ズビ
ZUBI (ZWING)
NOT THAT!!
HMM?
WE CAN PUT IT IN MY STOMACH STORAGE, SO IT'LL KEEP INDEFINITELY.

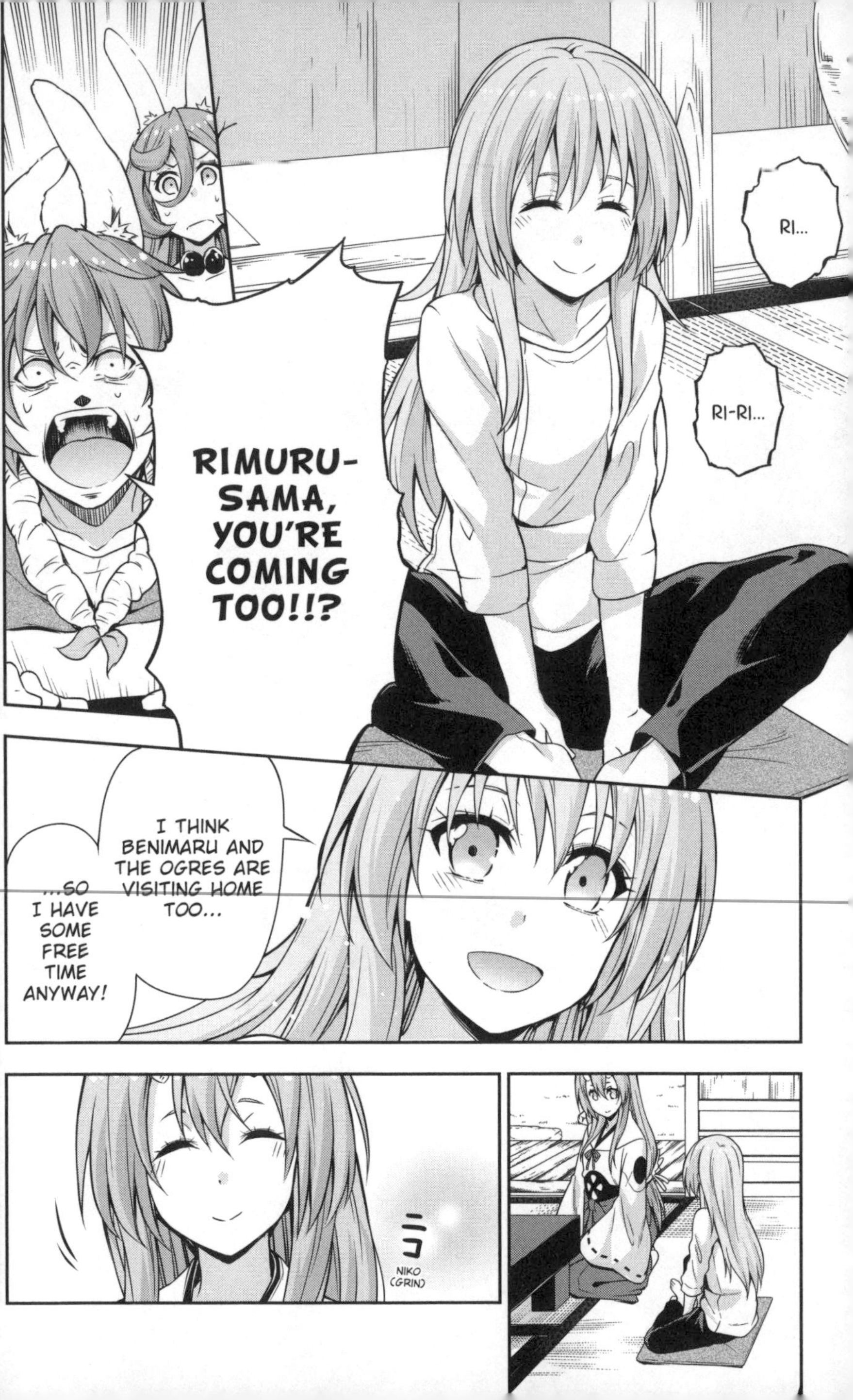
RI...
RI-RI...
RIMURU-SAMA, YOU'RE COMING TOO!!?
I THINK BENIMARU AND THE OGRES ARE VISITING HOME TOO...
...SO I HAVE SOME FREE TIME ANYWAY!
ニコ
NIKO (GRIN)

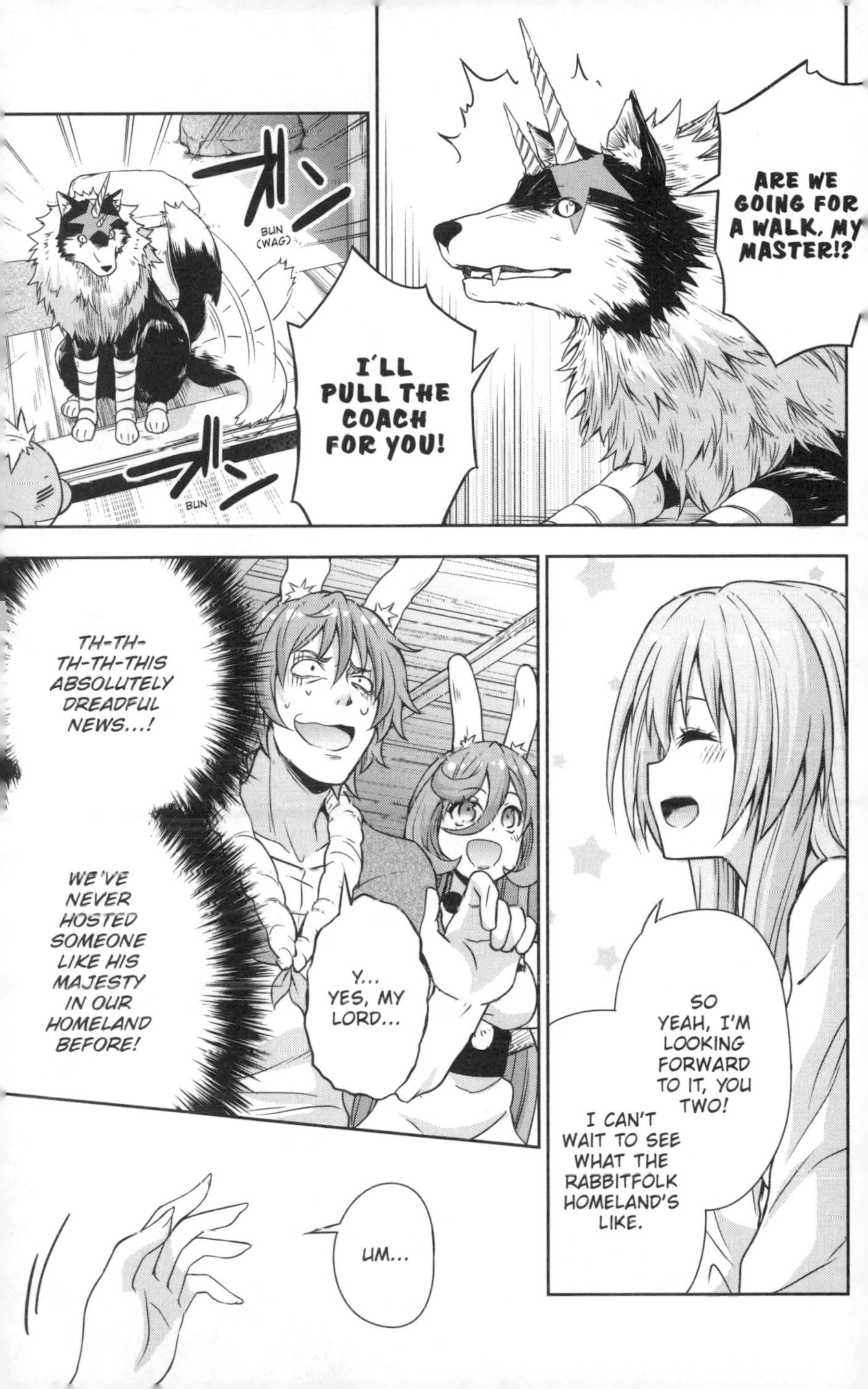

ARE WE GOING FOR A WALK, MY MASTER!?
I'LL PULL THE COACH FOR YOU!
BUN (WAG)
BUN
SO YEAH, I'M LOOKING FORWARD TO IT, YOU TWO!
I CAN'T WAIT TO SEE WHAT THE RABBITFOLK HOMELAND'S LIKE.
Y... YES, MY LORD...
TH-TH-TH-TH-THIS ABSOLUTELY DREADFUL NEWS...!
WE'VE NEVER HOSTED SOMEONE LIKE HIS MAJESTY IN OUR HOMELAND BEFORE!
UM...

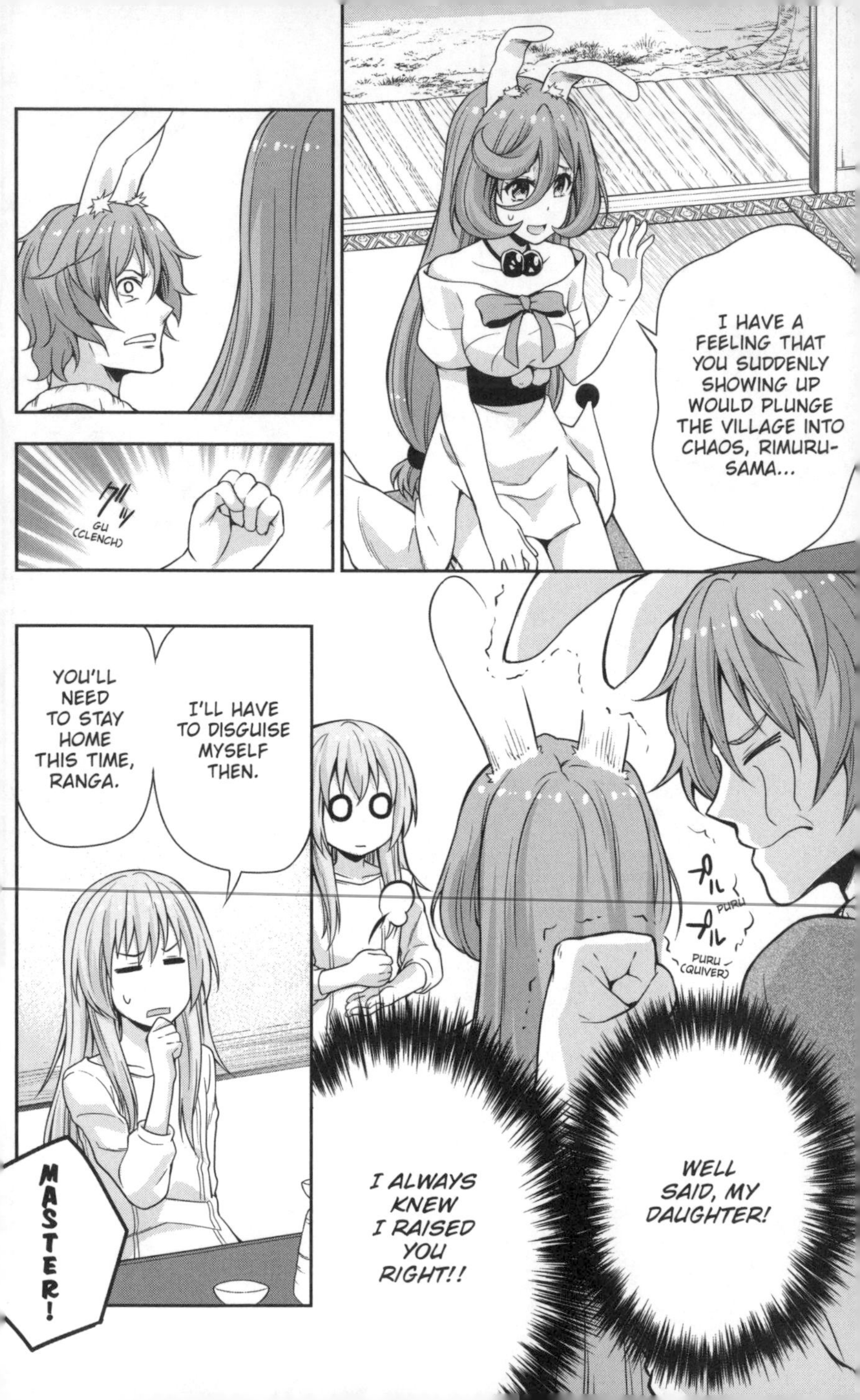
I HAVE A FEELING THAT YOU SUDDENLY SHOWING UP WOULD PLUNGE THE VILLAGE INTO CHAOS, RIMURU-SAMA...
グッ
GU (CLENCH)
プル
PURU
プル
PURU (QUIVER)
WELL SAID, MY DAUGHTER!
I ALWAYS KNEW I RAISED YOU RIGHT!!
I'LL HAVE TO DISGUISE MYSELF THEN.
YOU'LL NEED TO STAY HOME THIS TIME, RANGA.
MASTER!

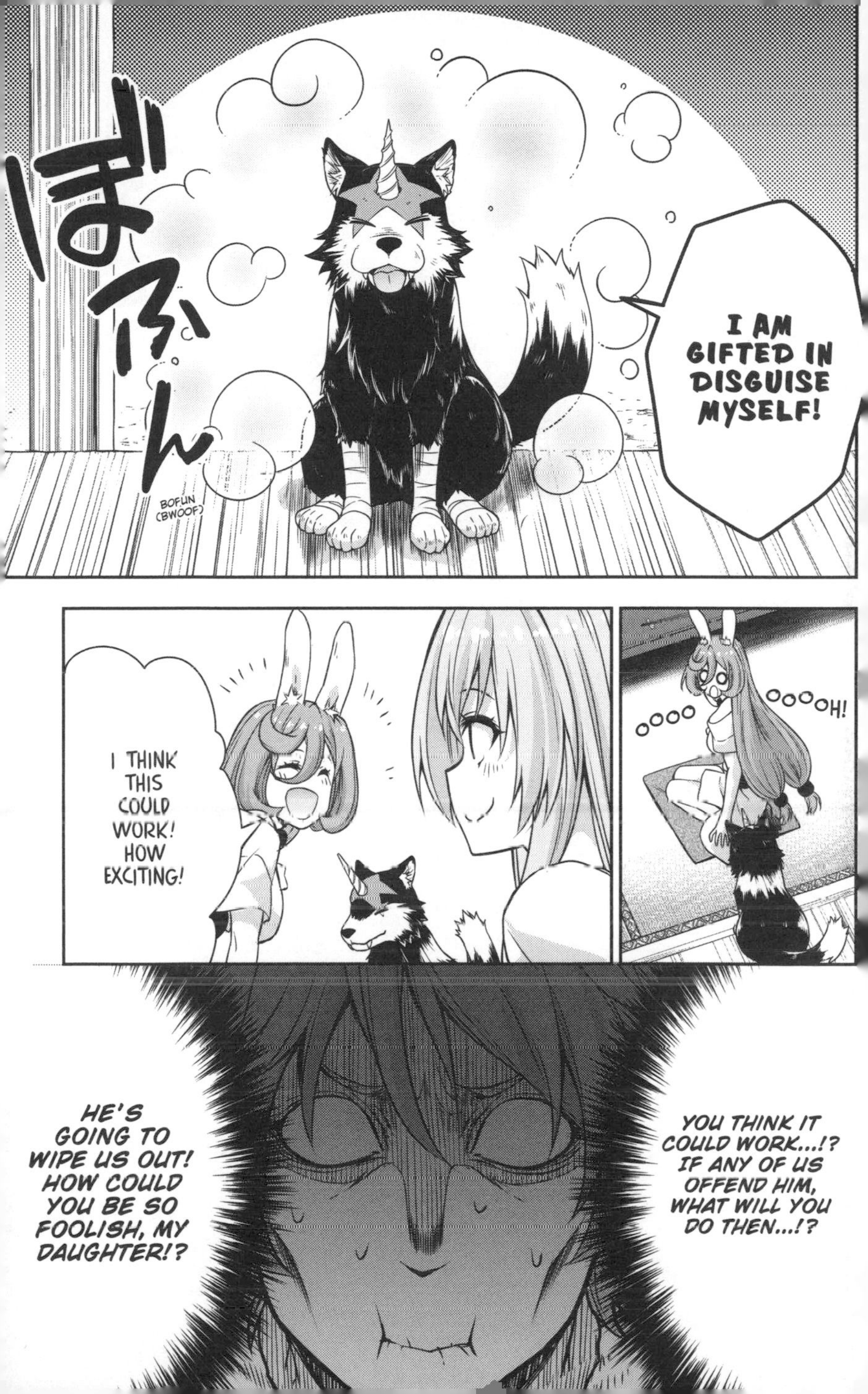
ぼふん
BOFUN (BWOOF)
I AM GIFTED IN DISGUISE MYSELF!
OOOO OOOOH!
I THINK THIS COULD WORK! HOW EXCITING!
YOU THINK IT COULD WORK...!? IF ANY OF US OFFEND HIM, WHAT WILL YOU DO THEN...!?
HE'S GOING TO WIPE US OUT! HOW COULD YOU BE SO FOOLISH, MY DAUGHTER!?

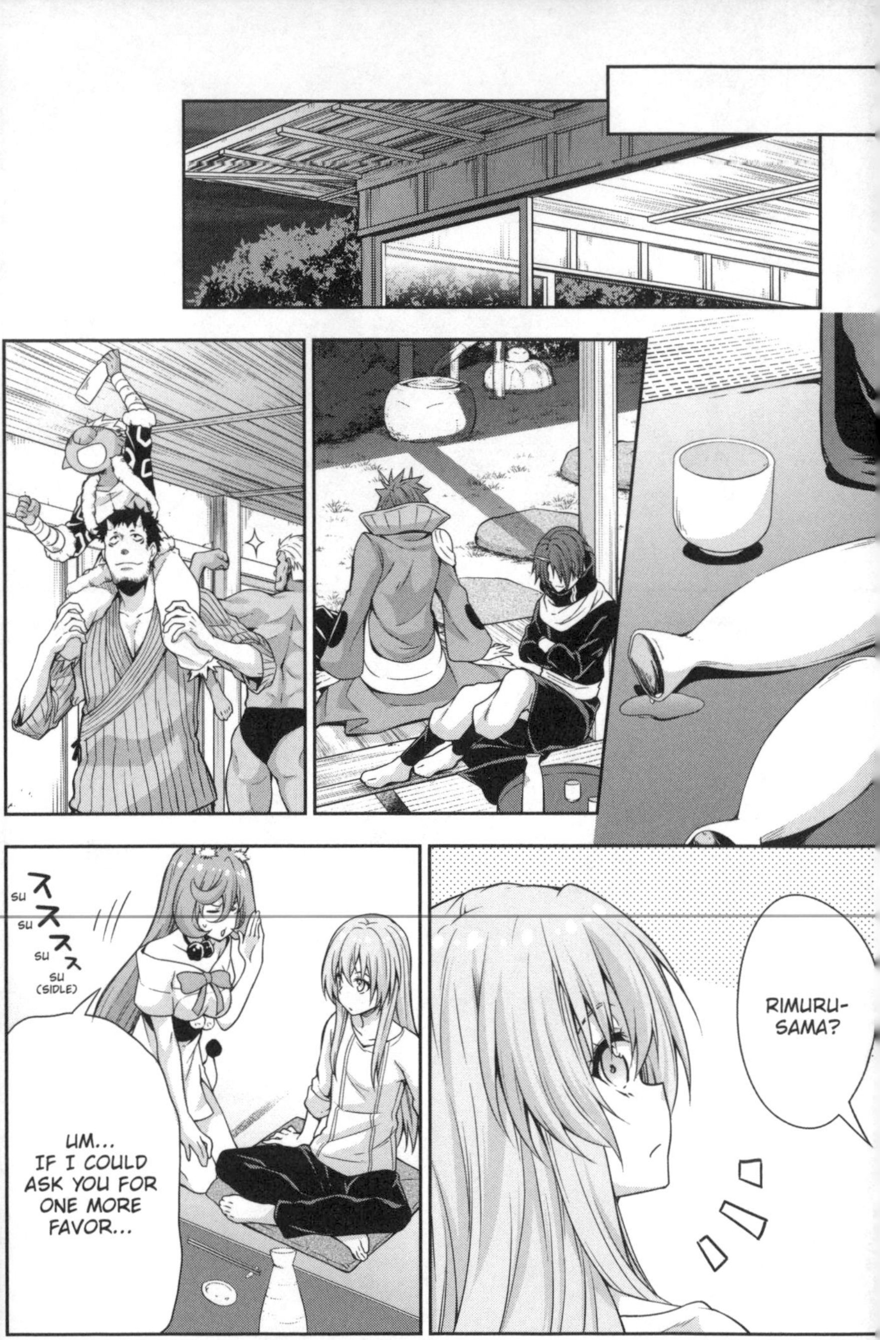
RIMURU-SAMA?
SU SU SU SU
(SIDLE)
UM... IF I COULD ASK YOU FOR ONE MORE FAVOR...

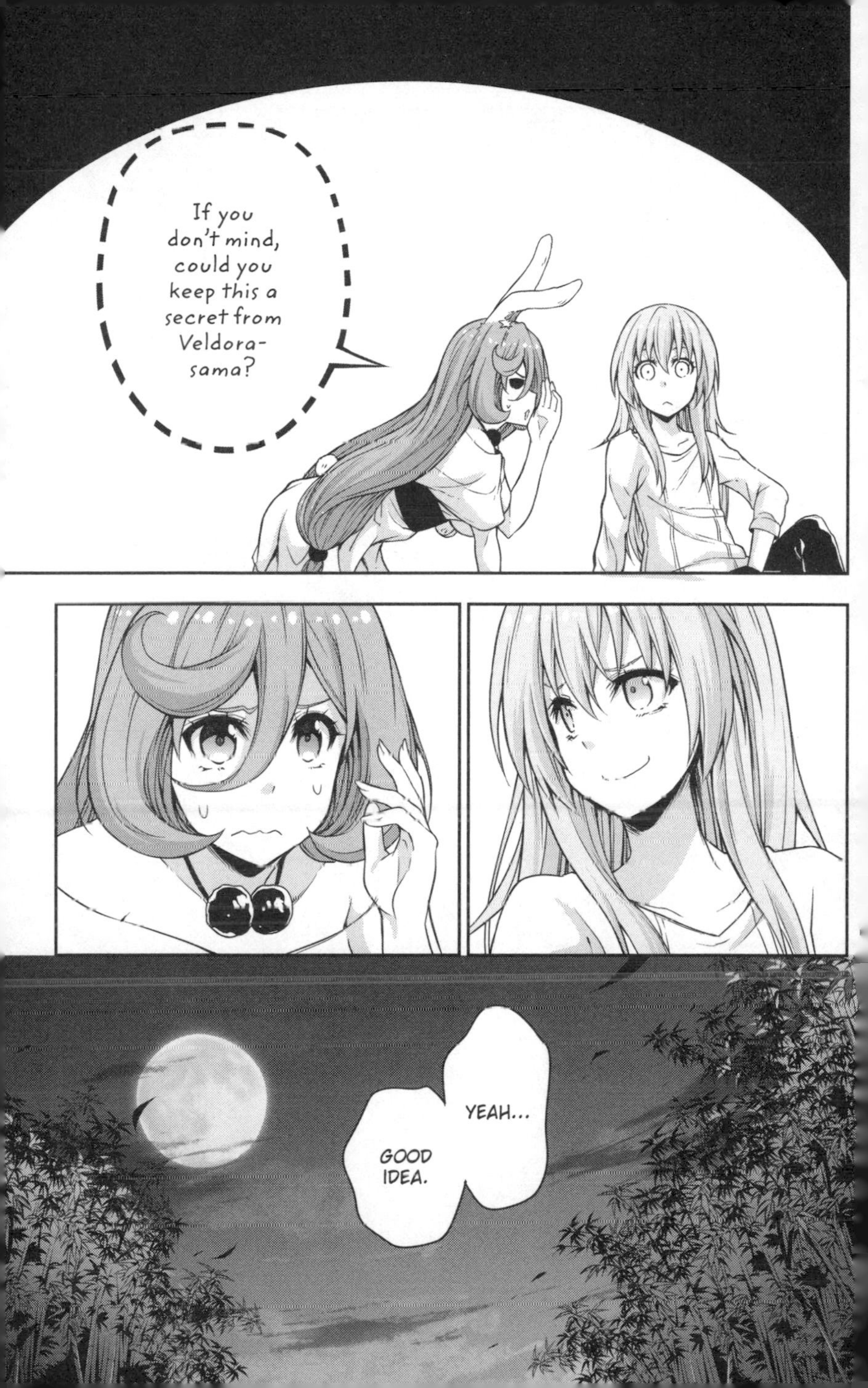
If you don't mind, could you keep this a secret from Veldora-sama?
YEAH...
GOOD IDEA.

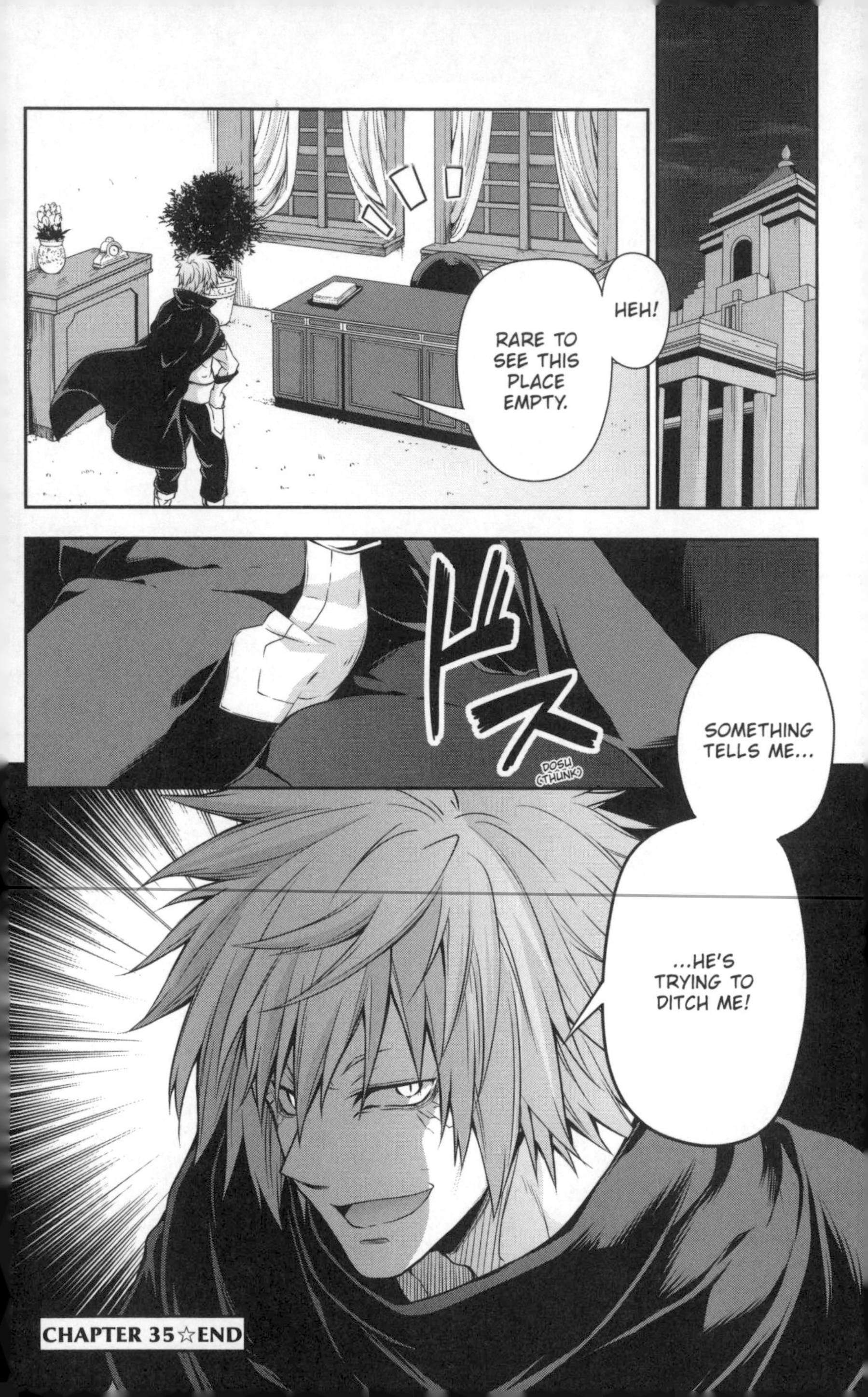
HEH!
RARE TO SEE THIS PLACE EMPTY.
DOSU (THUNK)
SOMETHING TELLS ME...
...HE'S TRYING TO DITCH ME!

CHAPTER 35☆END

That Time I Got
Reincarnated
as a SLIME
The Ways of the Monster Nation

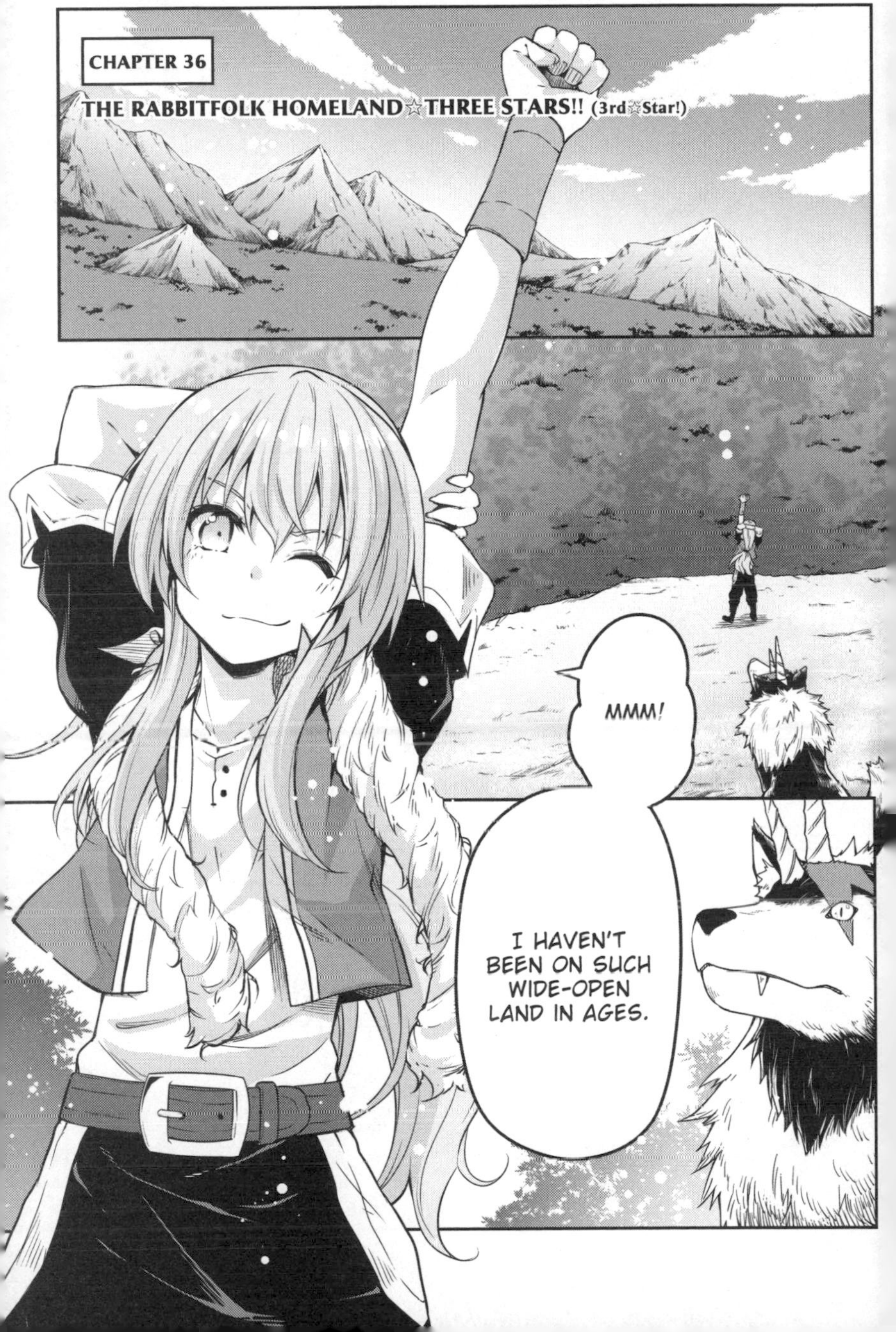
CHAPTER 36
THE RABBITFOLK HOMELAND☆THREE STARS!! (3rd☆Star!)
MMM!
I HAVEN'T BEEN ON SUCH WIDE-OPEN LAND IN AGES.

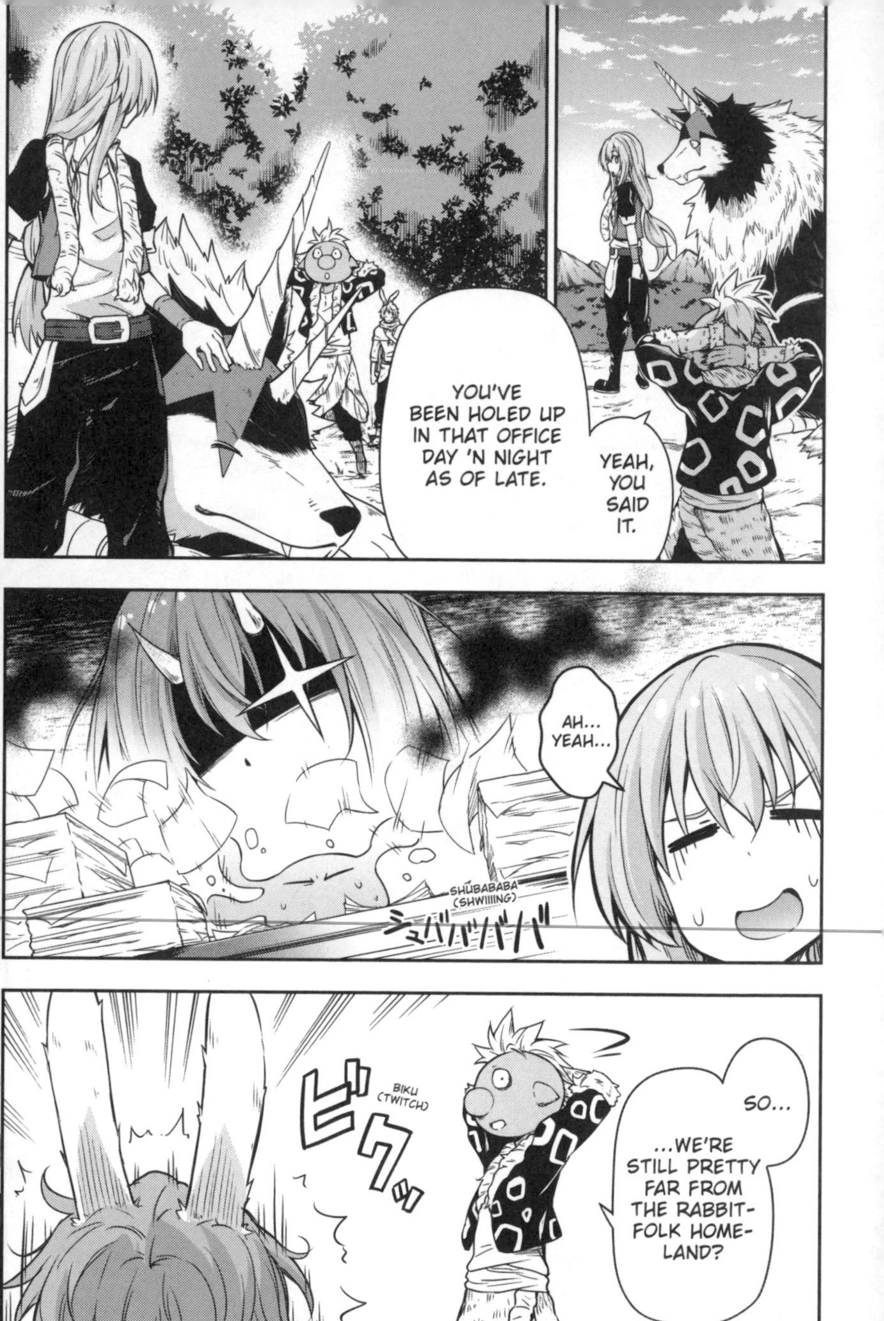

YOU'VE BEEN HOLED UP IN THAT OFFICE DAY 'N NIGHT AS OF LATE.
YEAH, YOU SAID IT.
AH... YEAH...
SHŪBABABA (SHWIIIING)
SO...
...WE'RE STILL PRETTY FAR FROM THE RABBIT-FOLK HOME-LAND?
BIKU (TWITCH)

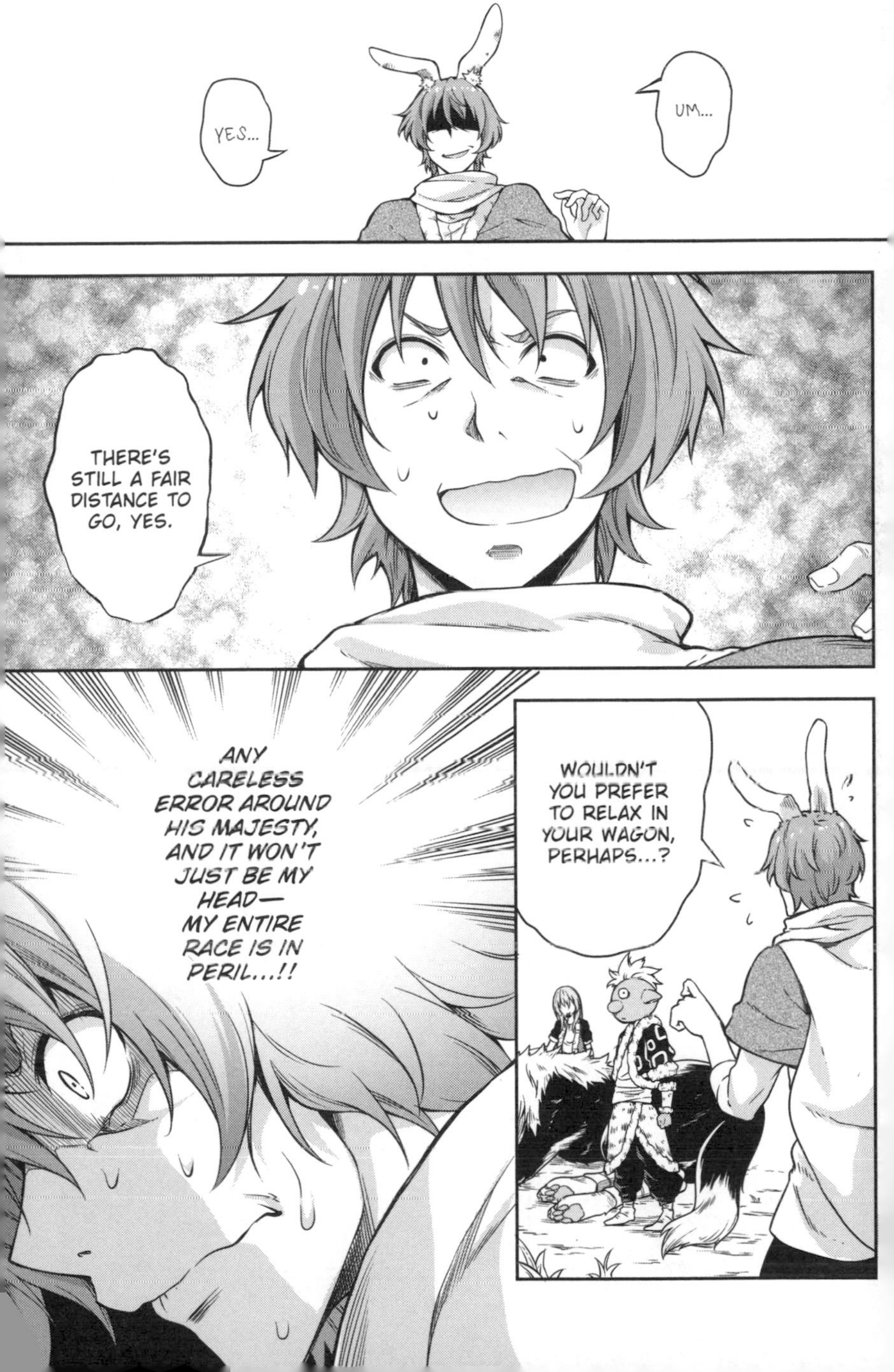
UM...
YES...
THERE'S STILL A FAIR DISTANCE TO GO, YES.
WOULDN'T YOU PREFER TO RELAX IN YOUR WAGON, PERHAPS...?
ANY CARELESS ERROR AROUND HIS MAJESTY, AND IT WON'T JUST BE MY HEAD— MY ENTIRE RACE IS IN PERIL...!!

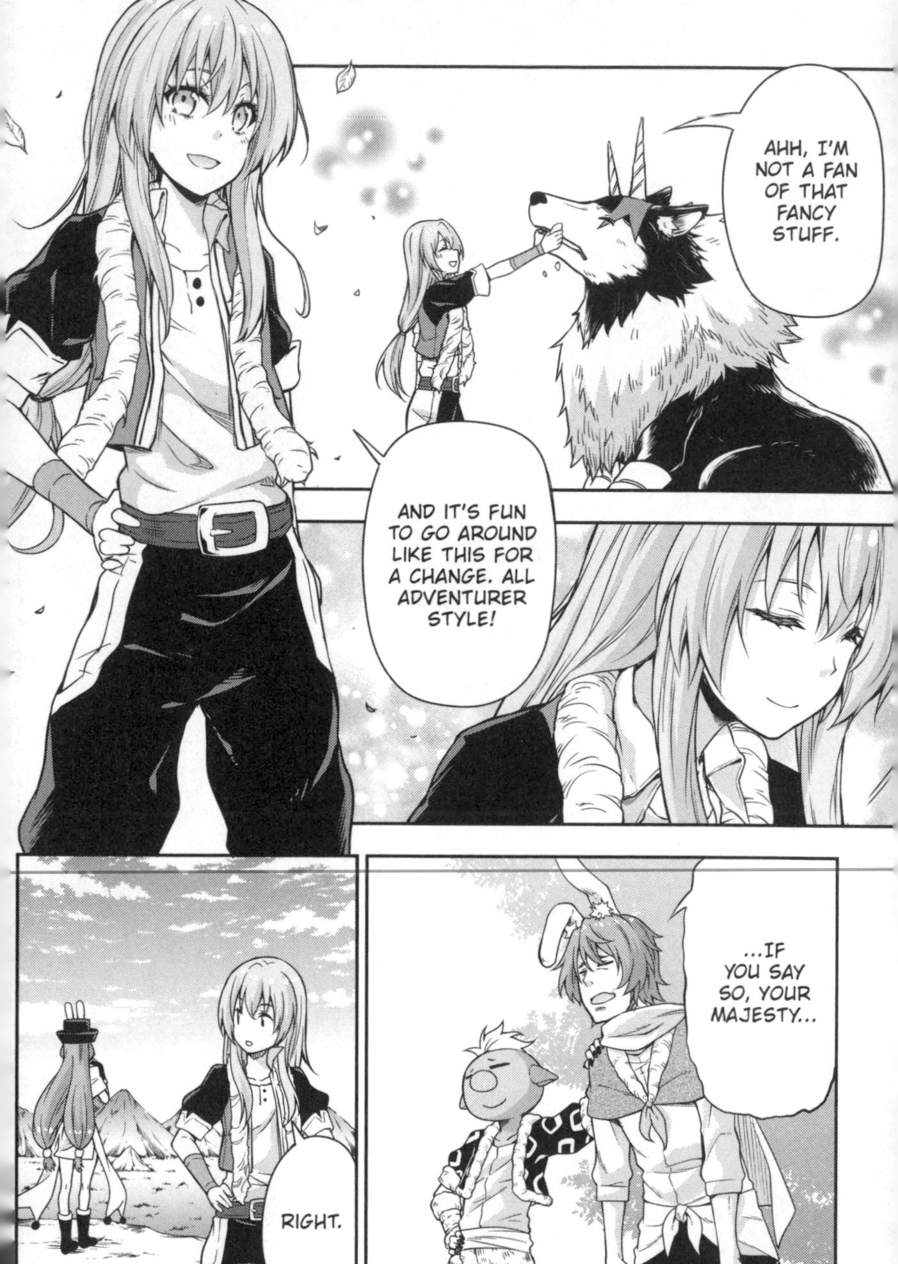
AHH, I'M NOT A FAN OF THAT FANCY STUFF.
AND IT'S FUN TO GO AROUND LIKE THIS FOR A CHANGE. ALL ADVENTURER STYLE!
...IF YOU SAY SO, YOUR MAJESTY...
RIGHT.

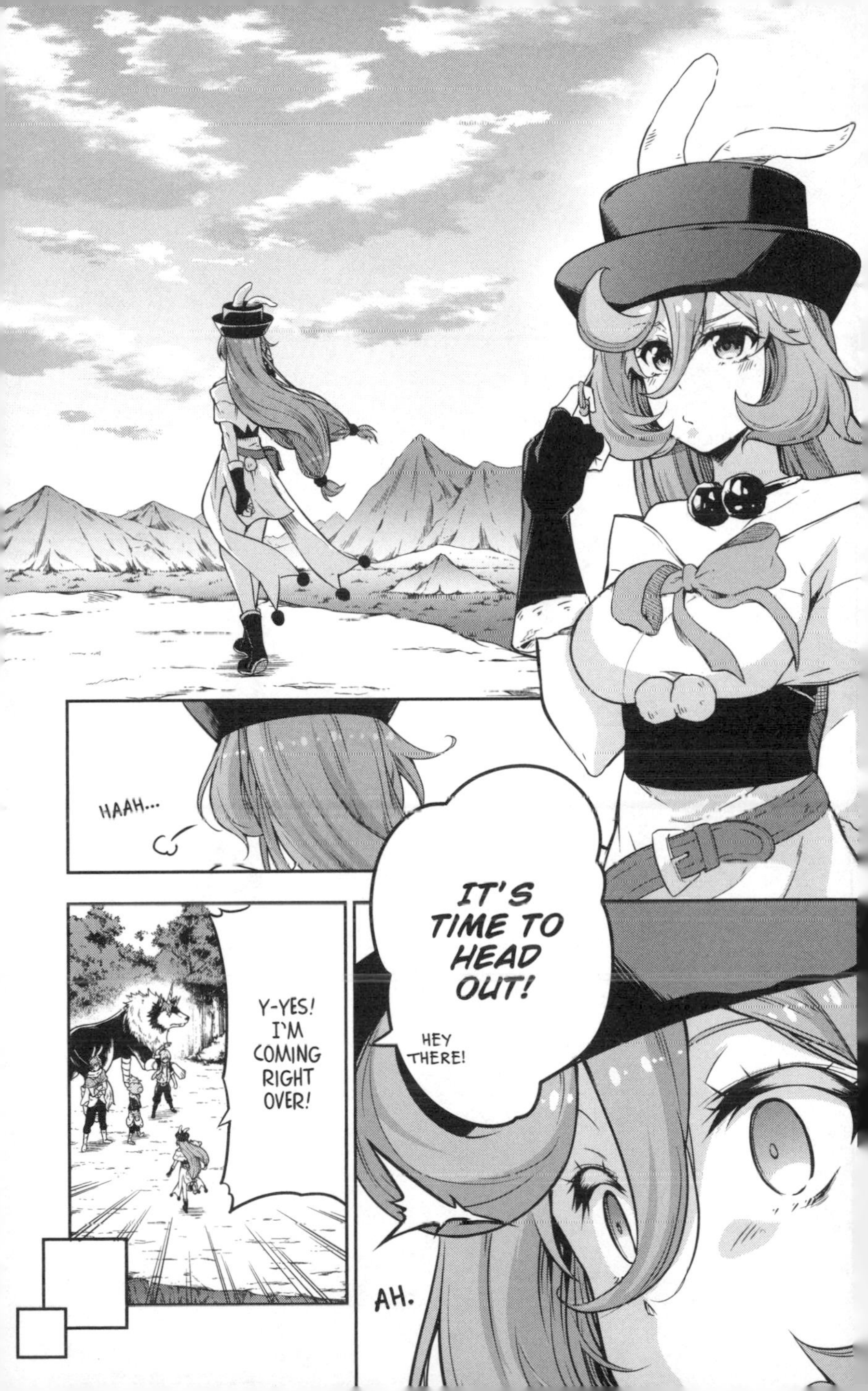
HAAH...
IT'S TIME TO HEAD OUT!
HEY THERE!
AH.
Y-YES! I'M COMING RIGHT OVER!

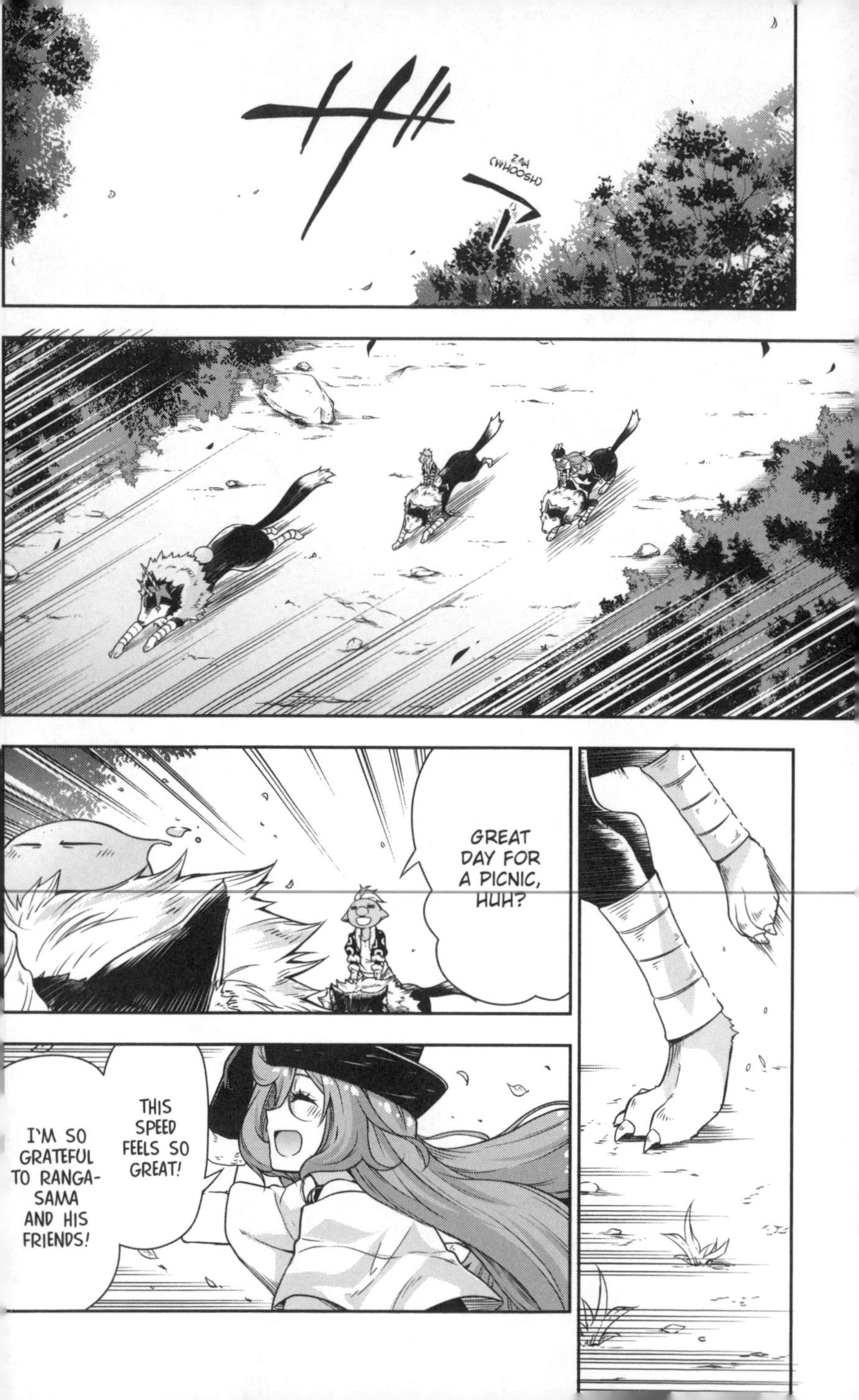
ZAH
(WHOOSH)
GREAT DAY FOR A PICNIC, HUH?
THIS SPEED FEELS SO GREAT!
I'M SO GRATEFUL TO RANGA-SAMA AND HIS FRIENDS!

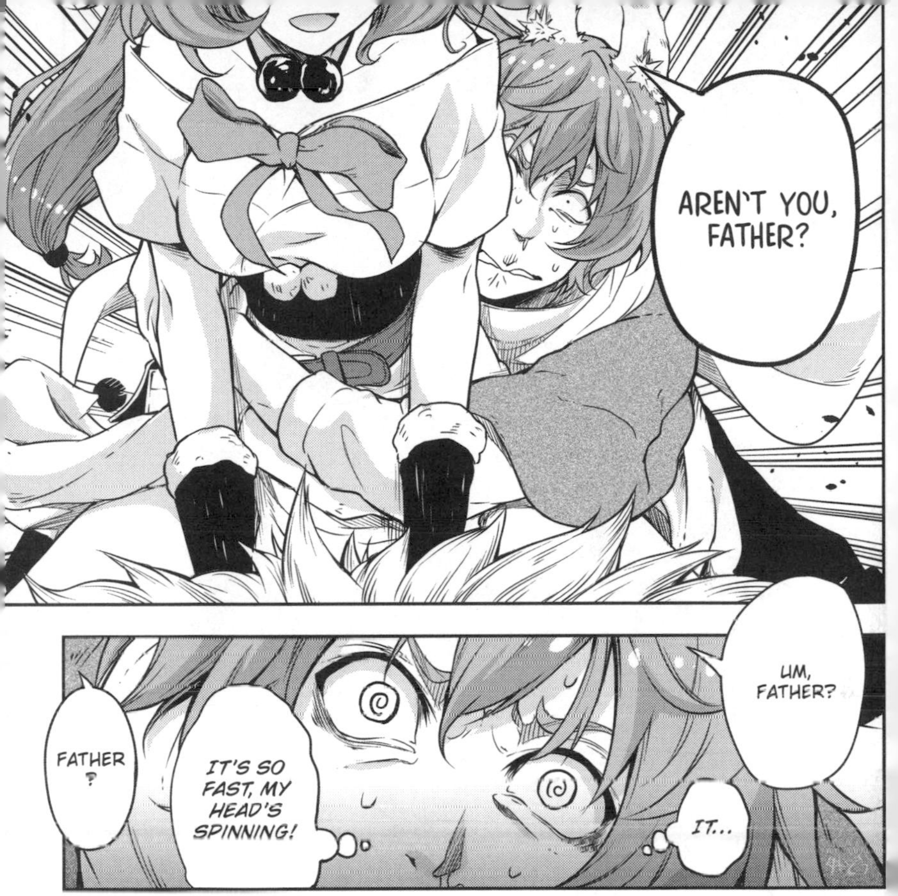
AREN'T YOU, FATHER?
UM, FATHER?
IT...
IT'S SO FAST, MY HEAD'S SPINNING!
FATHER?

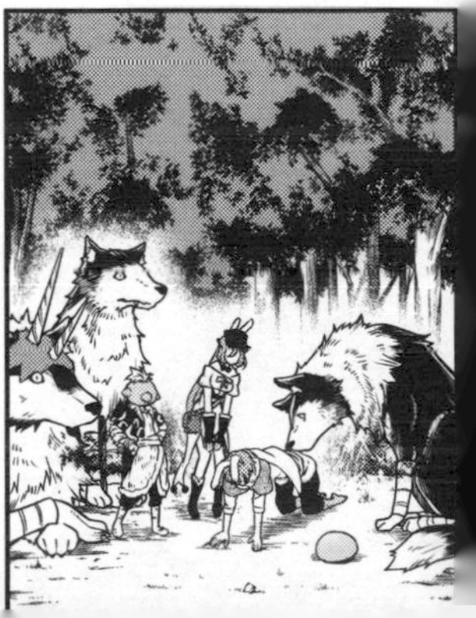

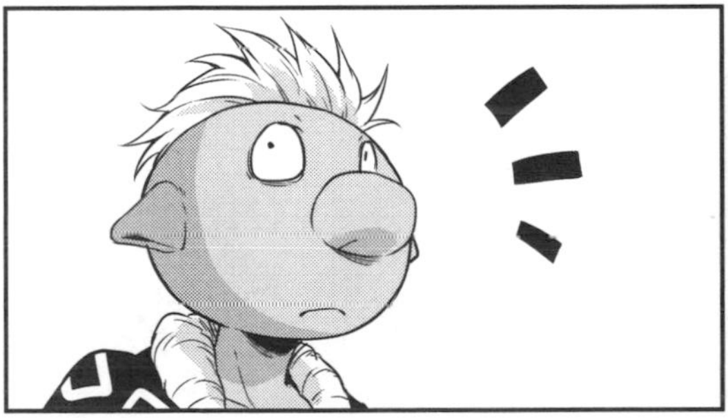

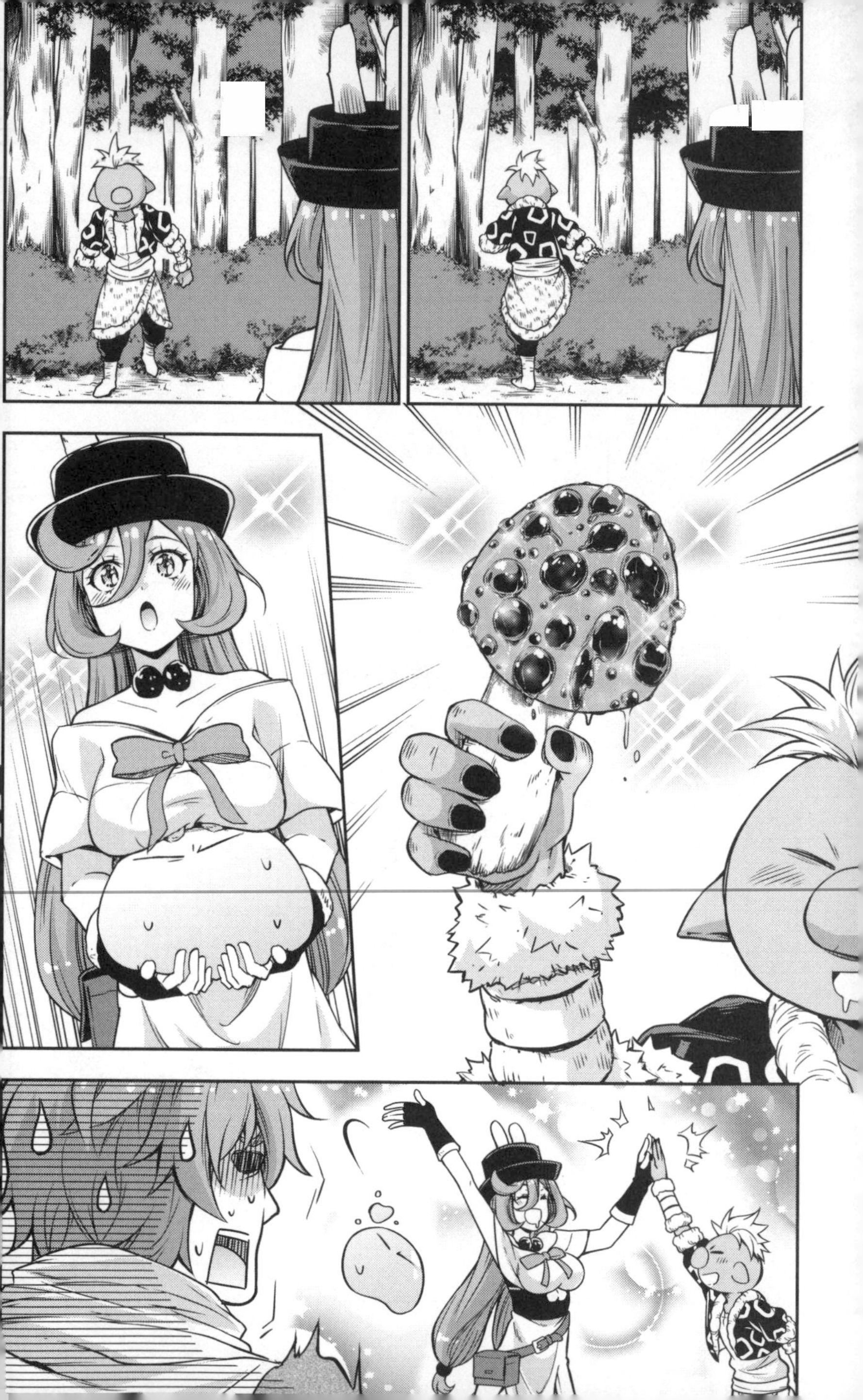

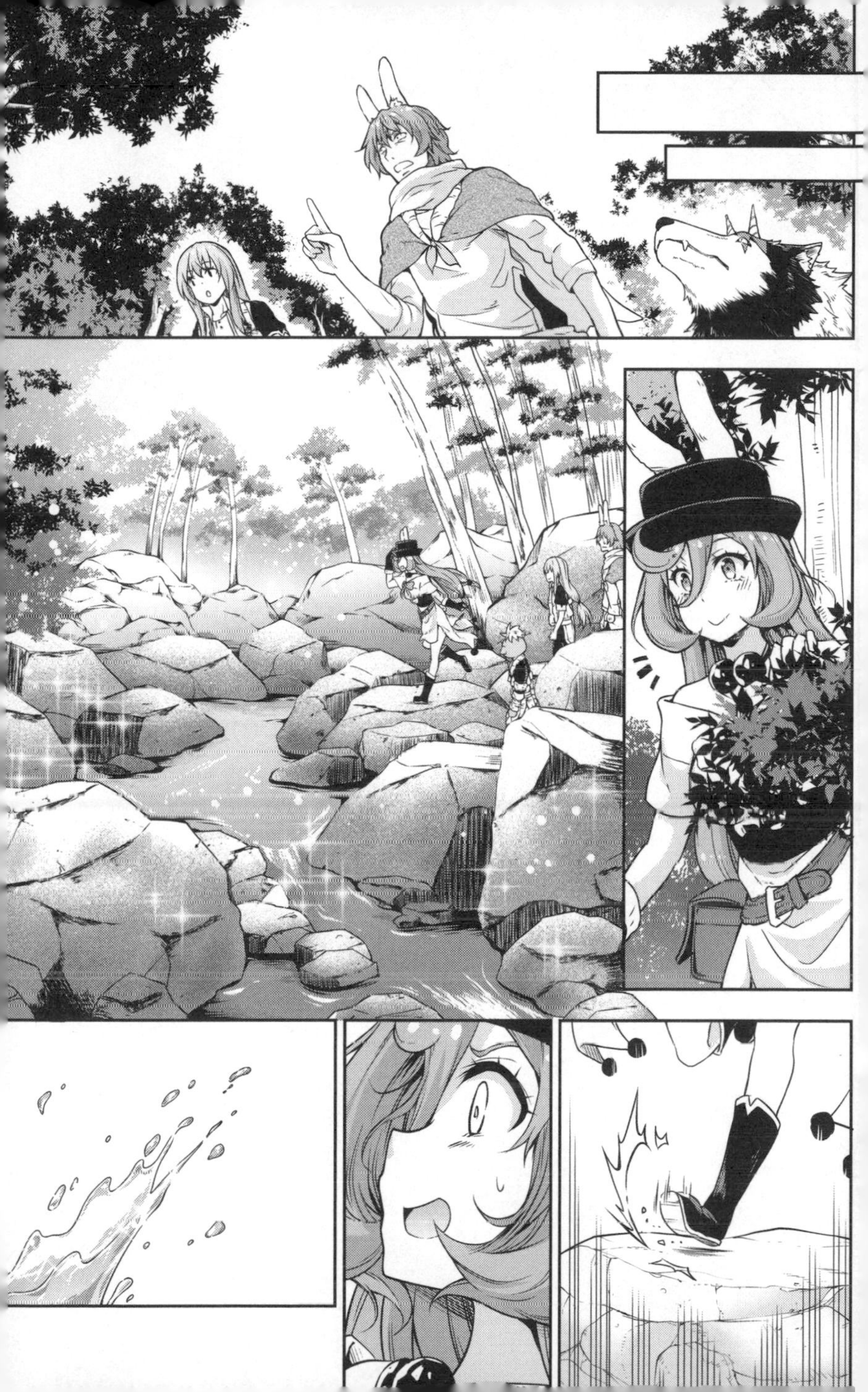

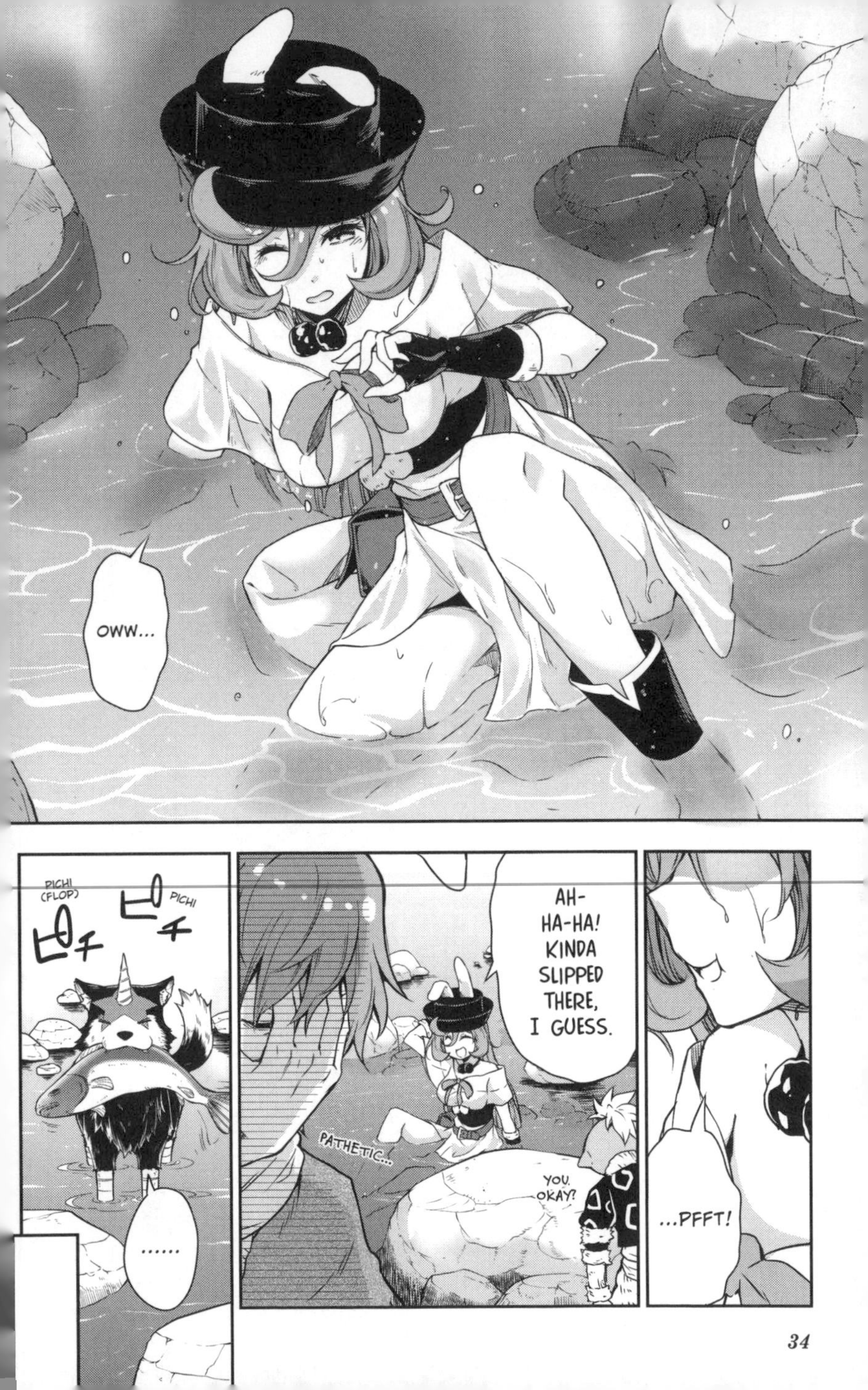
OWW...
...PFFT!
AH-HA-HA! KINDA SLIPPED THERE, I GUESS.
YOU. OKAY?
PATHETIC...
PICHI
PICHI (FLOP)
......

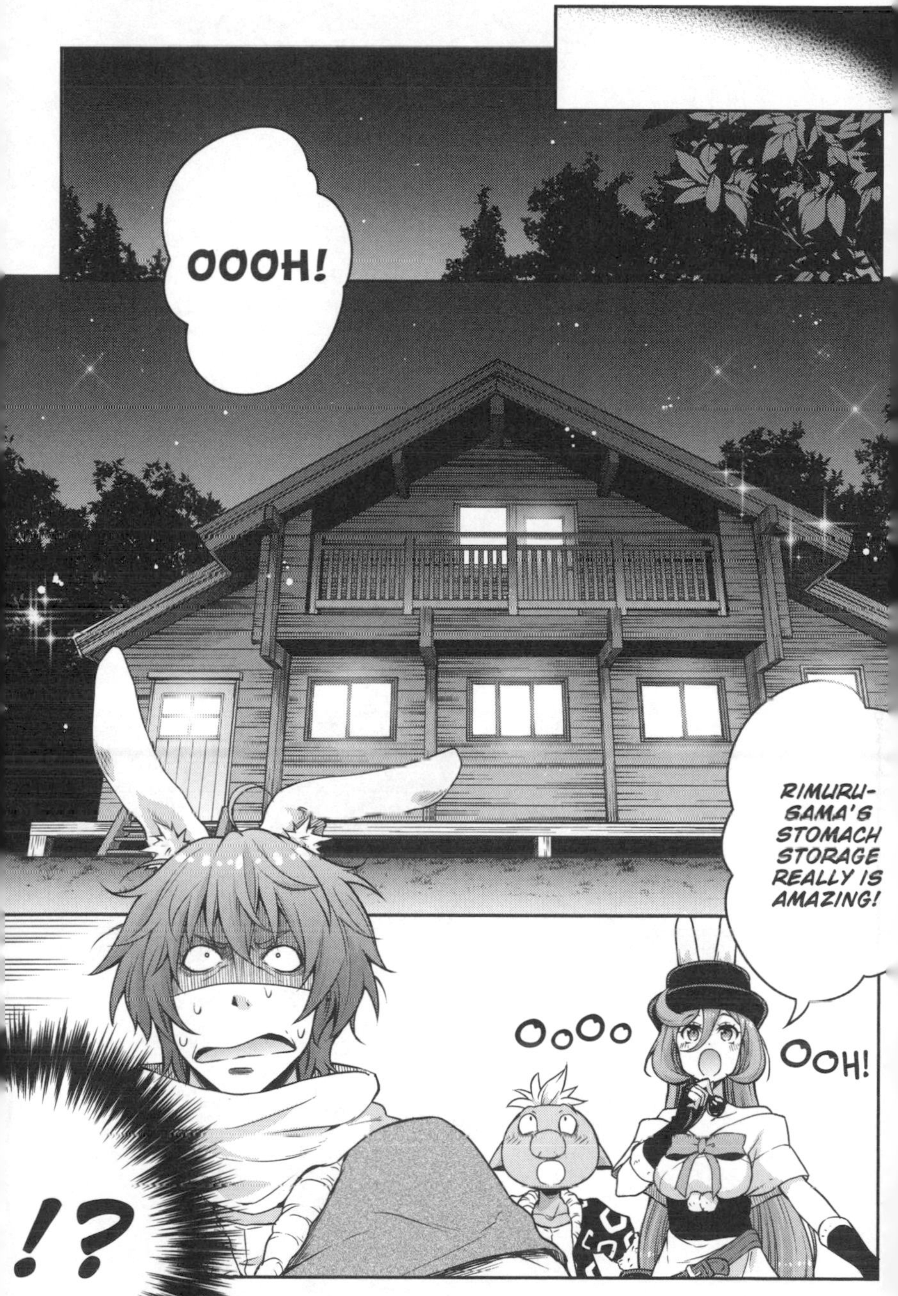
OOOH!
RIMURU-SAMA'S STOMACH STORAGE REALLY IS AMAZING!
OOOO
OOH!
!?

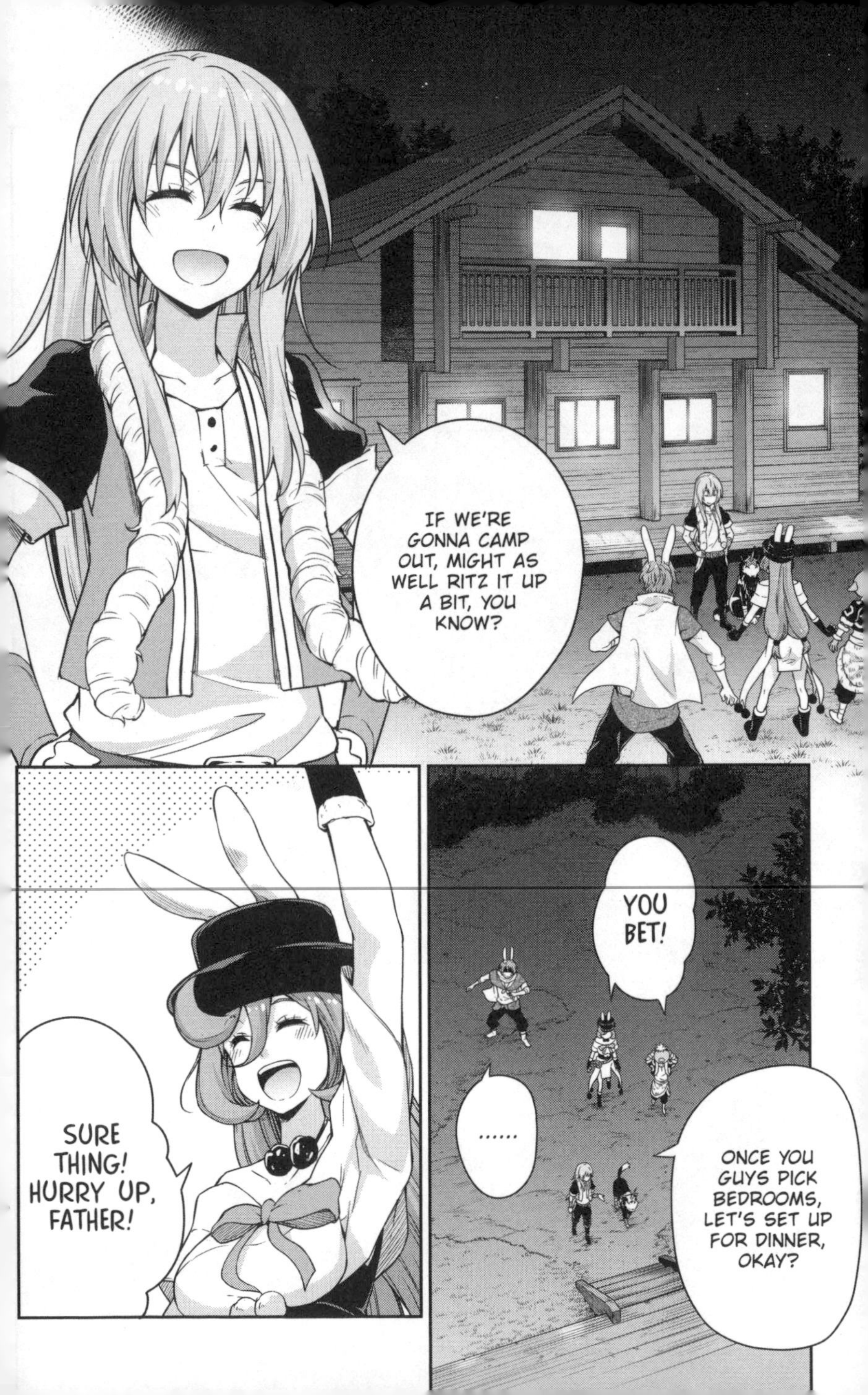
IF WE'RE GONNA CAMP OUT, MIGHT AS WELL RITZ IT UP A BIT, YOU KNOW?
YOU BET!
......
ONCE YOU GUYS PICK BEDROOMS, LET'S SET UP FOR DINNER, OKAY?
SURE THING! HURRY UP, FATHER!

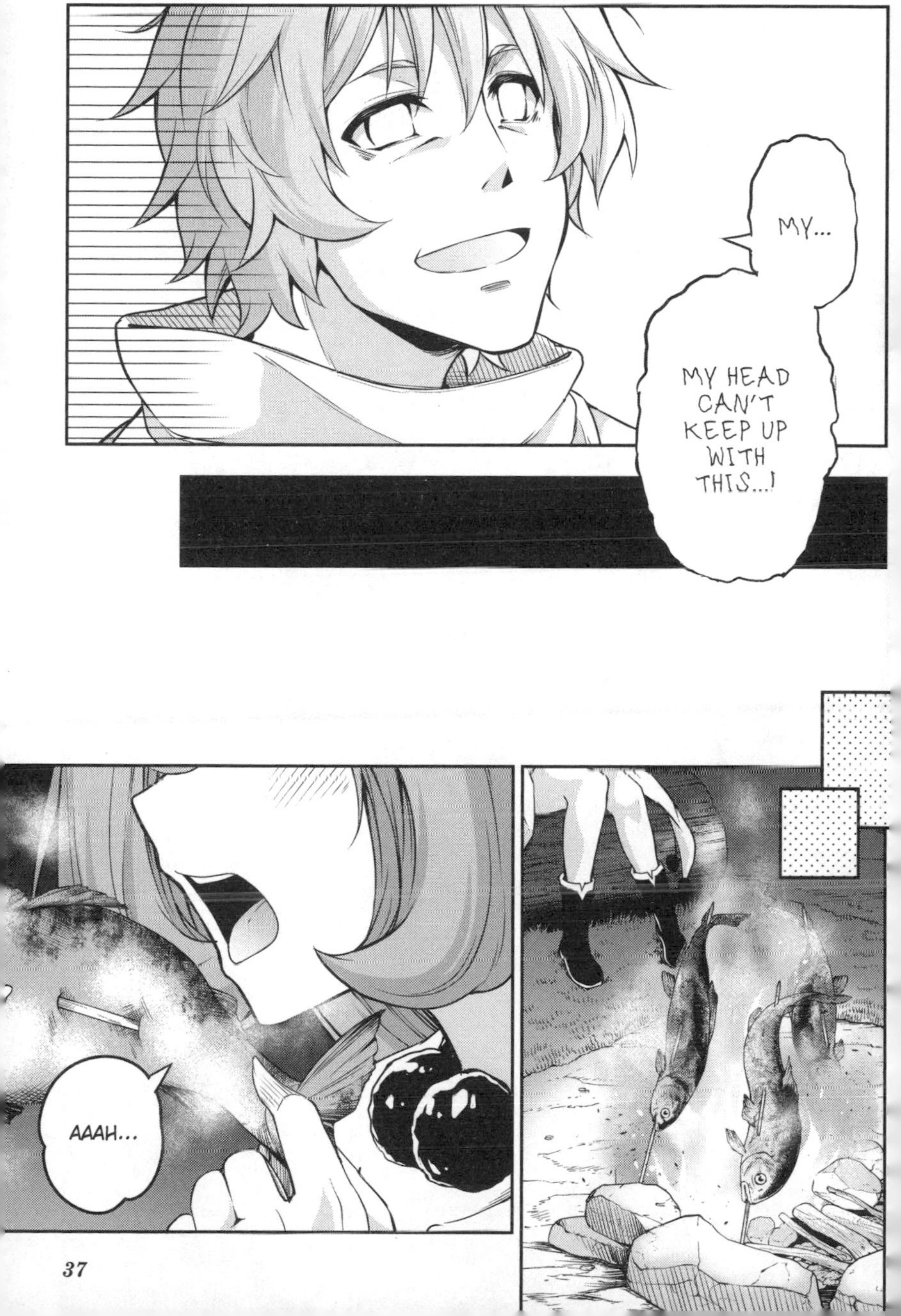
MY...
MY HEAD CAN'T KEEP UP WITH THIS...!
AAAH...

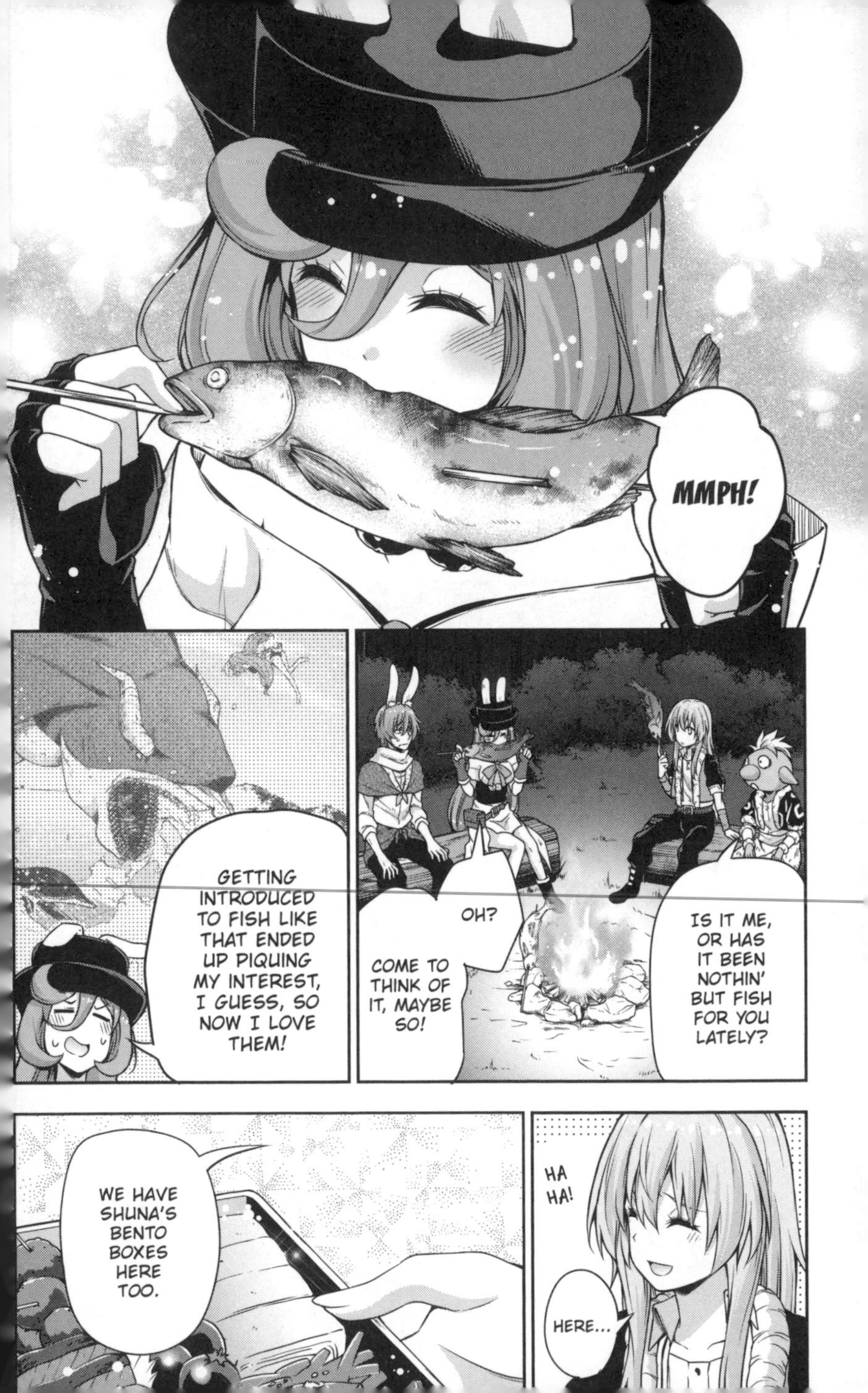
MMPH!
IS IT ME, OR HAS IT BEEN NOTHIN' BUT FISH FOR YOU LATELY?
OH?
COME TO THINK OF IT, MAYBE SO!
GETTING INTRODUCED TO FISH LIKE THAT ENDED UP PIQUING MY INTEREST, I GUESS, SO NOW I LOVE THEM!
HA HA!
HERE...
WE HAVE SHUNA'S BENTO BOXES HERE TOO.

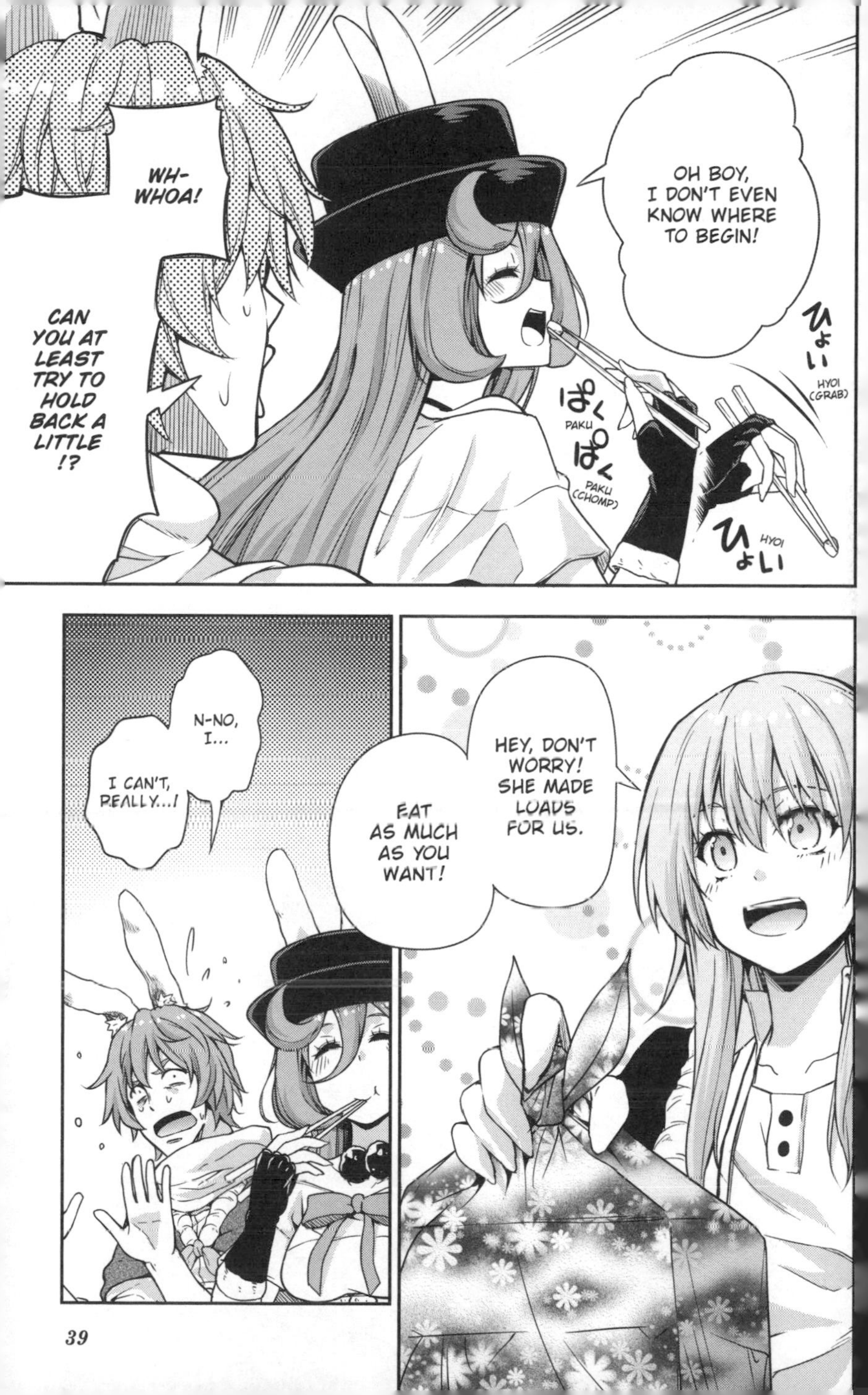
OH BOY, I DON'T EVEN KNOW WHERE TO BEGIN!
ひょい
HYOI (GRAB)
ぱく
PAKU
ぱく
PAKU (CHOMP)
ひょい
HYOI
WH- WHOA!
CAN YOU AT LEAST TRY TO HOLD BACK A LITTLE !?
HEY, DON'T WORRY! SHE MADE LOADS FOR US.
EAT AS MUCH AS YOU WANT!
N-NO, I...
I CAN'T, REALLY...!

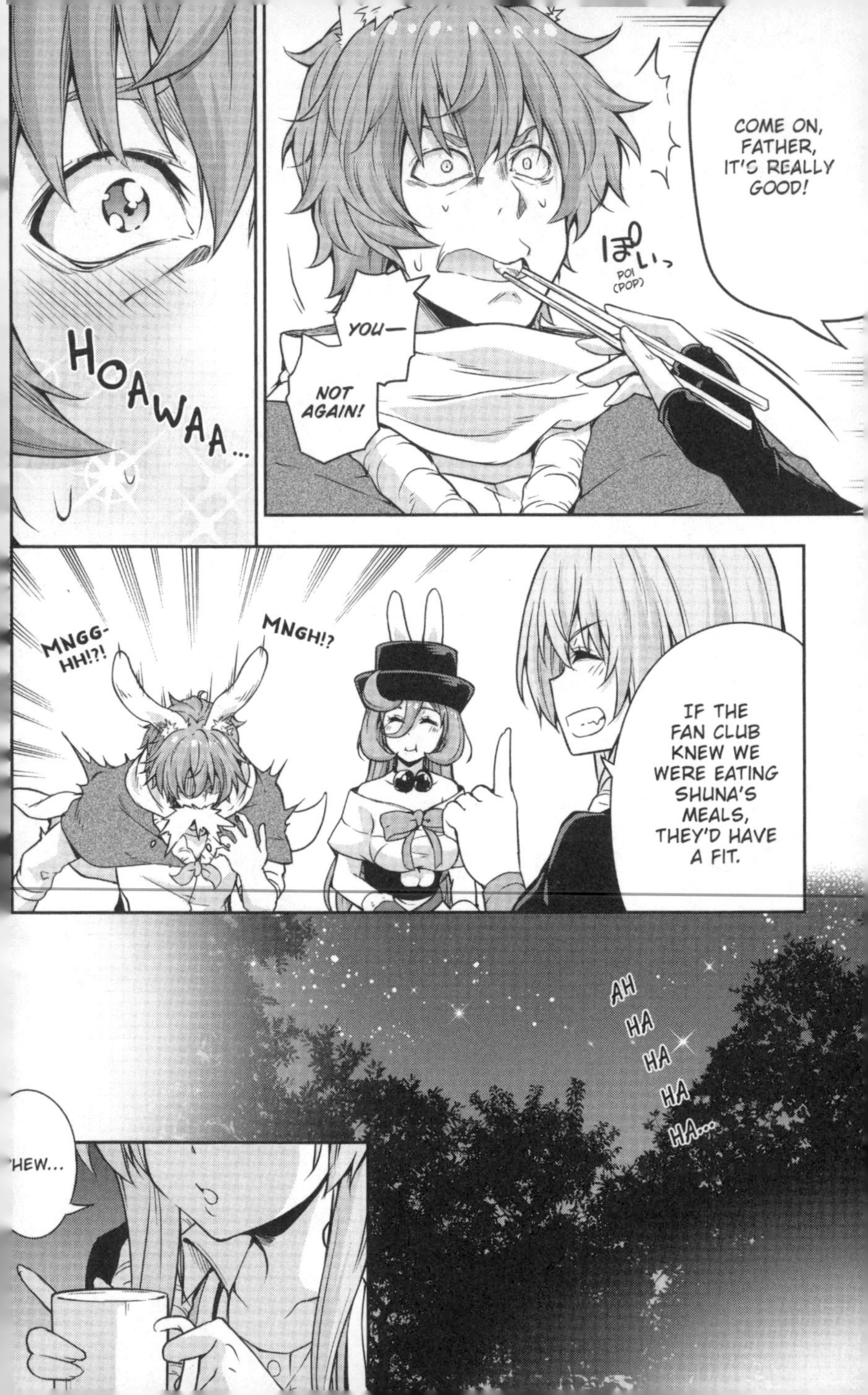
COME ON, FATHER, IT'S REALLY GOOD!
ぽいっ
POI (POP)
YOU—
NOT AGAIN!
HOAWAA...
IF THE FAN CLUB KNEW WE WERE EATING SHUNA'S MEALS, THEY'D HAVE A FIT.
MNGH!?
MNGG-HH!?!
AH HA HA HA HA HA...
HEW...

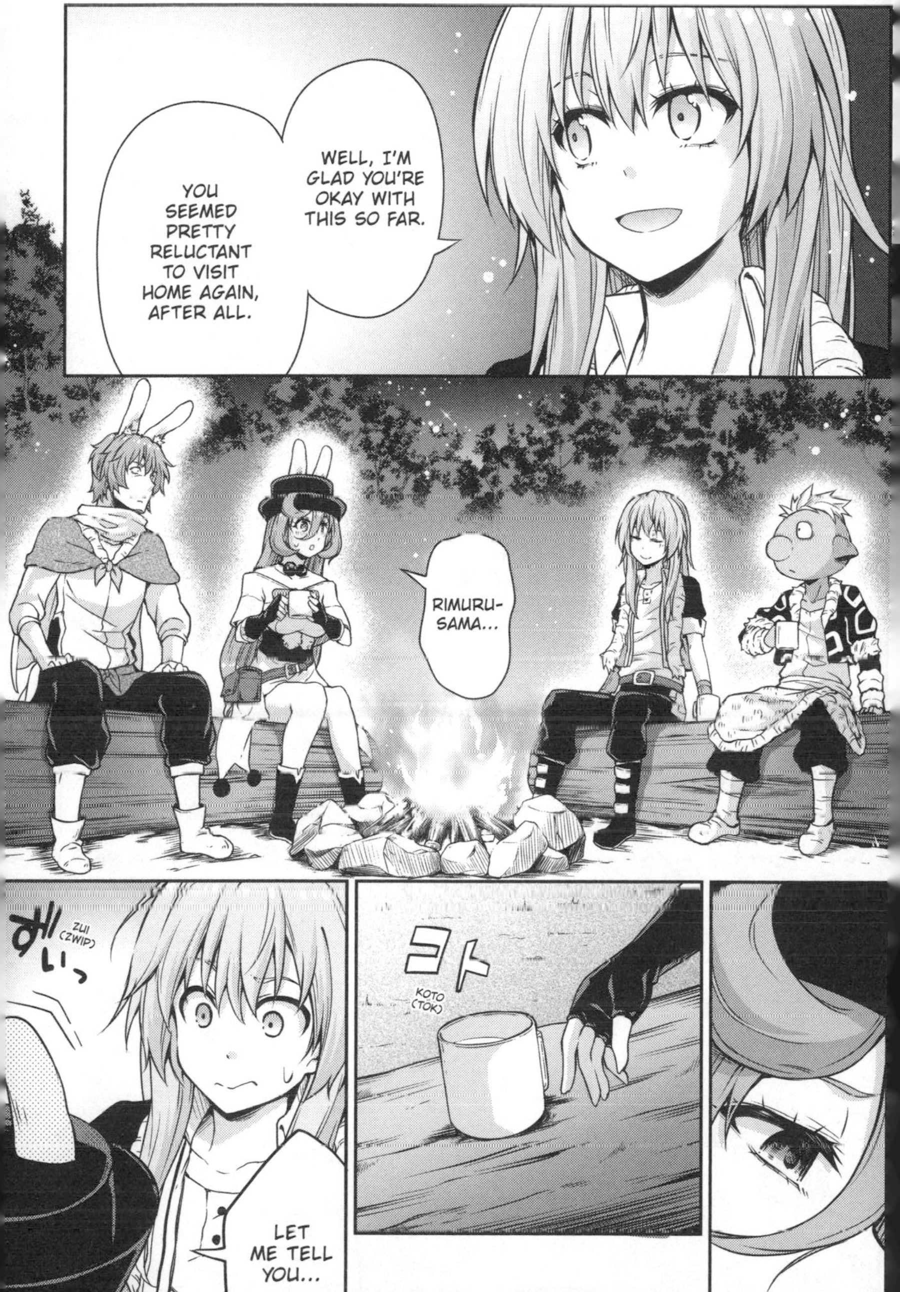

WELL, I'M GLAD YOU'RE OKAY WITH THIS SO FAR.
YOU SEEMED PRETTY RELUCTANT TO VISIT HOME AGAIN, AFTER ALL.
RIMURU-SAMA...
コト
KOTO (TOK)
ずいっ
ZUI (ZWIP)
LET ME TELL YOU...

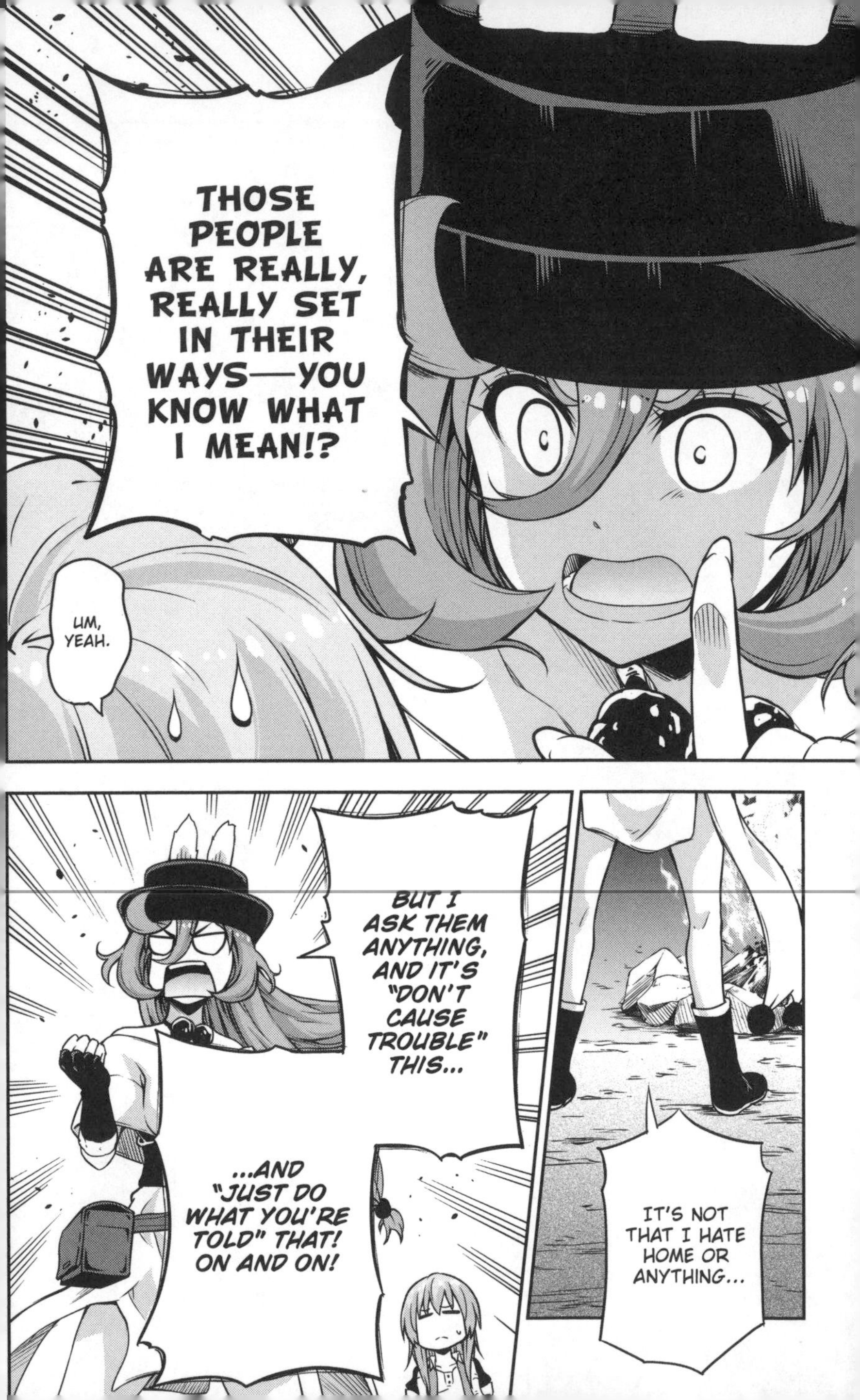
THOSE PEOPLE ARE REALLY, REALLY SET IN THEIR WAYS—YOU KNOW WHAT I MEAN!?
UM, YEAH.
IT'S NOT THAT I HATE HOME OR ANYTHING...
BUT I ASK THEM ANYTHING, AND IT'S "DON'T CAUSE TROUBLE" THIS...
...AND "JUST DO WHAT YOU'RE TOLD" THAT! ON AND ON!

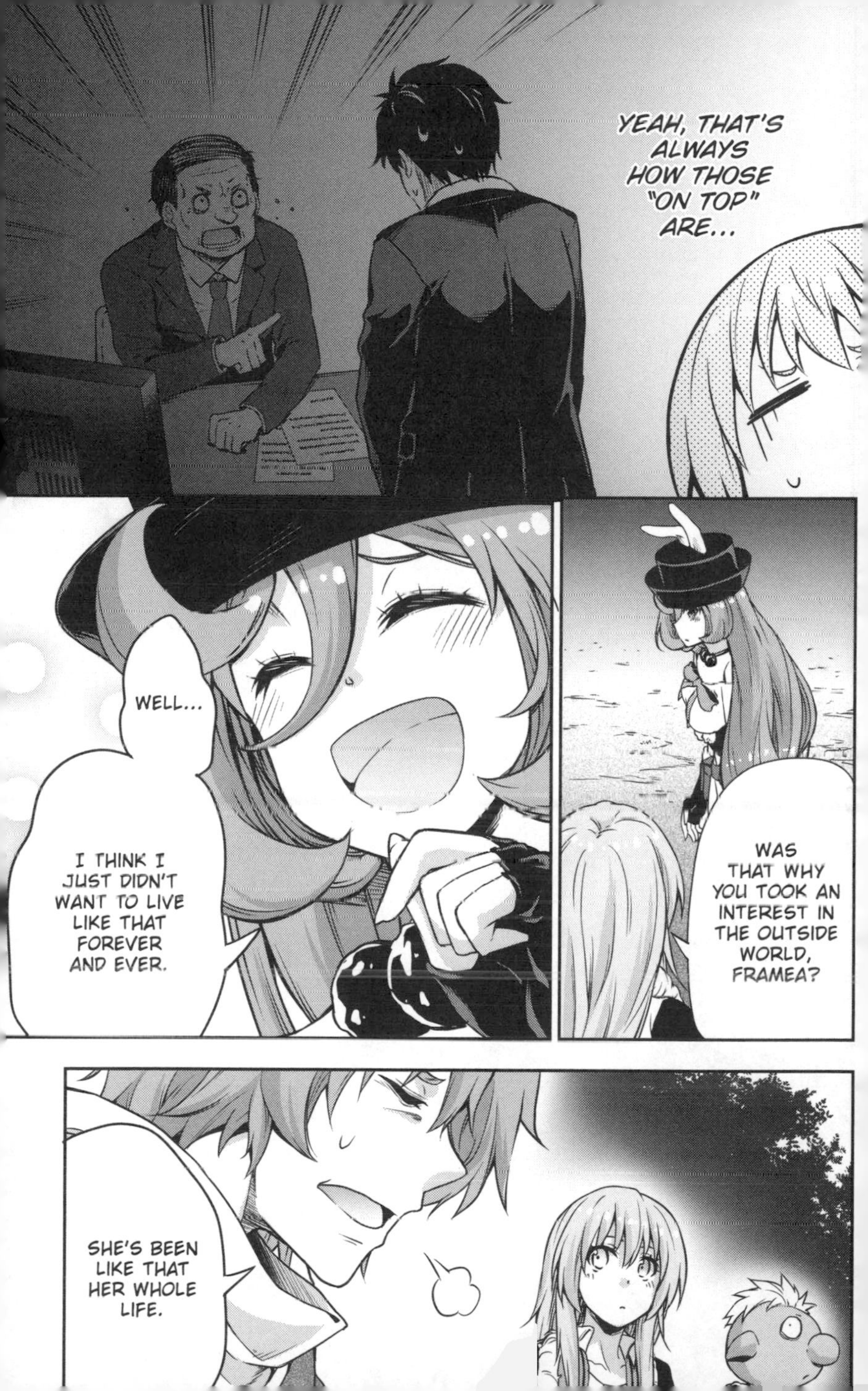
YEAH, THAT'S ALWAYS HOW THOSE "ON TOP" ARE...
WAS THAT WHY YOU TOOK AN INTEREST IN THE OUTSIDE WORLD, FRAMEA?
WELL...
I THINK I JUST DIDN'T WANT TO LIVE LIKE THAT FOREVER AND EVER.
SHE'S BEEN LIKE THAT HER WHOLE LIFE.

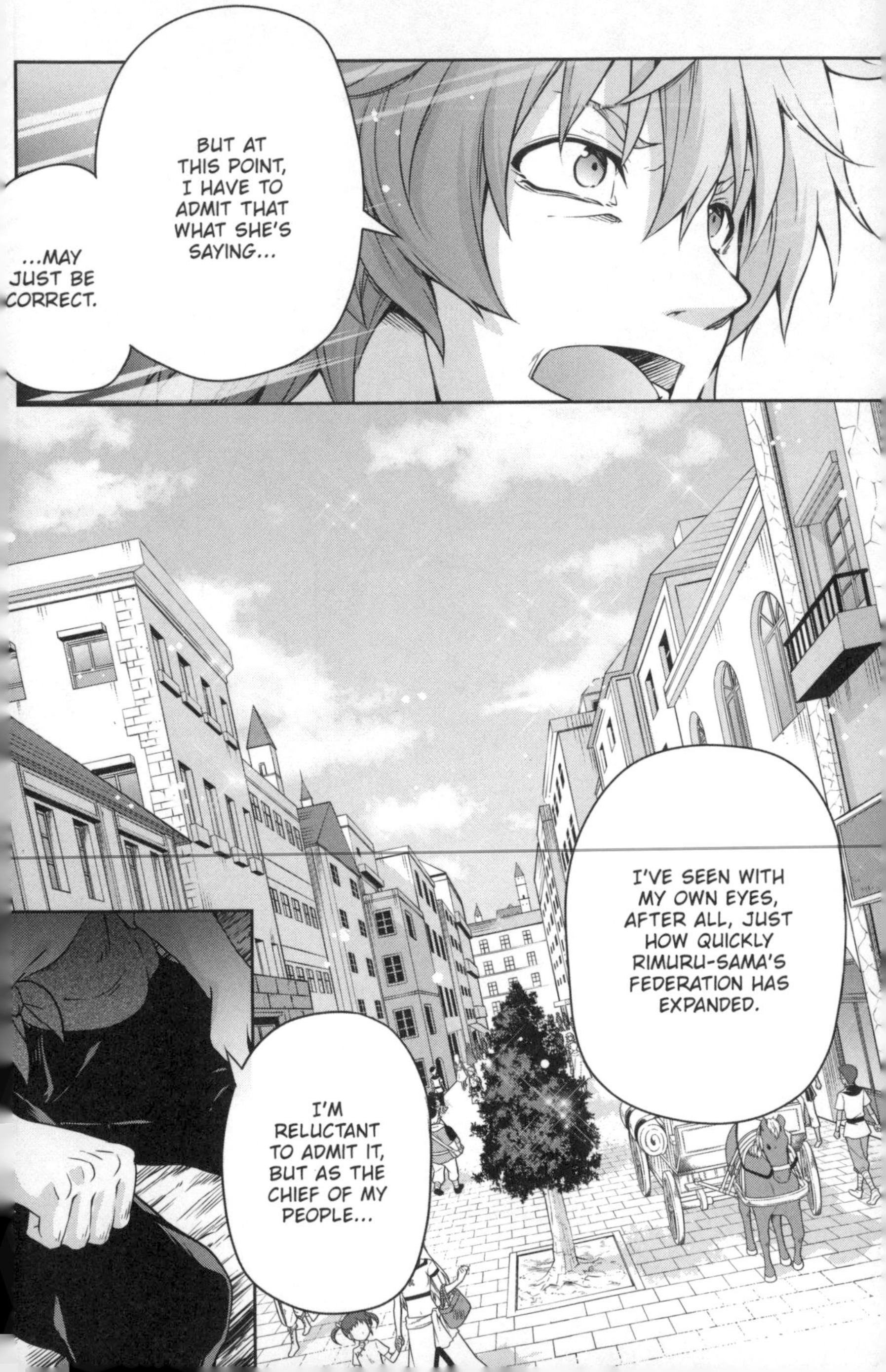
BUT AT THIS POINT, I HAVE TO ADMIT THAT WHAT SHE'S SAYING...
...MAY JUST BE CORRECT.
I'VE SEEN WITH MY OWN EYES, AFTER ALL, JUST HOW QUICKLY RIMURU-SAMA'S FEDERATION HAS EXPANDED.
I'M RELUCTANT TO ADMIT IT, BUT AS THE CHIEF OF MY PEOPLE...

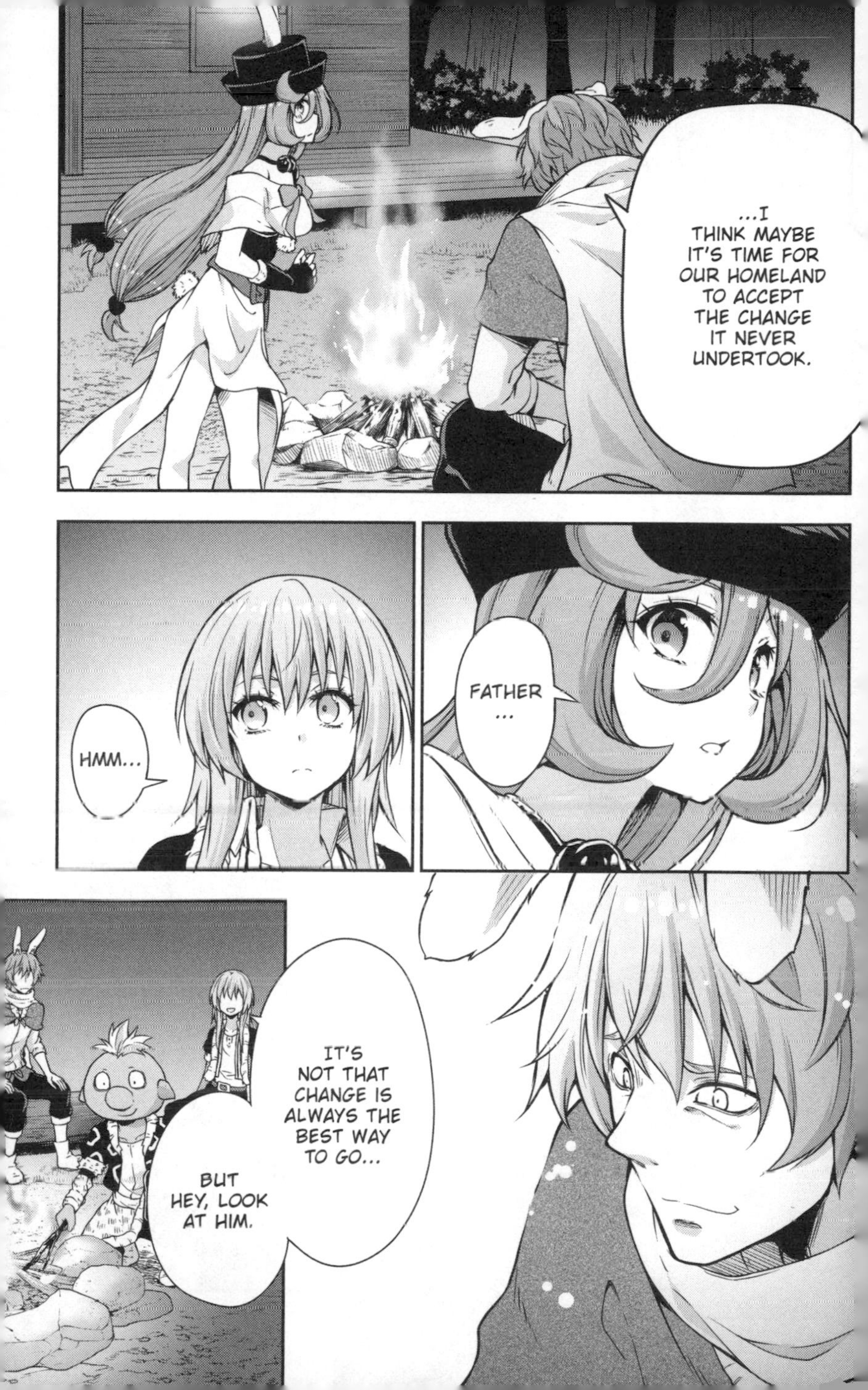
...I THINK MAYBE IT'S TIME FOR OUR HOMELAND TO ACCEPT THE CHANGE IT NEVER UNDERTOOK.
FATHER ...
HMM...
IT'S NOT THAT CHANGE IS ALWAYS THE BEST WAY TO GO...
BUT HEY, LOOK AT HIM.

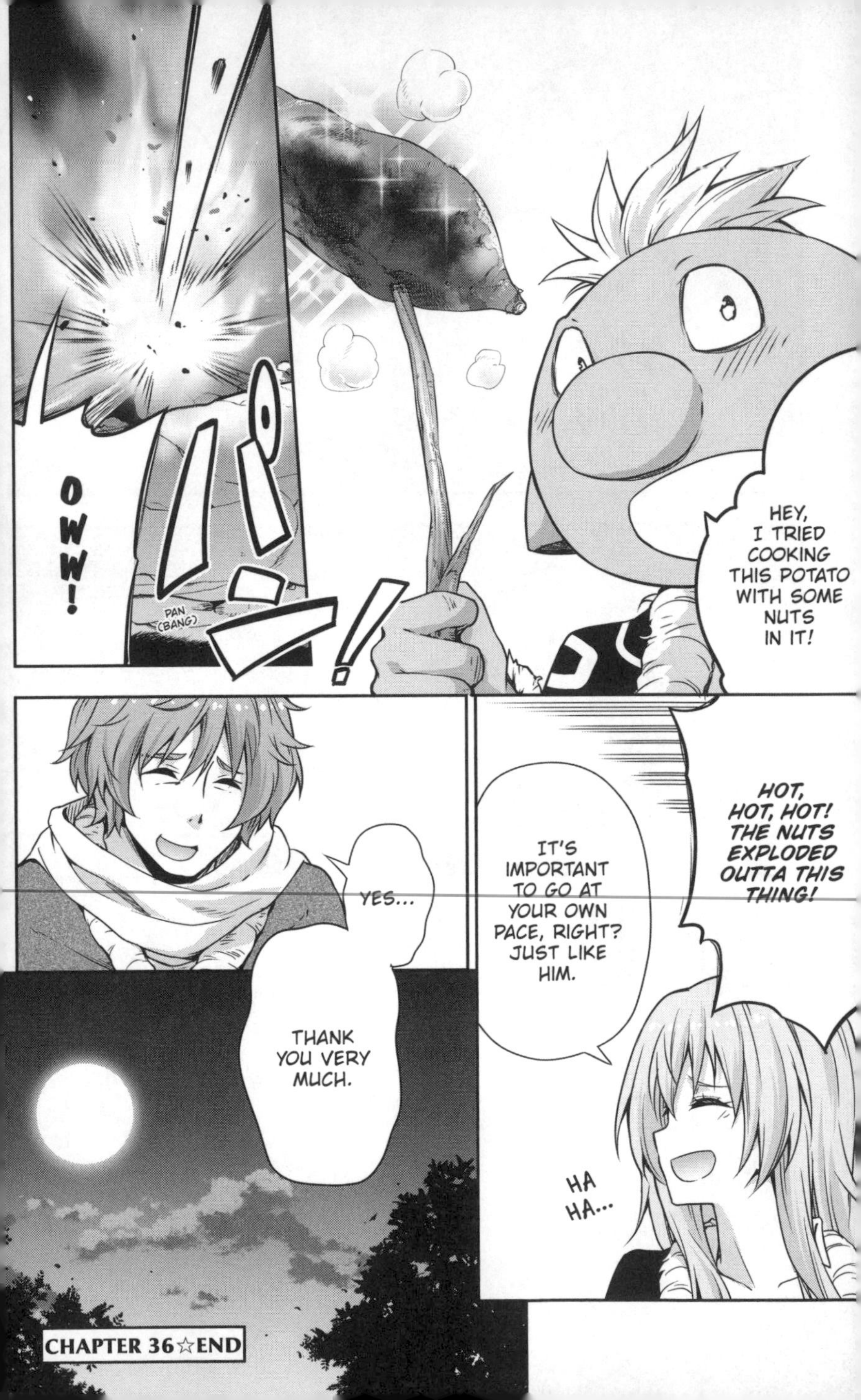
HEY, I TRIED COOKING THIS POTATO WITH SOME NUTS IN IT!
PAN (BANG)
OWW!
HOT, HOT, HOT! THE NUTS EXPLODED OUTTA THIS THING!
IT'S IMPORTANT TO GO AT YOUR OWN PACE, RIGHT? JUST LIKE HIM.
HA HA...
YES...
THANK YOU VERY MUCH.
CHAPTER 36☆END

That **Time I Got**
Rèincarnated
as SLIME
a
The Ways of the Monster Nation

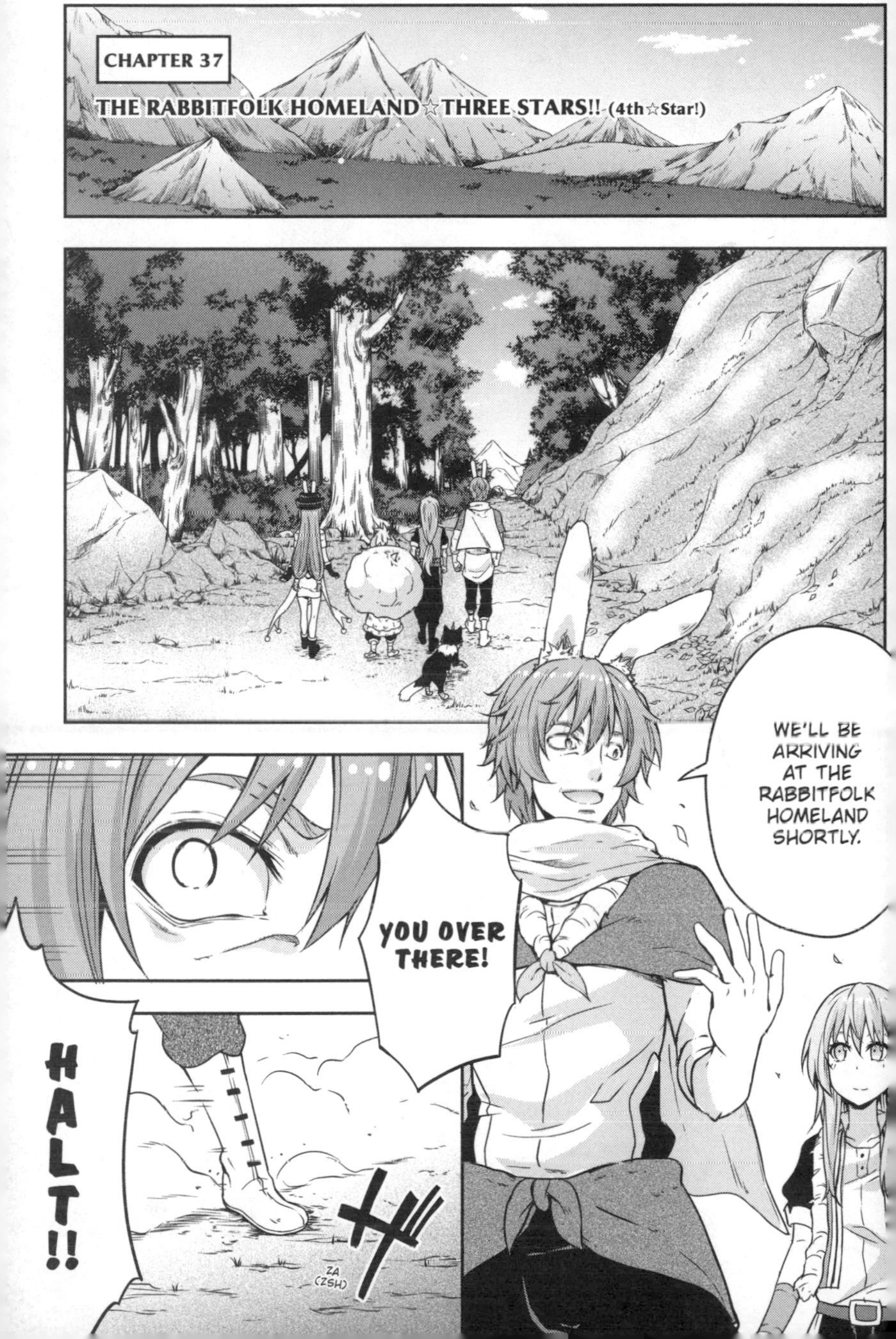
CHAPTER 37
THE RABBITFOLK HOMELAND☆THREE STARS!! (4th☆Star!)
WE'LL BE ARRIVING AT THE RABBITFOLK HOMELAND SHORTLY.
YOU OVER THERE!
HALT!!
ZA (ZSH)

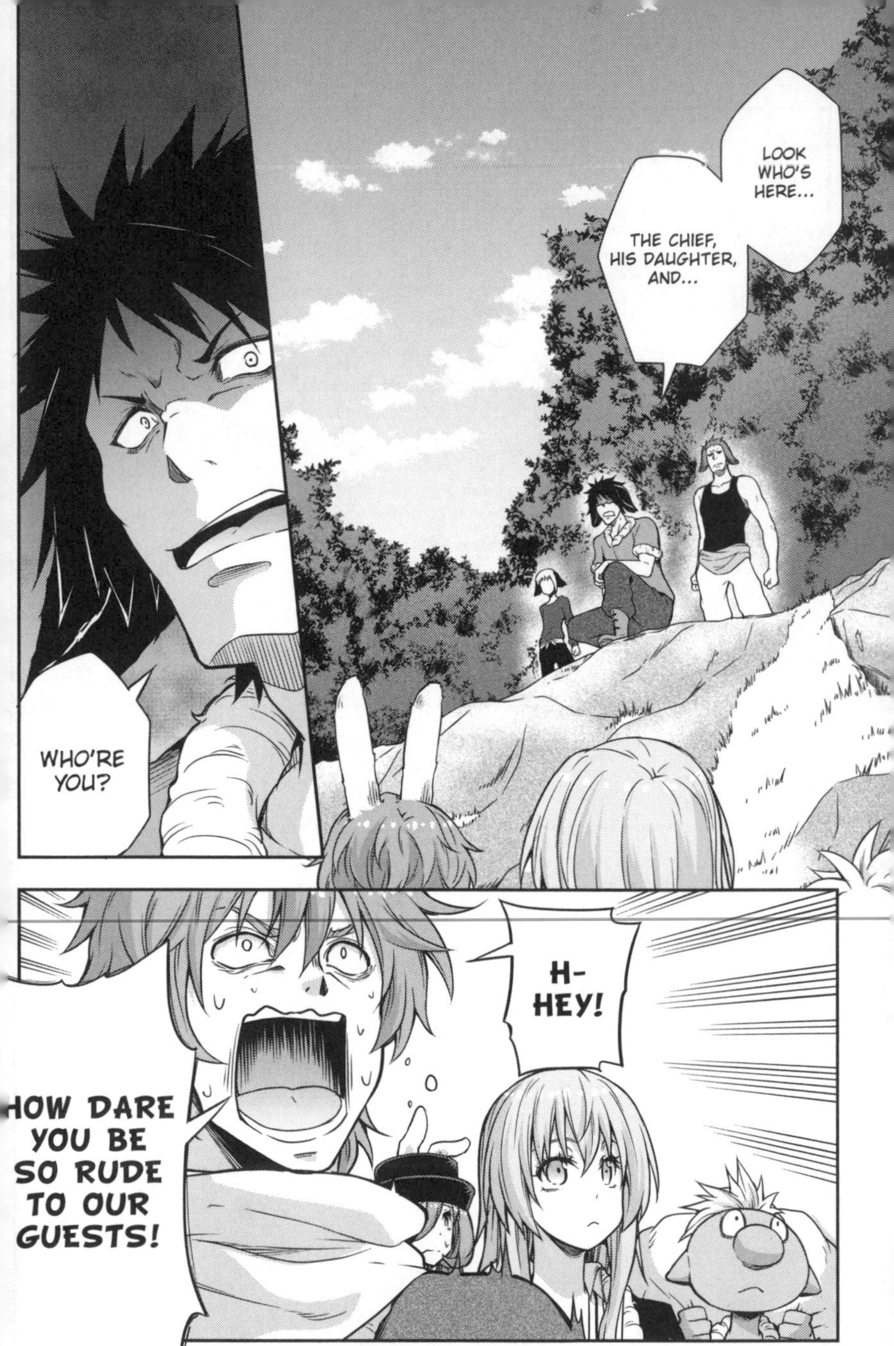
LOOK WHO'S HERE...
THE CHIEF, HIS DAUGHTER, AND...
WHO'RE YOU?
H-HEY!
HOW DARE YOU BE SO RUDE TO OUR GUESTS!

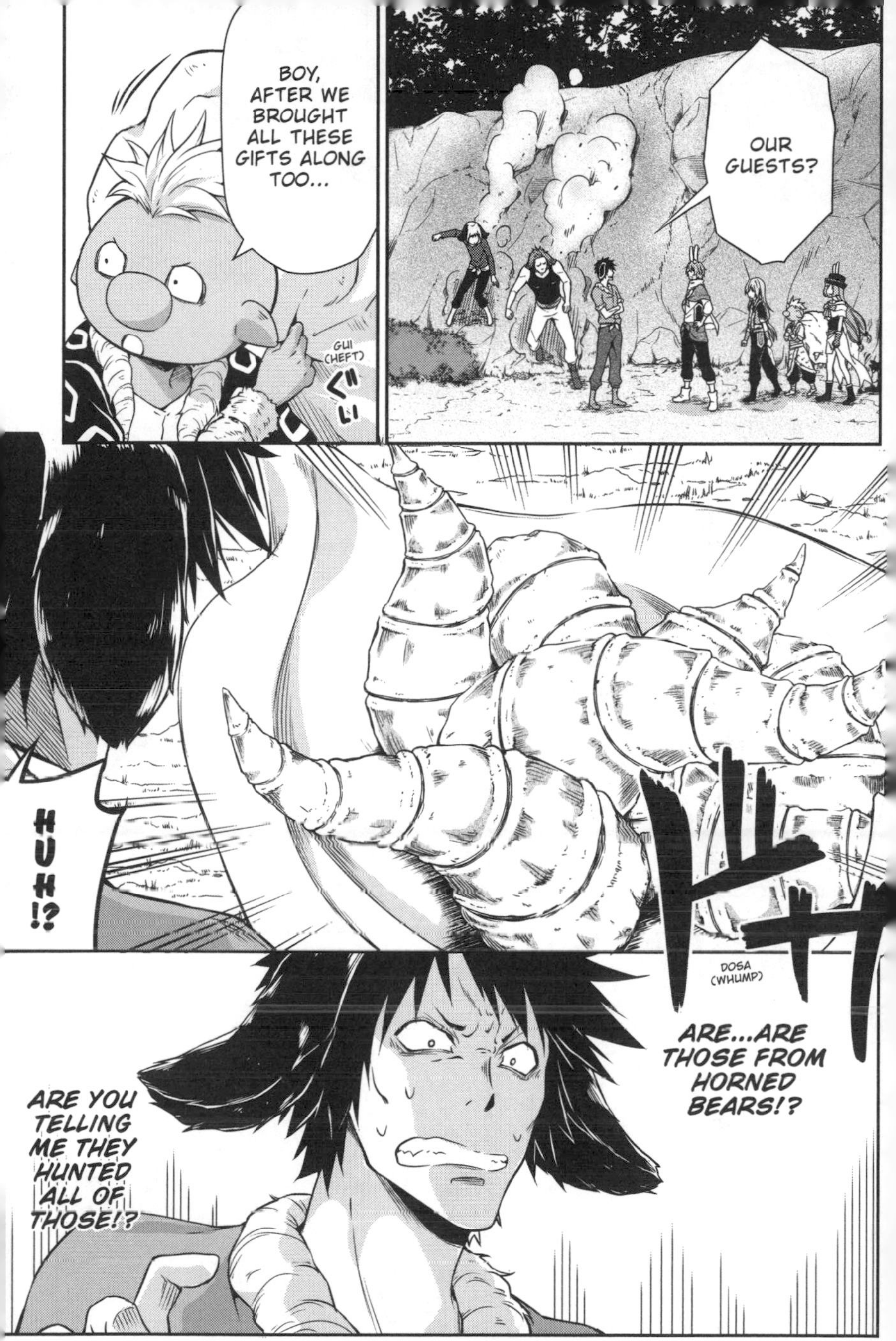
OUR GUESTS?
BOY, AFTER WE BROUGHT ALL THESE GIFTS ALONG TOO...
ぐい
GUI (HEFT)
ドサッ
DOSA (WHUMP)
HUH!?
ARE...ARE THOSE FROM HORNED BEARS!?
ARE YOU TELLING ME THEY HUNTED ALL OF THOSE!?

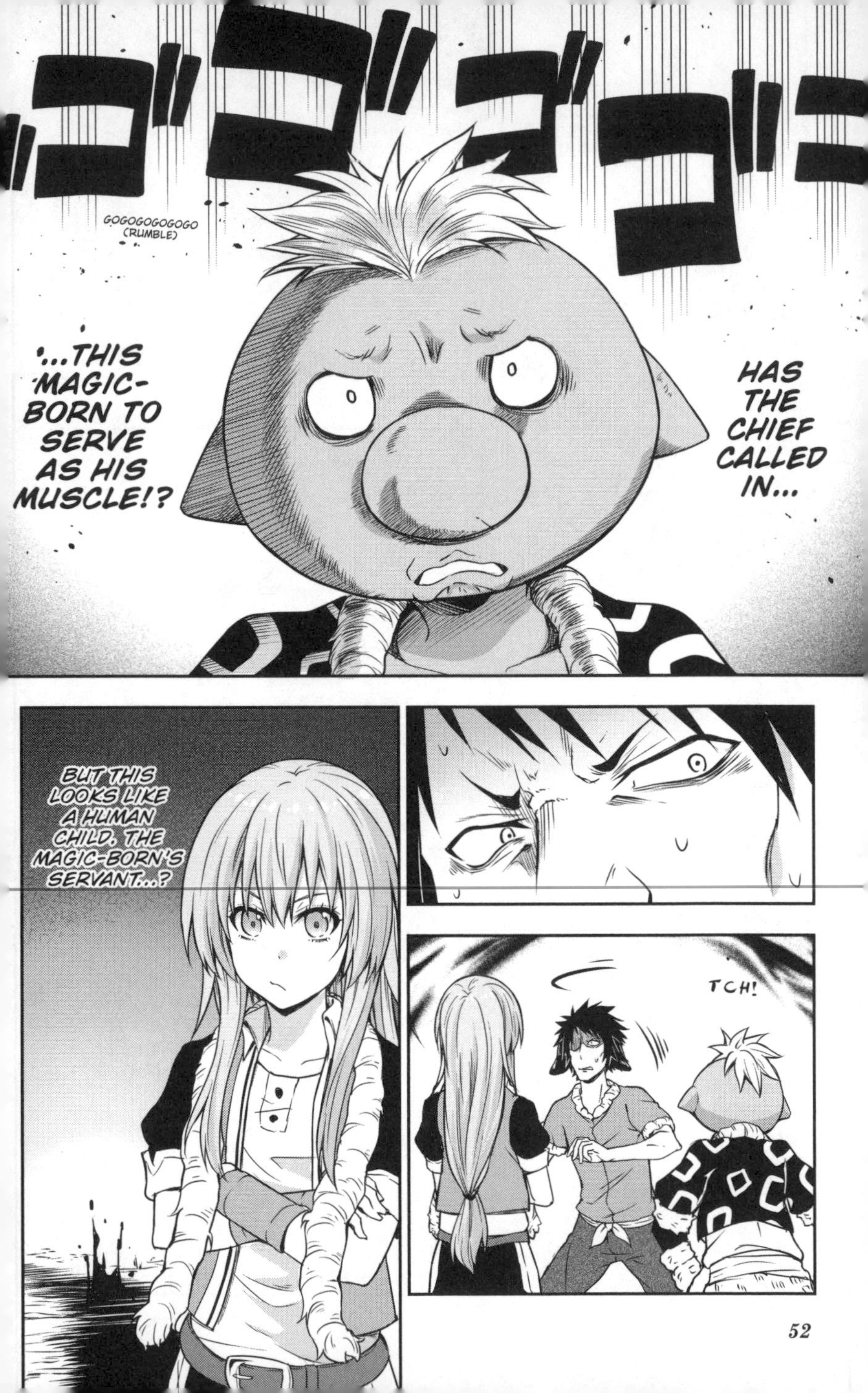
GOGOGOGOGOGO (RUMBLE)
HAS THE CHIEF CALLED IN...
...THIS MAGIC-BORN TO SERVE AS HIS MUSCLE!?
TCH!
BUT THIS LOOKS LIKE A HUMAN CHILD. THE MAGIC-BORN'S SERVANT...?

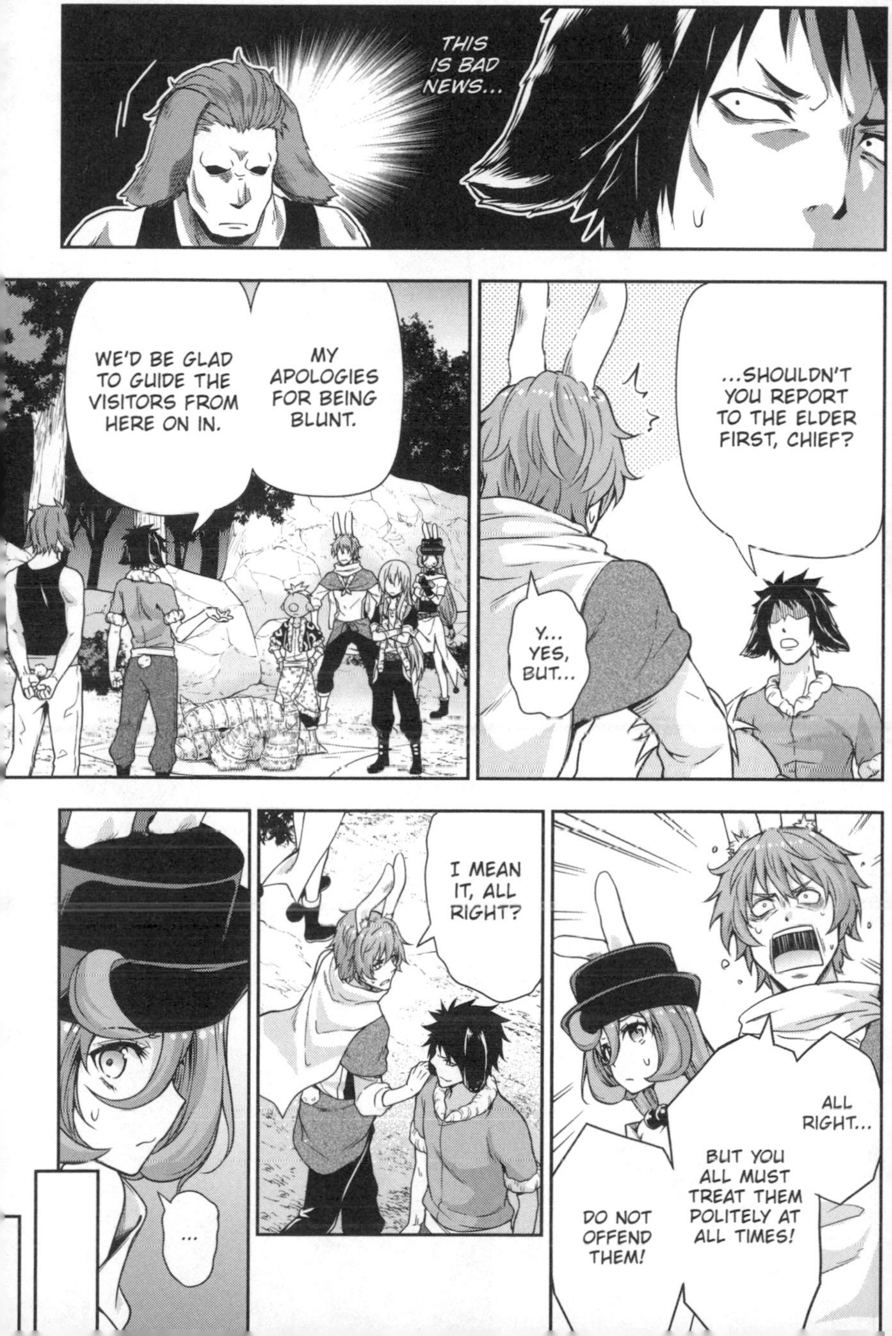
THIS IS BAD NEWS...
...SHOULDN'T YOU REPORT TO THE ELDER FIRST, CHIEF?
Y... YES, BUT...
MY APOLOGIES FOR BEING BLUNT.
WE'D BE GLAD TO GUIDE THE VISITORS FROM HERE ON IN.
ALL RIGHT...
BUT YOU ALL MUST TREAT THEM POLITELY AT ALL TIMES!
DO NOT OFFEND THEM!
I MEAN IT, ALL RIGHT?
...

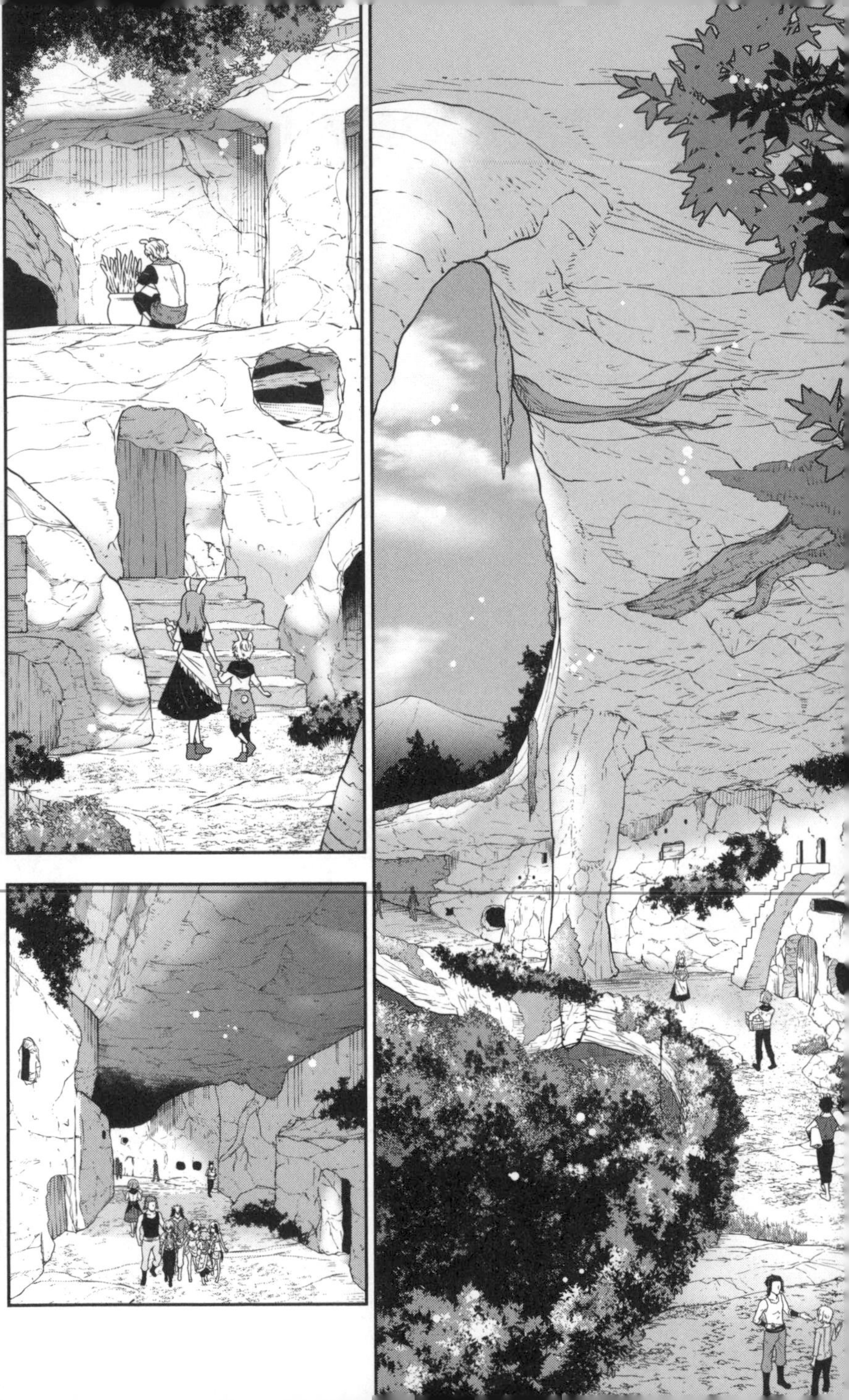

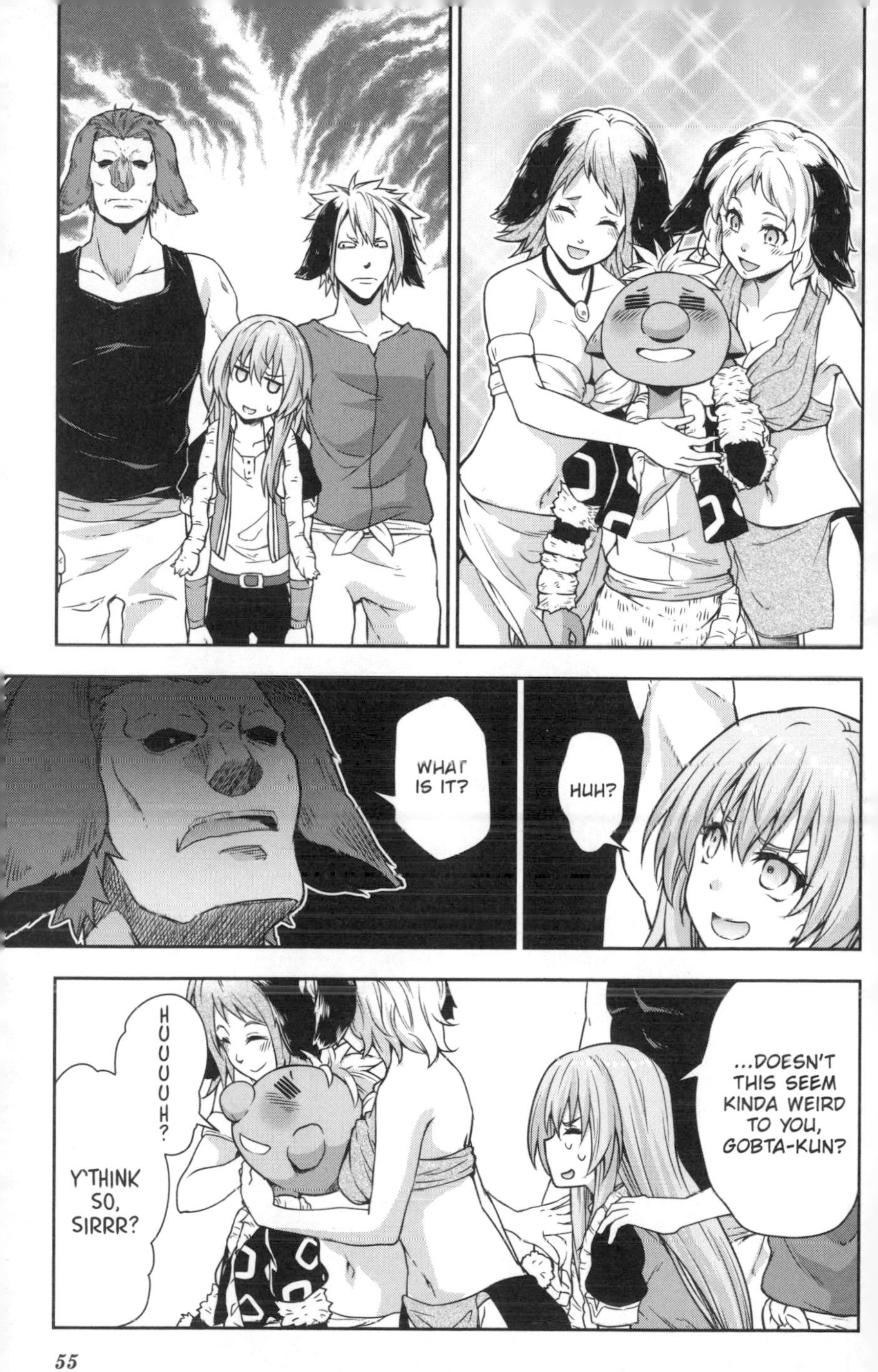
HUH?
WHAT IS IT?
...DOESN'T THIS SEEM KINDA WEIRD TO YOU, GOBTA-KUN?
HUUUUH?
Y'THINK SO, SIRRR?

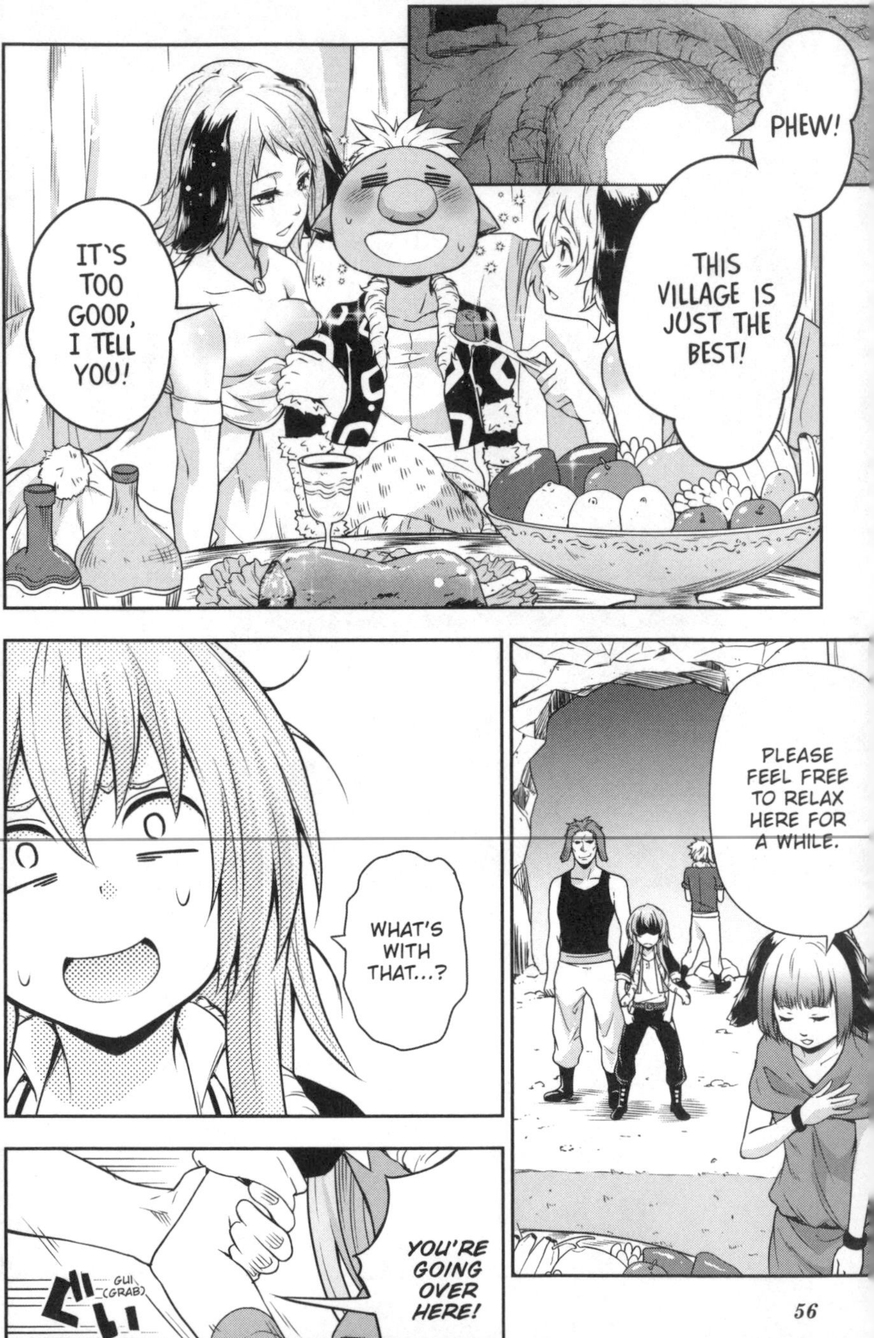
PHEW!
THIS VILLAGE IS JUST THE BEST!
IT'S TOO GOOD, I TELL YOU!
PLEASE FEEL FREE TO RELAX HERE FOR A WHILE.
WHAT'S WITH THAT...?
YOU'RE GOING OVER HERE!
GUI (GRAB)

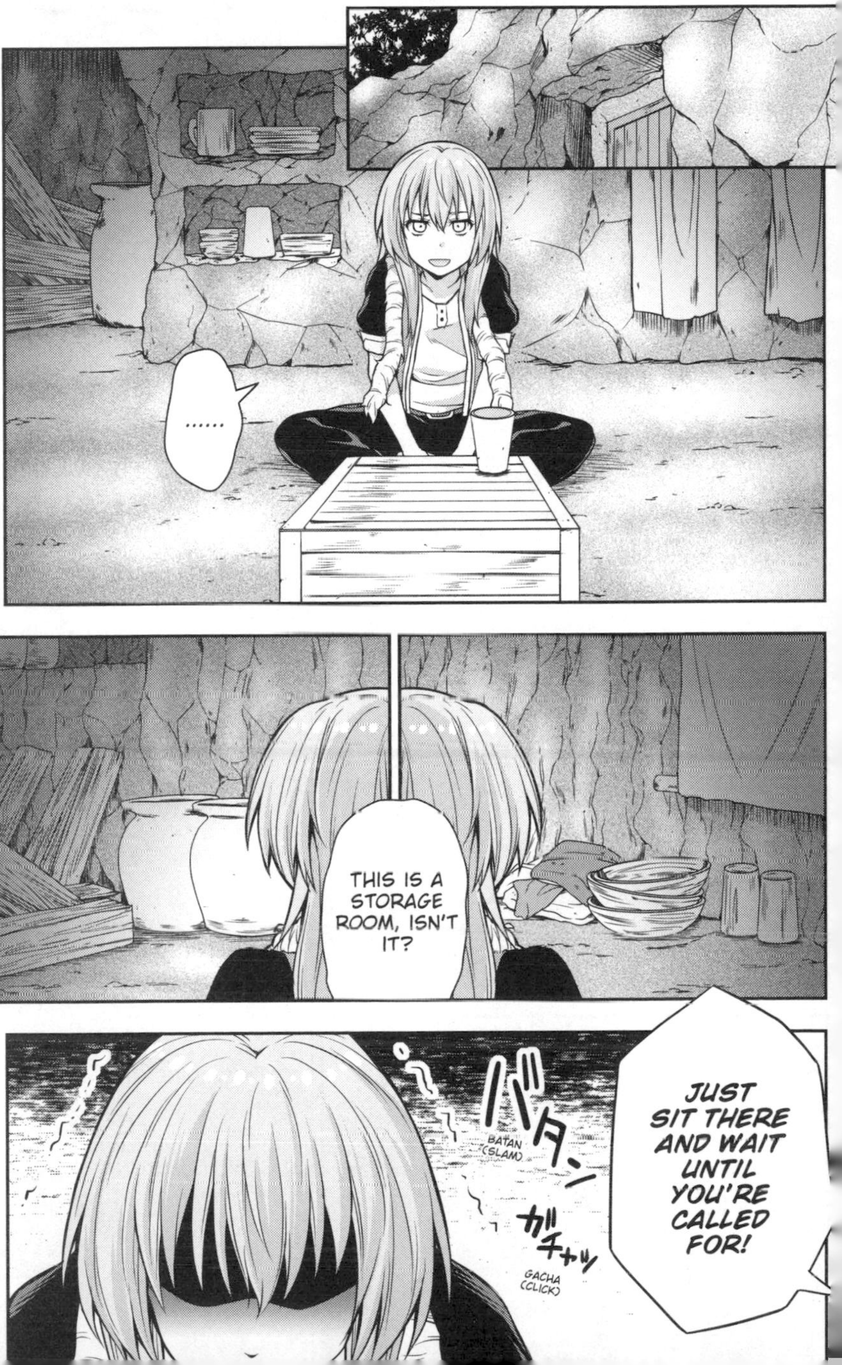
......
THIS IS A STORAGE ROOM, ISN'T IT?
JUST SIT THERE AND WAIT UNTIL YOU'RE CALLED FOR!
バタン
BATAN (SLAM)
ガチャッ
GACHA (CLICK)

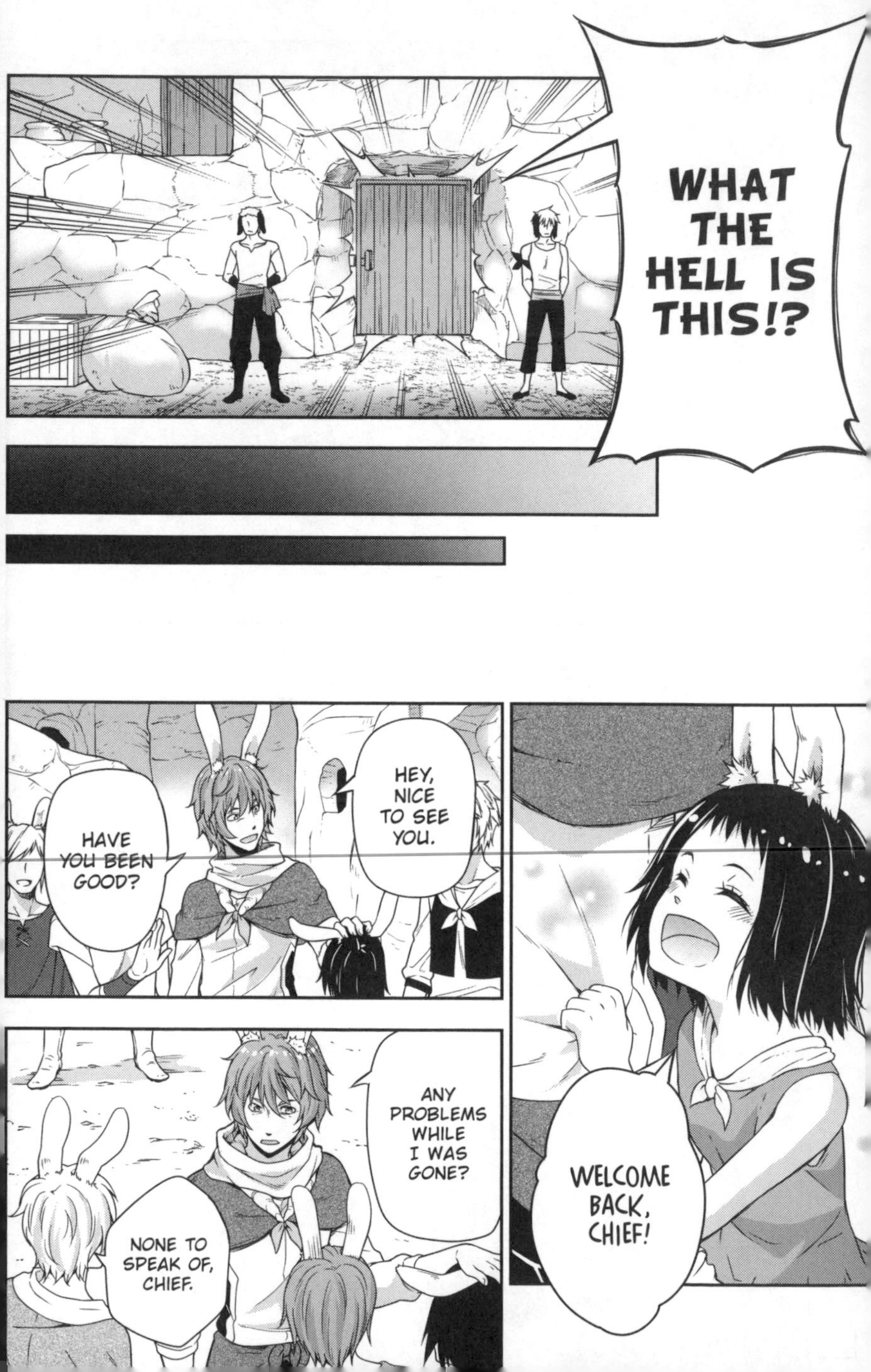
WHAT THE HELL IS THIS!?
WELCOME BACK, CHIEF!
HEY, NICE TO SEE YOU.
HAVE YOU BEEN GOOD?
ANY PROBLEMS WHILE I WAS GONE?
NONE TO SPEAK OF, CHIEF.

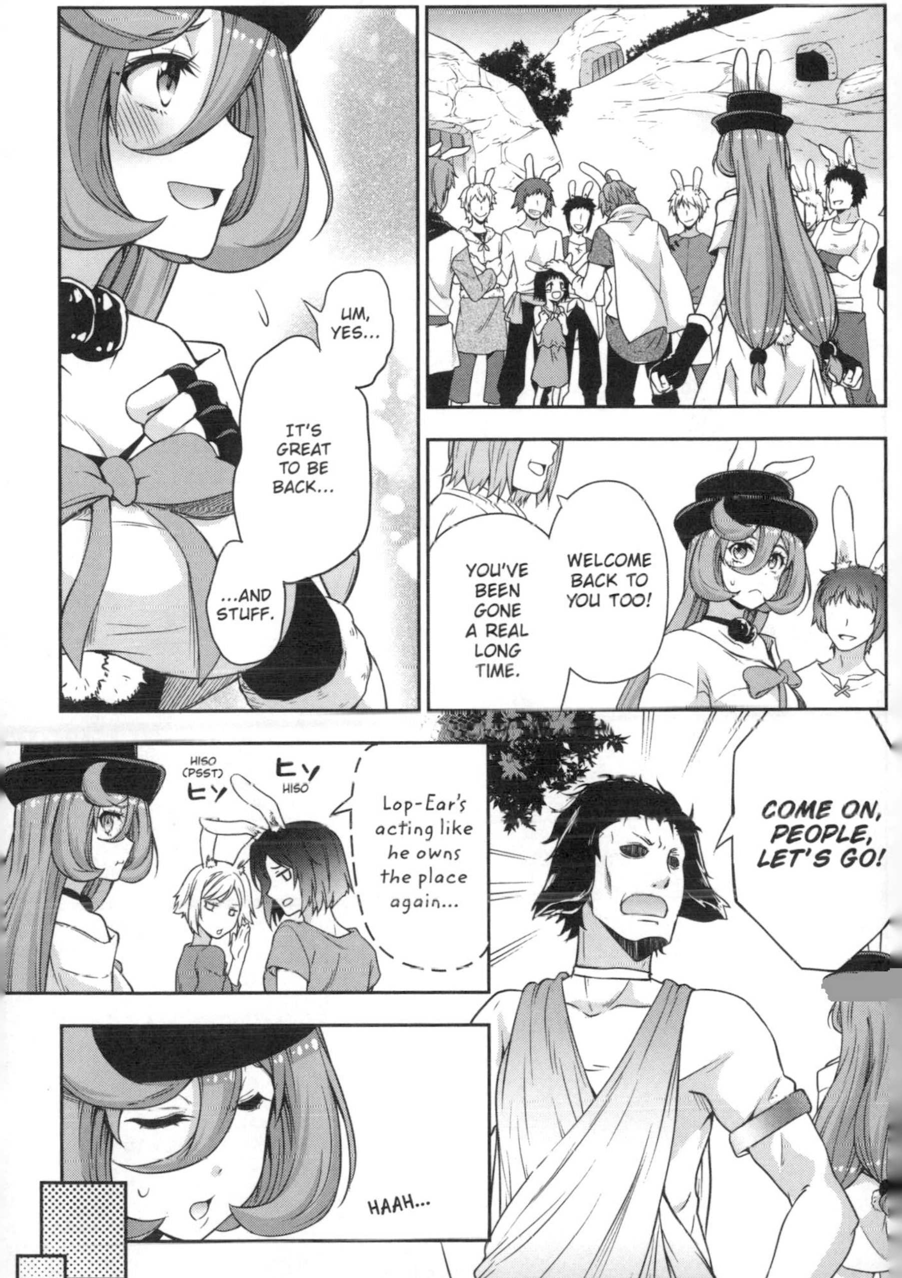
WELCOME BACK TO YOU TOO!
YOU'VE BEEN GONE A REAL LONG TIME.
UM, YES...
IT'S GREAT TO BE BACK...
...AND STUFF.
COME ON, PEOPLE, LET'S GO!
ヒソ HISO
ヒソ HISO (PSST)
Lop-Ear's acting like he owns the place again...
HAAH...

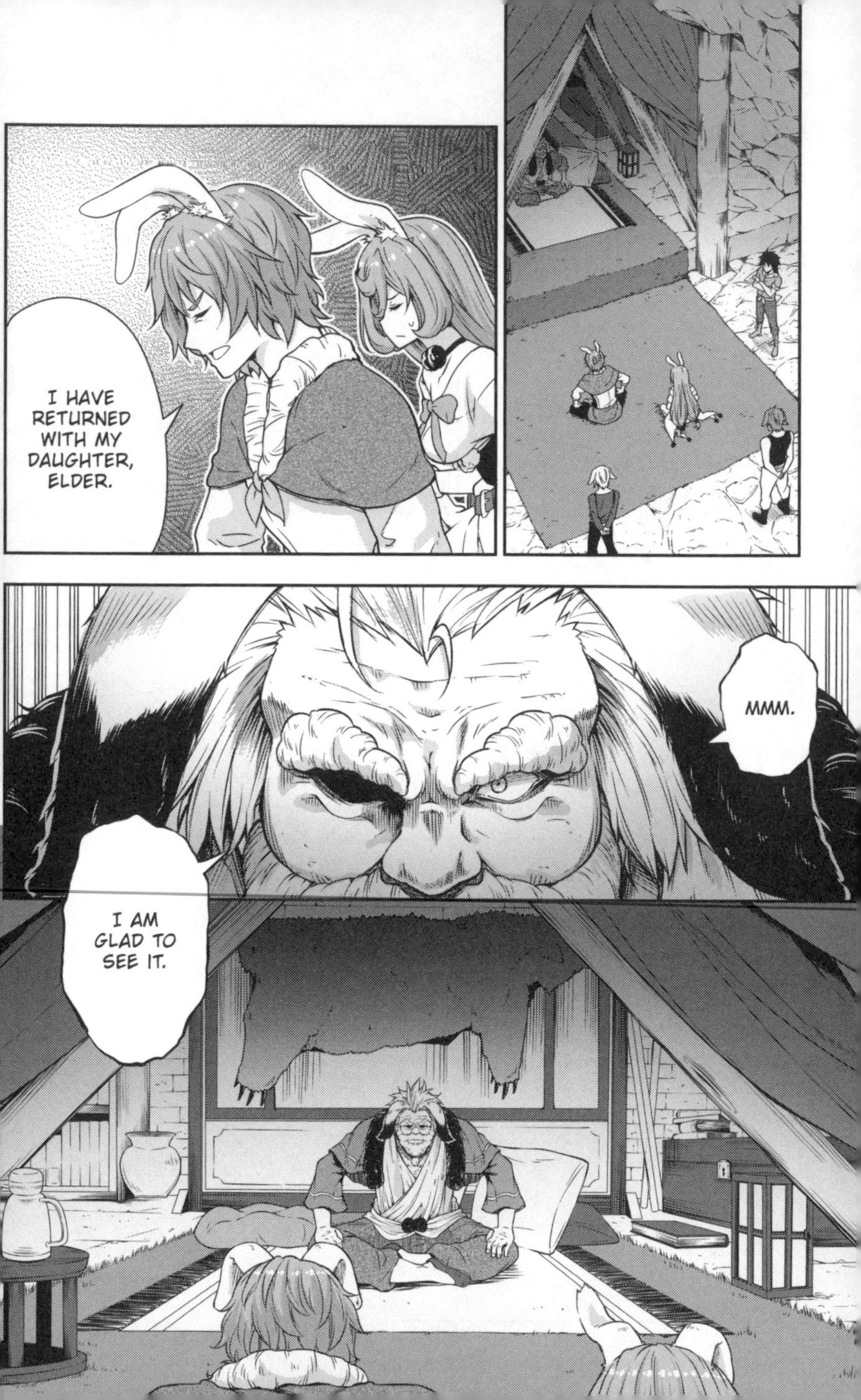
I HAVE RETURNED WITH MY DAUGHTER, ELDER.
MMM.
I AM GLAD TO SEE IT.

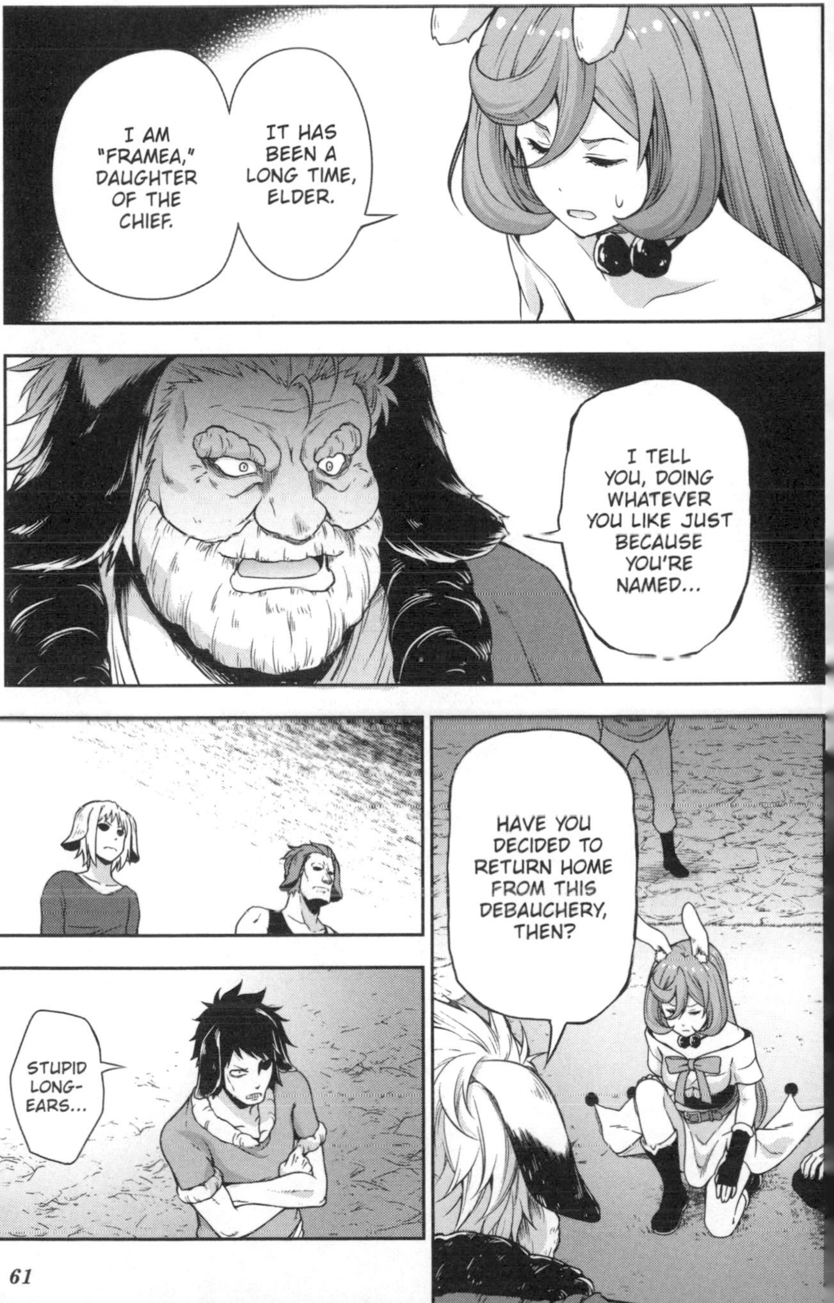
IT HAS BEEN A LONG TIME, ELDER.
I AM "FRAMEA," DAUGHTER OF THE CHIEF.
I TELL YOU, DOING WHATEVER YOU LIKE JUST BECAUSE YOU'RE NAMED...
HAVE YOU DECIDED TO RETURN HOME FROM THIS DEBAUCHERY, THEN?
STUPID LONG-EARS...

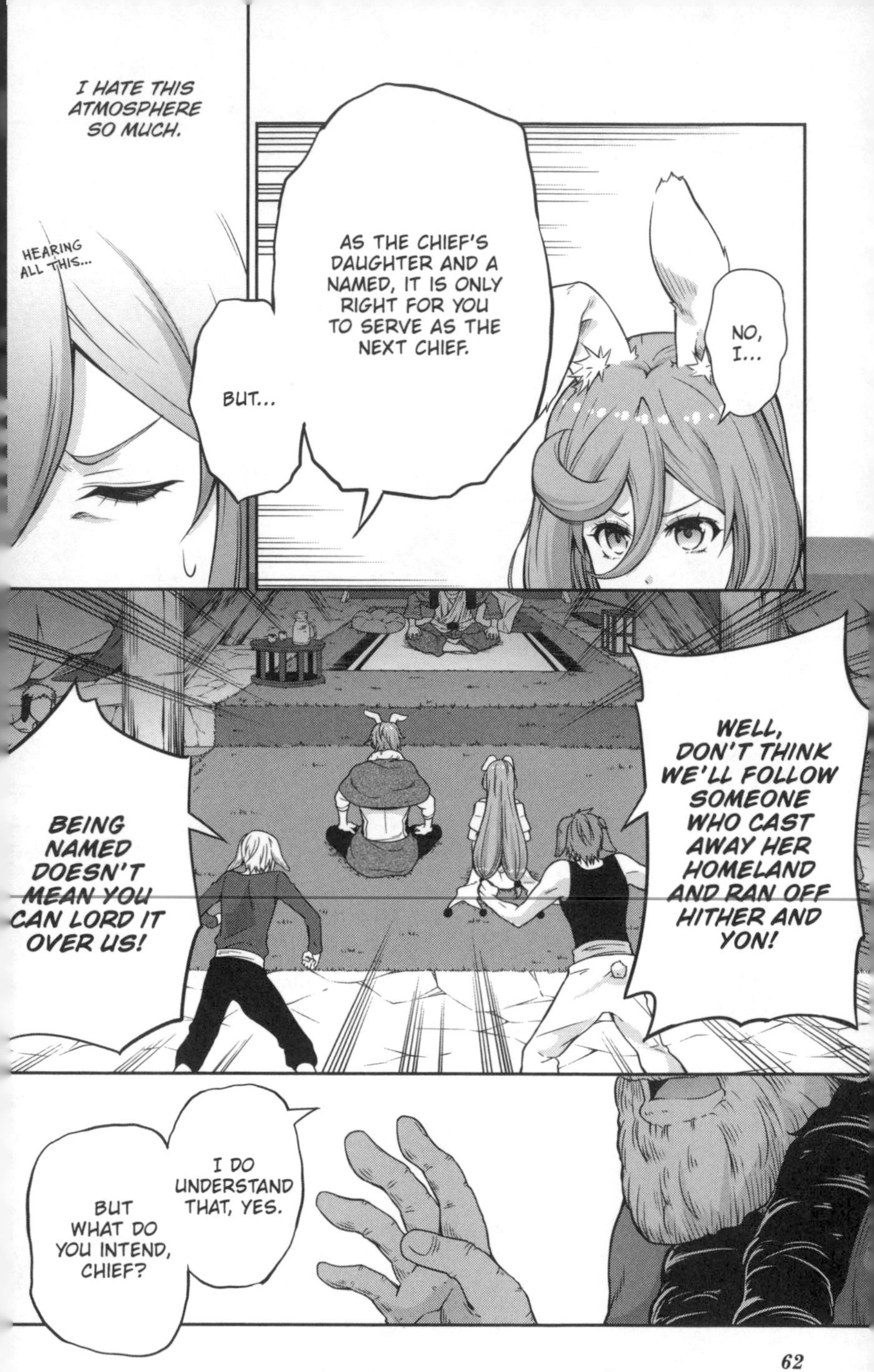
AS THE CHIEF'S DAUGHTER AND A NAMED, IT IS ONLY RIGHT FOR YOU TO SERVE AS THE NEXT CHIEF.
NO, I...
BUT...
I HATE THIS ATMOSPHERE SO MUCH.
HEARING ALL THIS...
WELL, DON'T THINK WE'LL FOLLOW SOMEONE WHO CAST AWAY HER HOMELAND AND RAN OFF HITHER AND YON!
BEING NAMED DOESN'T MEAN YOU CAN LORD IT OVER US!
I DO UNDERSTAND THAT, YES.
BUT WHAT DO YOU INTEND, CHIEF?

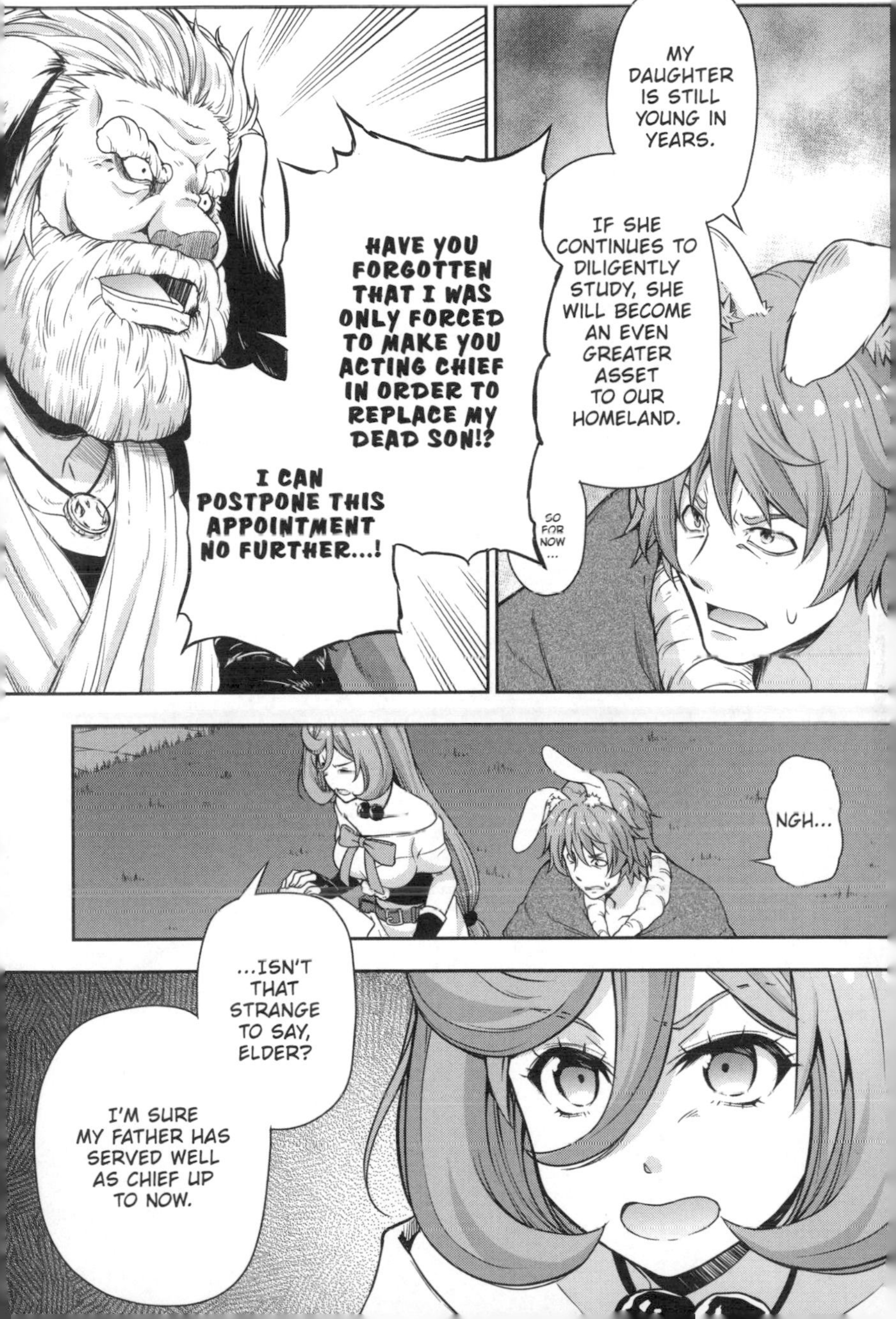
MY DAUGHTER IS STILL YOUNG IN YEARS.
IF SHE CONTINUES TO DILIGENTLY STUDY, SHE WILL BECOME AN EVEN GREATER ASSET TO OUR HOMELAND.
SO FOR NOW...
HAVE YOU FORGOTTEN THAT I WAS ONLY FORCED TO MAKE YOU ACTING CHIEF IN ORDER TO REPLACE MY DEAD SON!?
I CAN POSTPONE THIS APPOINTMENT NO FURTHER...!
NGH...
...ISN'T THAT STRANGE TO SAY, ELDER?
I'M SURE MY FATHER HAS SERVED WELL AS CHIEF UP TO NOW.

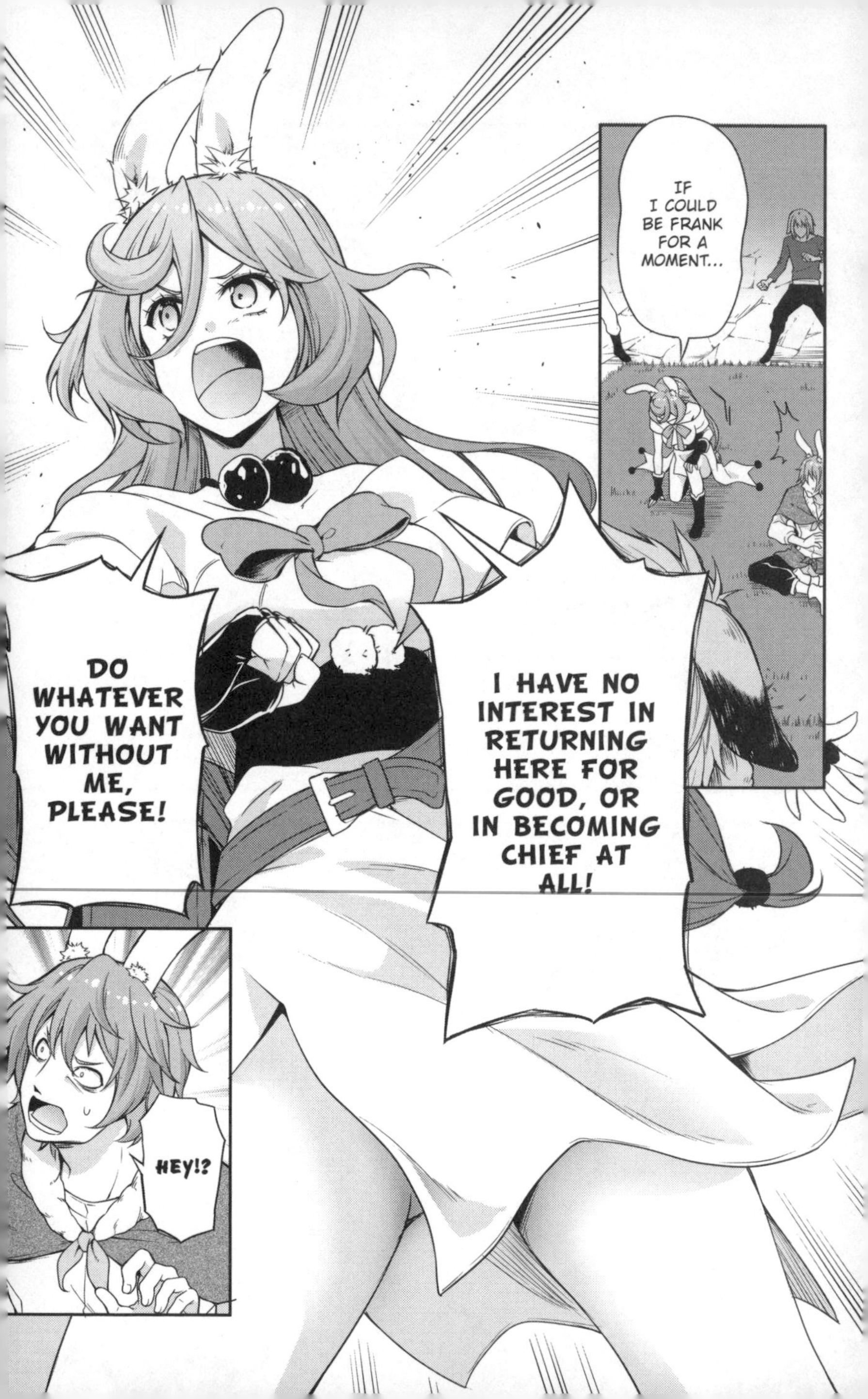
IF I COULD BE FRANK FOR A MOMENT...
I HAVE NO INTEREST IN RETURNING HERE FOR GOOD, OR IN BECOMING CHIEF AT ALL!
DO WHATEVER YOU WANT WITHOUT ME, PLEASE!
HEY!?

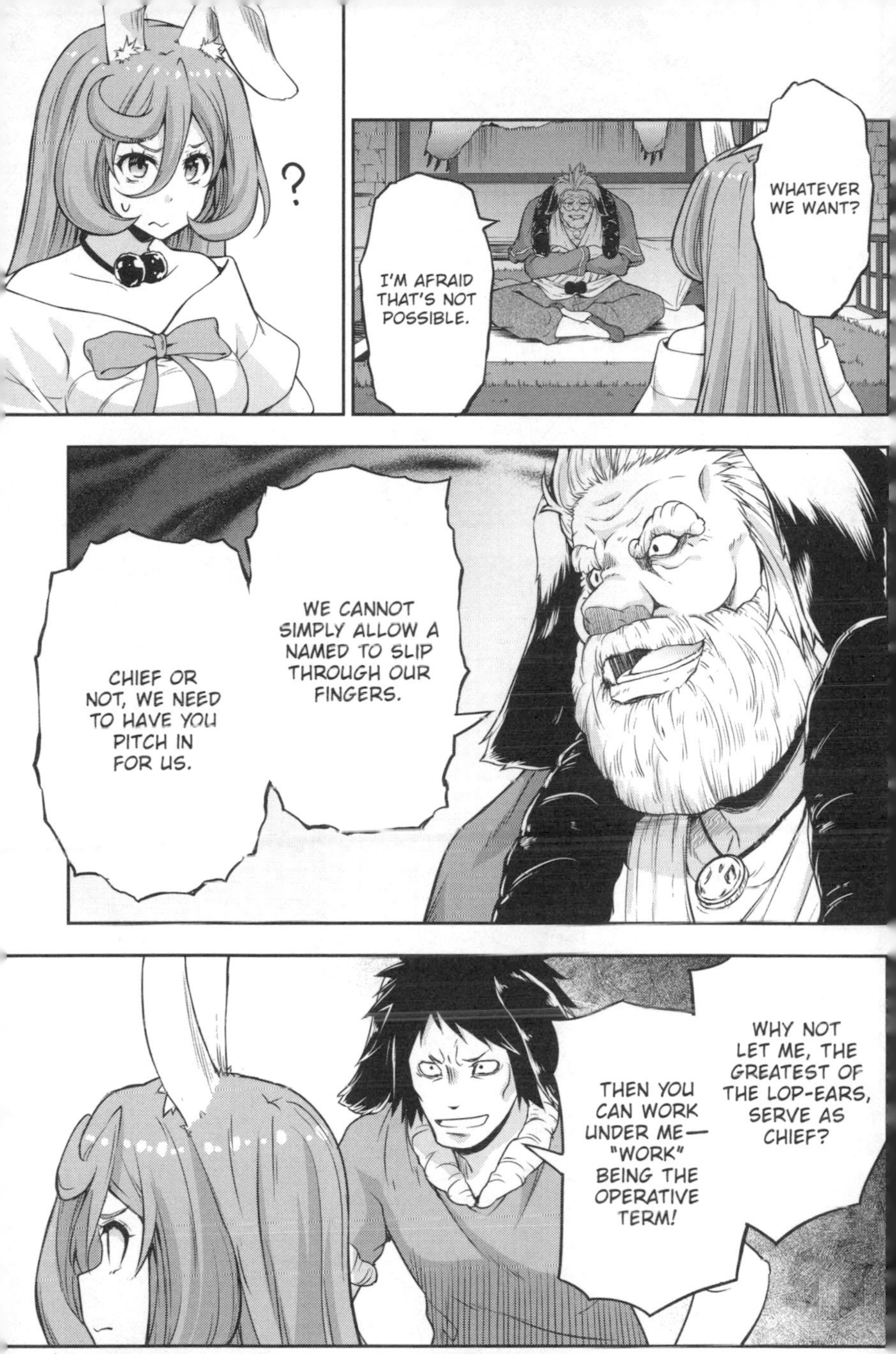
WHATEVER WE WANT?
I'M AFRAID THAT'S NOT POSSIBLE.
?
WE CANNOT SIMPLY ALLOW A NAMED TO SLIP THROUGH OUR FINGERS.
CHIEF OR NOT, WE NEED TO HAVE YOU PITCH IN FOR US.
WHY NOT LET ME, THE GREATEST OF THE LOP-EARS, SERVE AS CHIEF?
THEN YOU CAN WORK UNDER ME— "WORK" BEING THE OPERATIVE TERM!

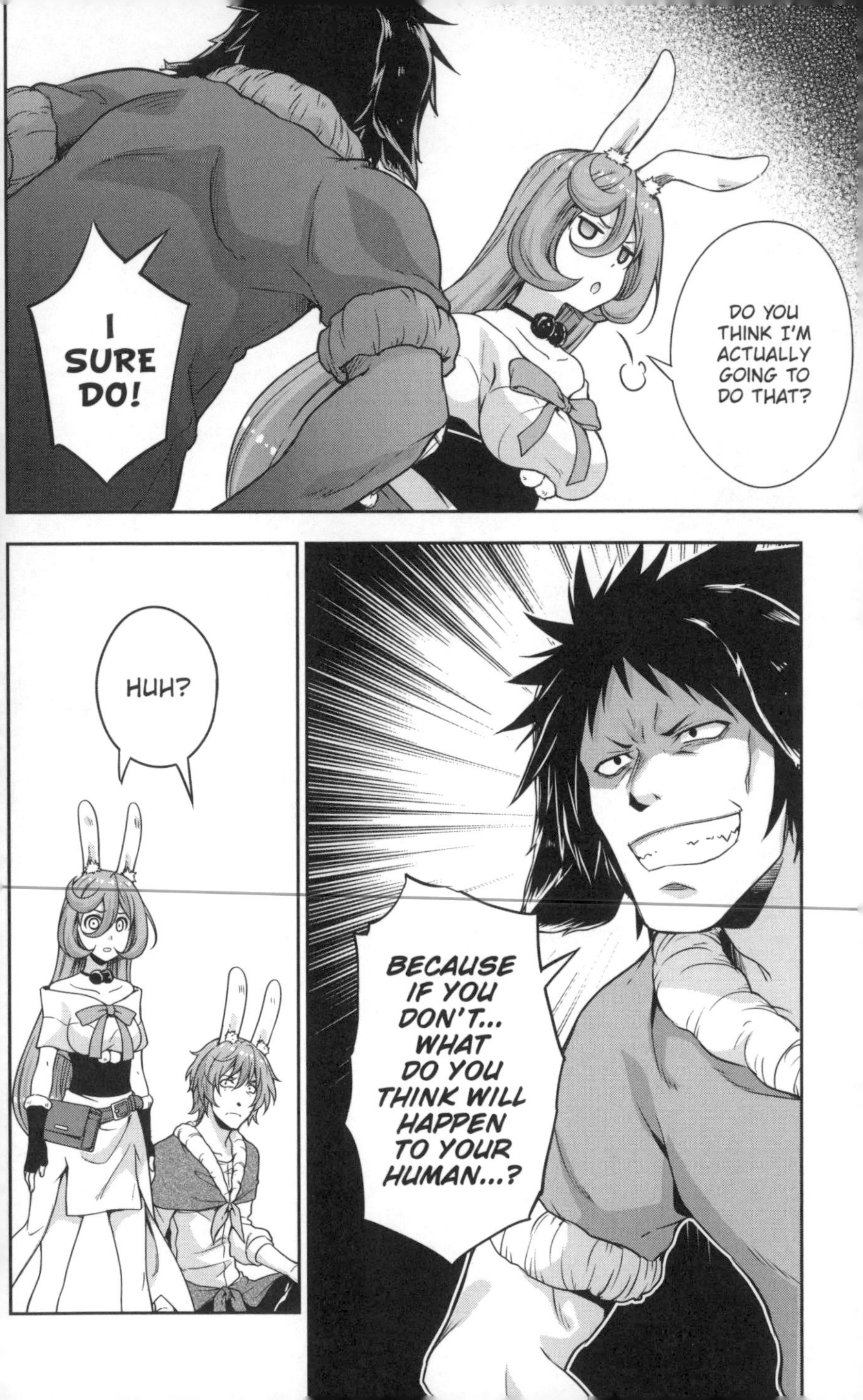
DO YOU THINK I'M ACTUALLY GOING TO DO THAT?
I SURE DO!
BECAUSE IF YOU DON'T... WHAT DO YOU THINK WILL HAPPEN TO YOUR HUMAN...?
HUH?

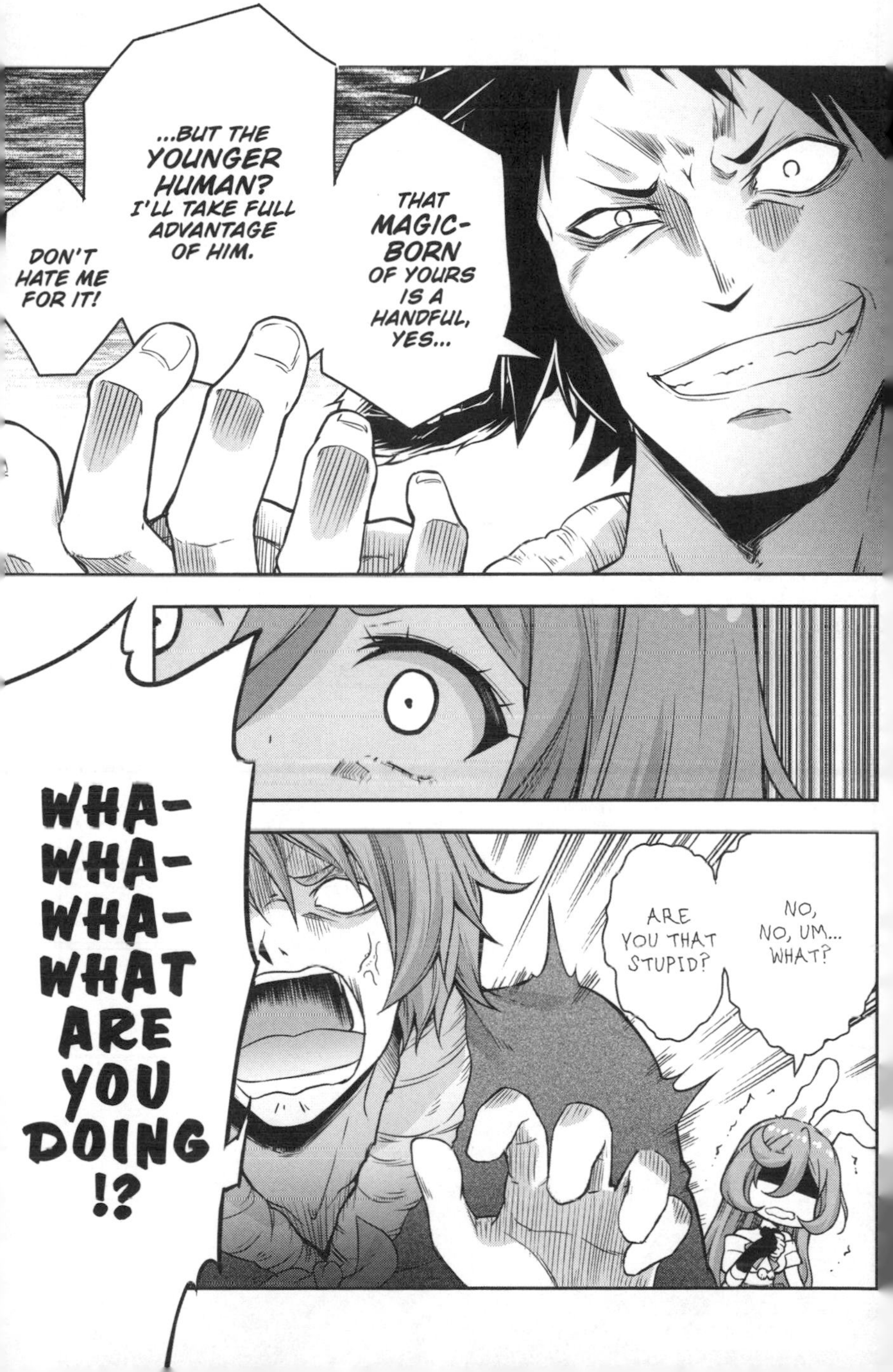
THAT MAGIC-BORN OF YOURS IS A HANDFUL, YES...
...BUT THE YOUNGER HUMAN? I'LL TAKE FULL ADVANTAGE OF HIM.
DON'T HATE ME FOR IT!
WHA-WHA-WHA-WHAT ARE YOU DOING!?
NO, NO, UM... WHAT?
ARE YOU THAT STUPID?

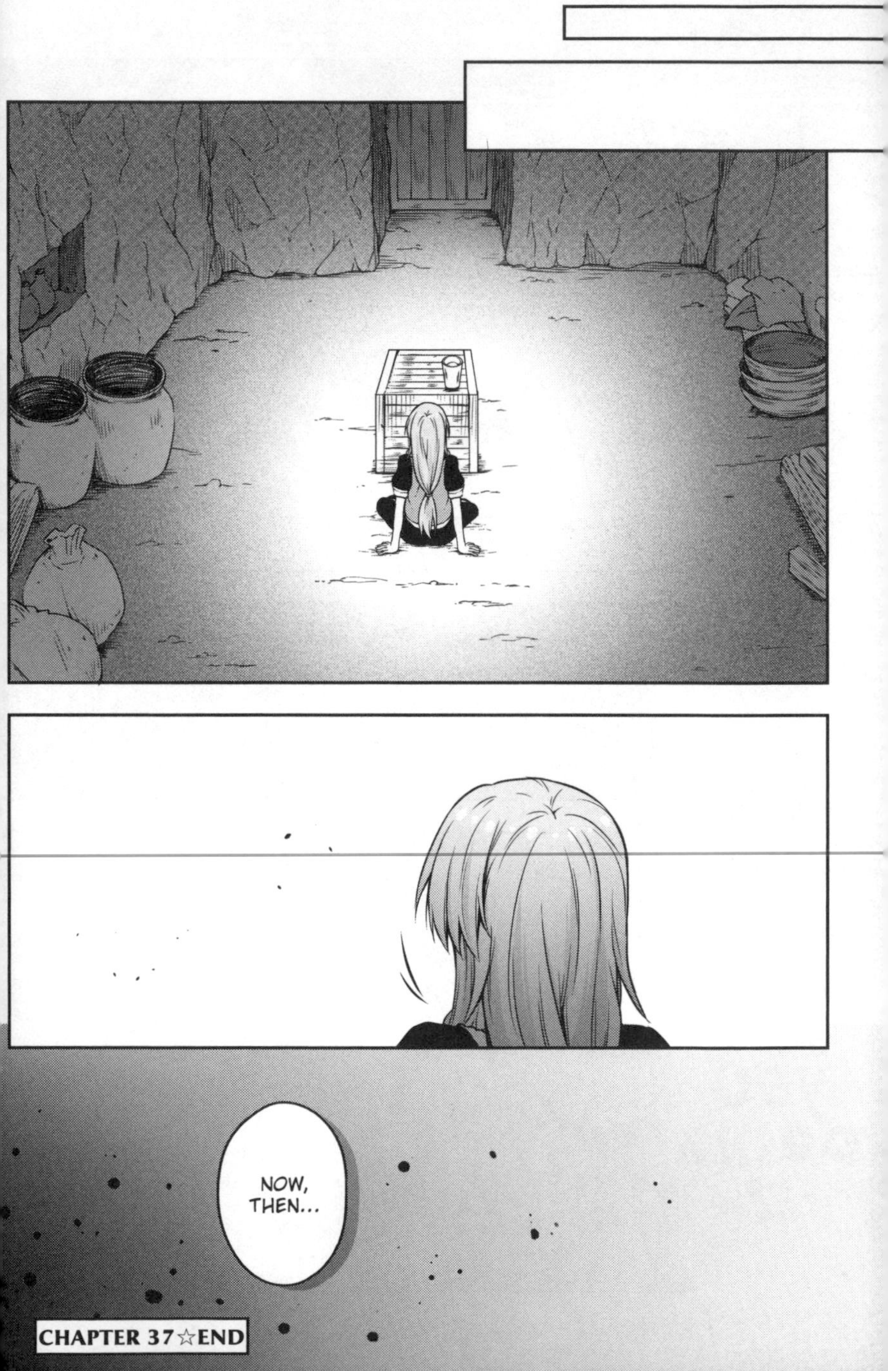
NOW, THEN...
CHAPTER 37☆END

That Time I Got Reìncarnated as a SLIME

The Ways of the Monster Nation

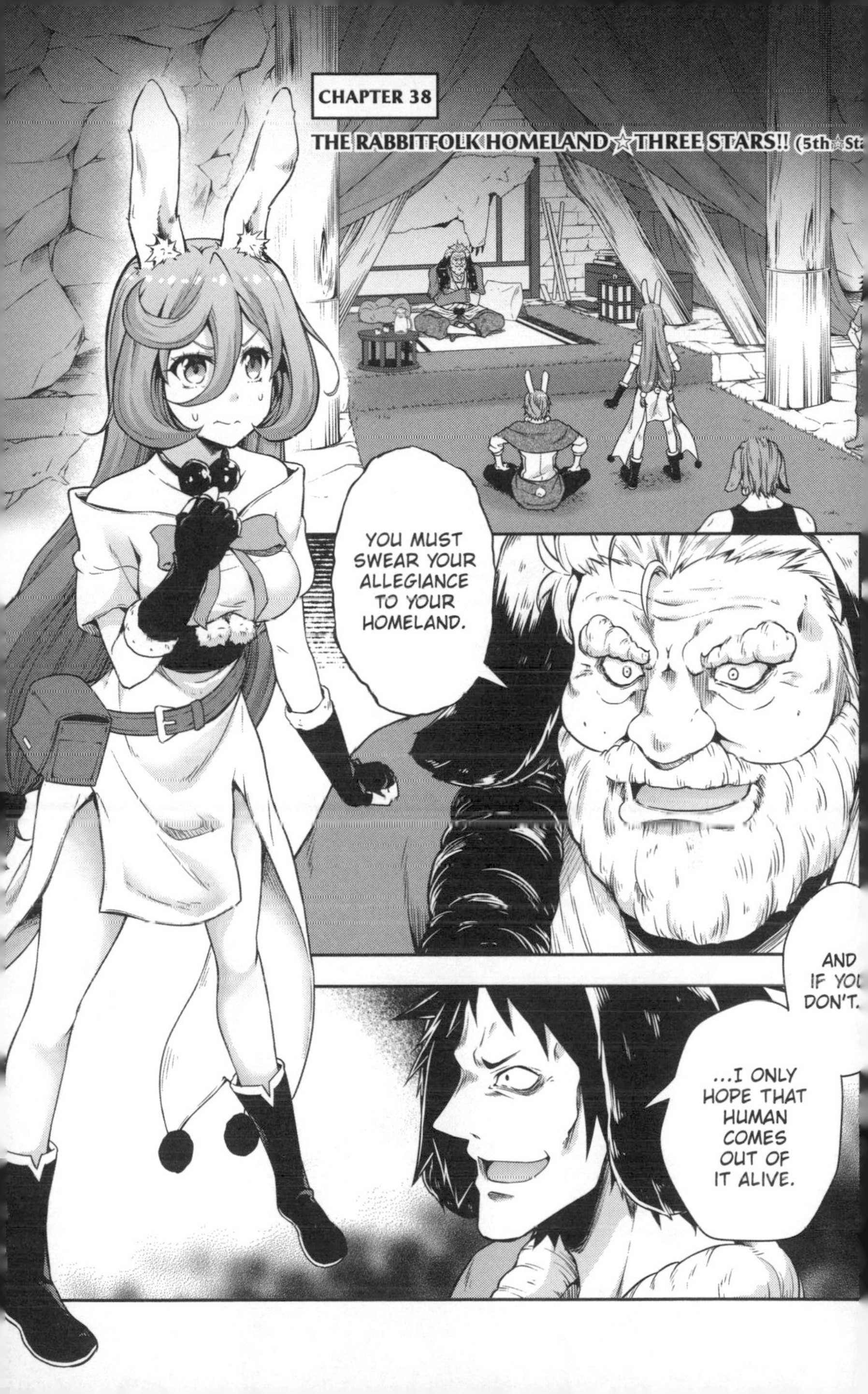
CHAPTER 38
THE RABBITFOLK HOMELAND☆THREE STARS!! (5th☆St
YOU MUST SWEAR YOUR ALLEGIANCE TO YOUR HOMELAND.
AND IF YOU DON'T.
...I ONLY HOPE THAT HUMAN COMES OUT OF IT ALIVE.

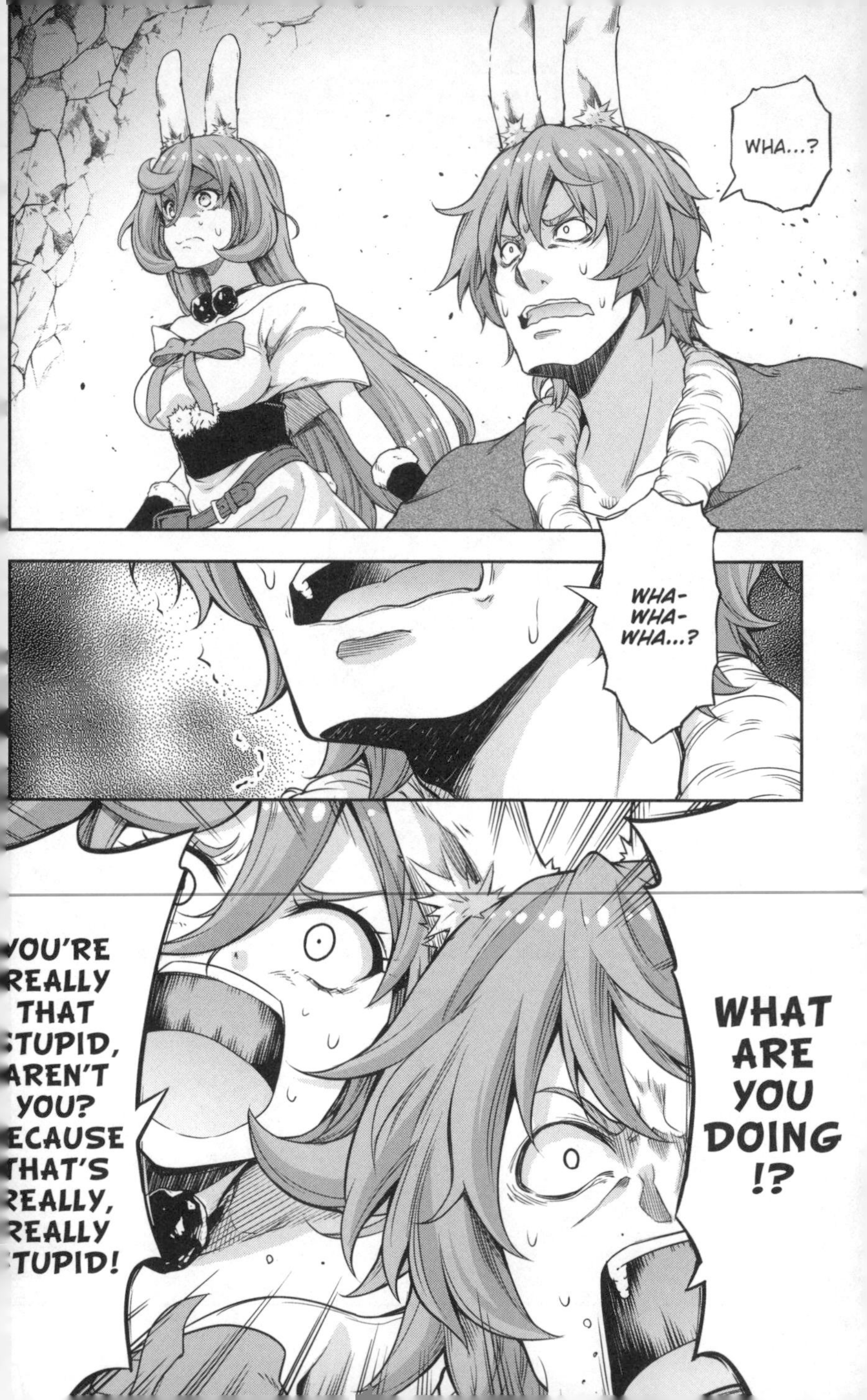
WHA...?
WHA-WHA-WHA...?
WHAT ARE YOU DOING!?
OU'RE REALLY THAT TUPID, AREN'T YOU? ECAUSE HAT'S REALLY, REALLY TUPID!

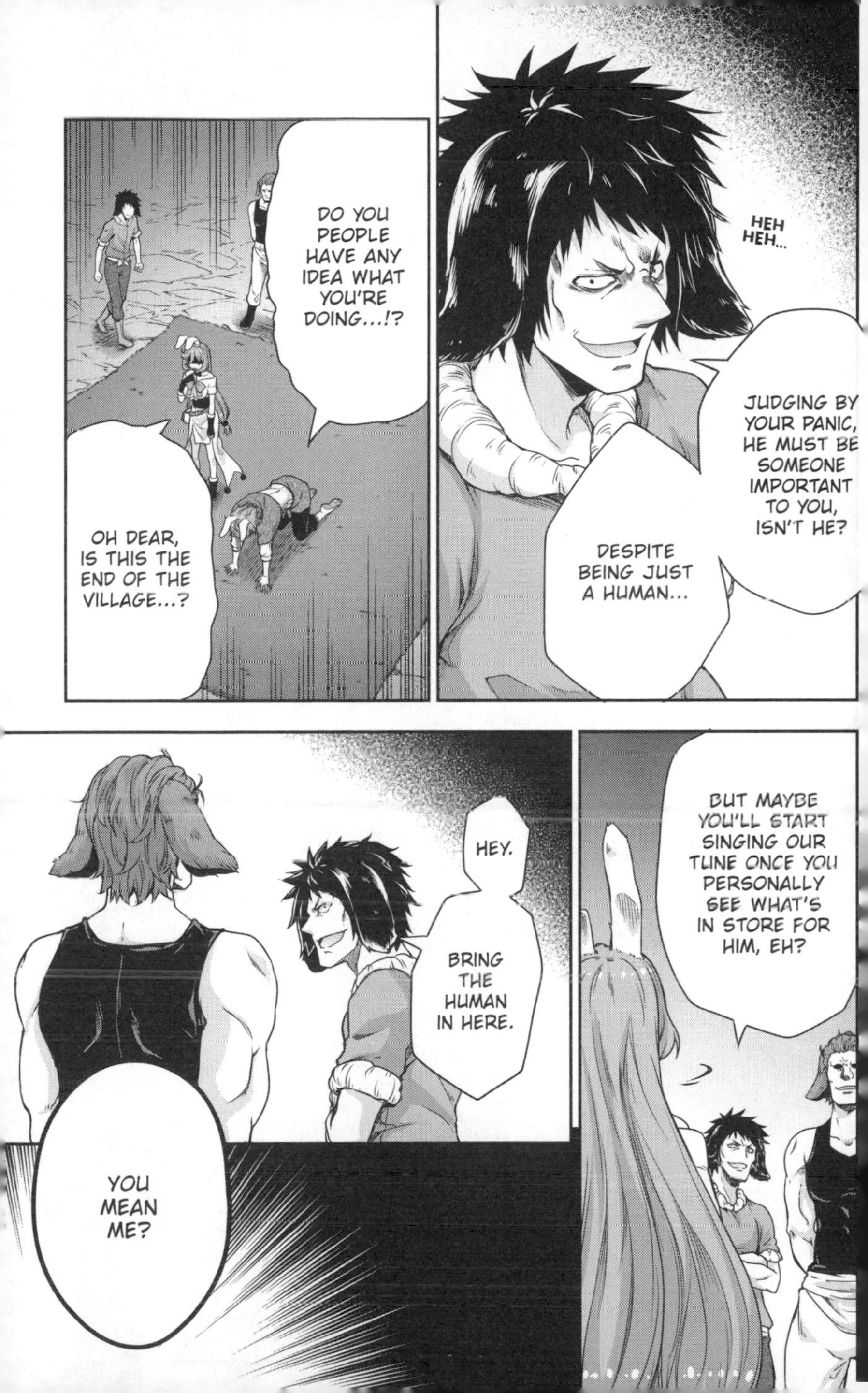
HEH HEH...
JUDGING BY YOUR PANIC, HE MUST BE SOMEONE IMPORTANT TO YOU, ISN'T HE?
DESPITE BEING JUST A HUMAN...
DO YOU PEOPLE HAVE ANY IDEA WHAT YOU'RE DOING...!?
OH DEAR, IS THIS THE END OF THE VILLAGE...?
BUT MAYBE YOU'LL START SINGING OUR TUNE ONCE YOU PERSONALLY SEE WHAT'S IN STORE FOR HIM, EH?
HEY.
BRING THE HUMAN IN HERE.
YOU MEAN ME?

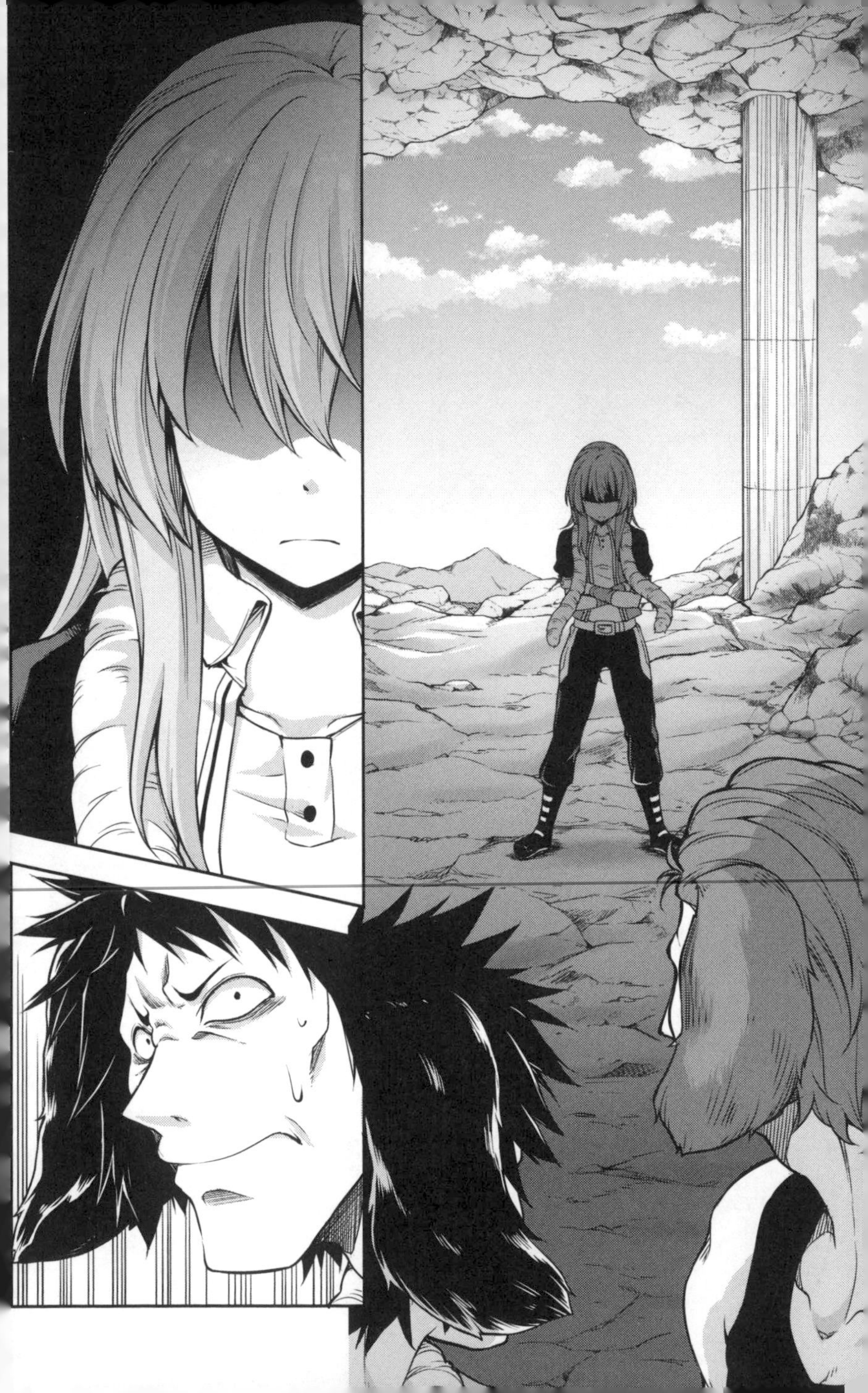

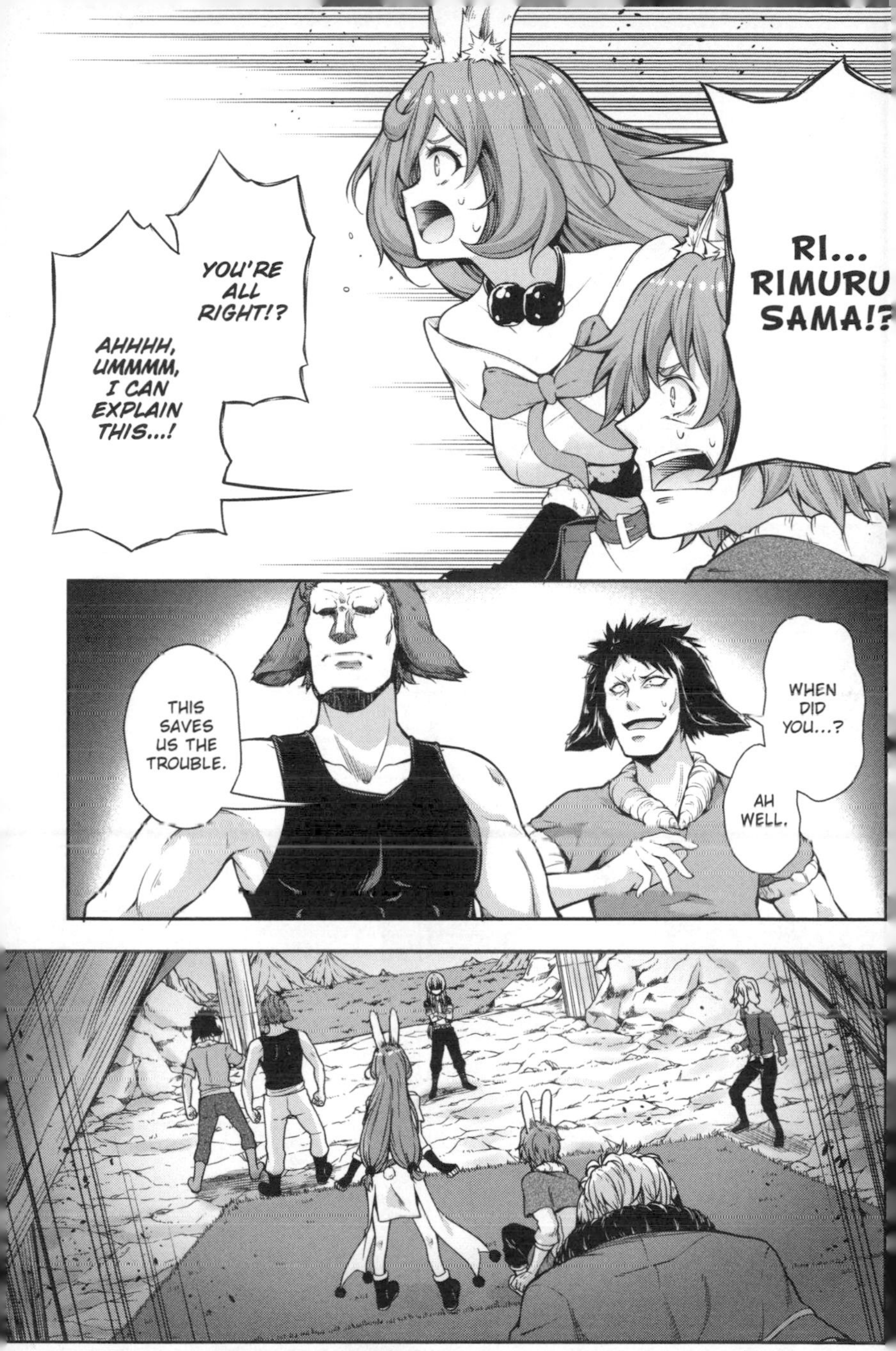
RI... RIMURU SAMA!?
YOU'RE ALL RIGHT!?
AHHHH, UMMMM, I CAN EXPLAIN THIS...!
WHEN DID YOU...?
AH WELL.
THIS SAVES US THE TROUBLE.

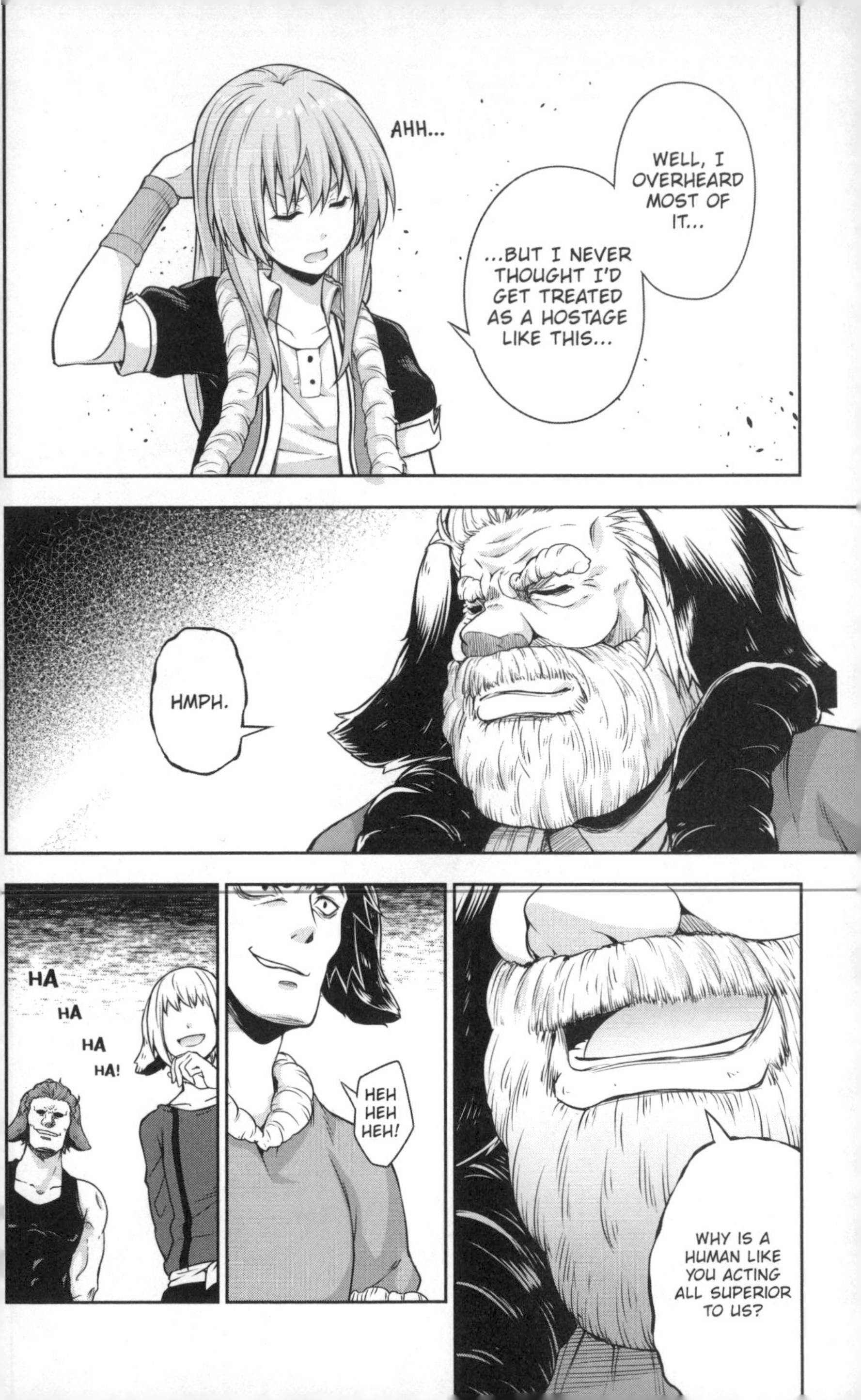
AHH...
WELL, I OVERHEARD MOST OF IT...
...BUT I NEVER THOUGHT I'D GET TREATED AS A HOSTAGE LIKE THIS...
HMPH.
WHY IS A HUMAN LIKE YOU ACTING ALL SUPERIOR TO US?
HEH HEH HEH!
HA HA HA HA!

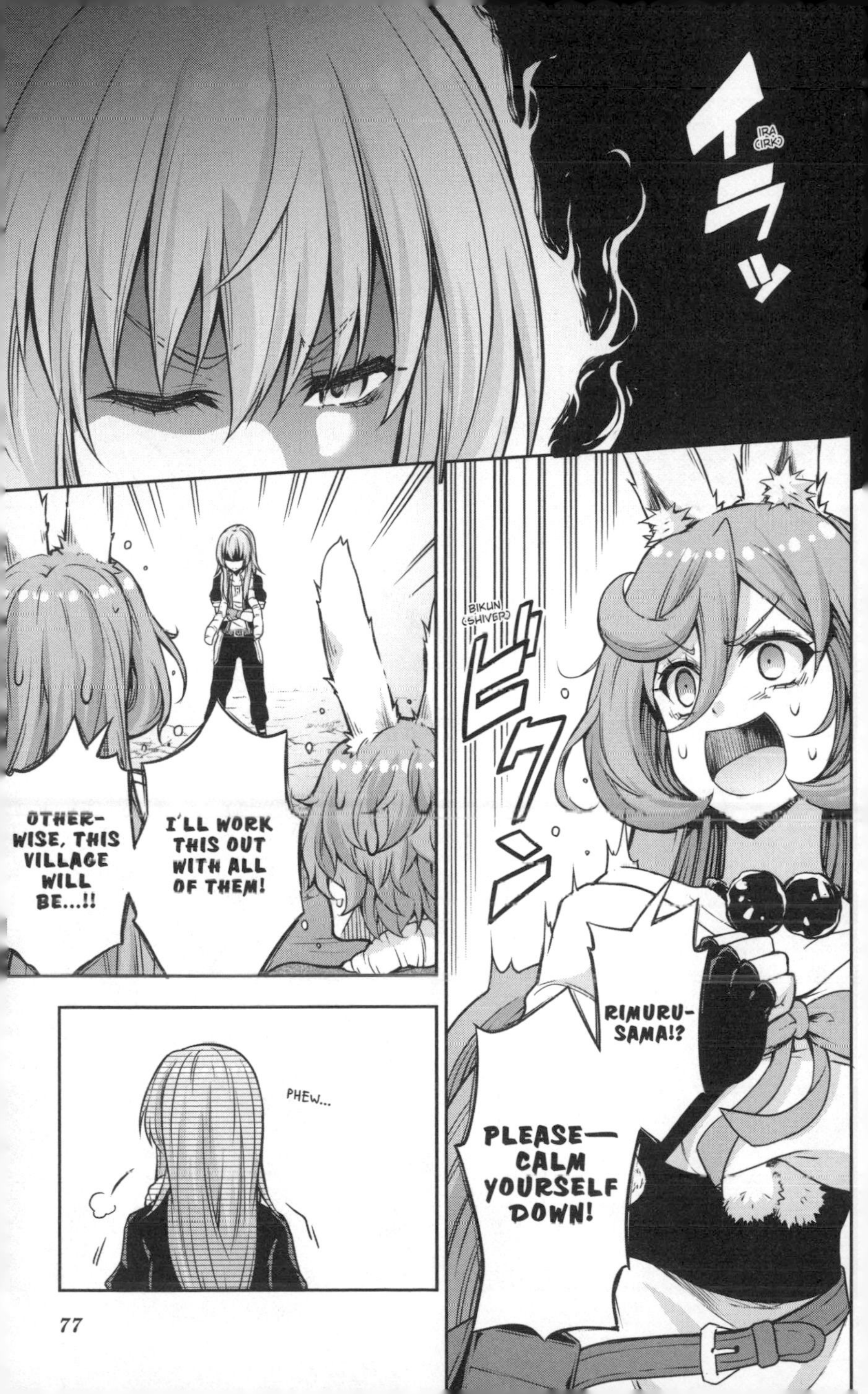
IRA (IRK)
BIKUN (SHIVER)
RIMURU-SAMA!?
PLEASE—CALM YOURSELF DOWN!
I'LL WORK THIS OUT WITH ALL OF THEM!
OTHER-WISE, THIS VILLAGE WILL BE...!!
PHEW...

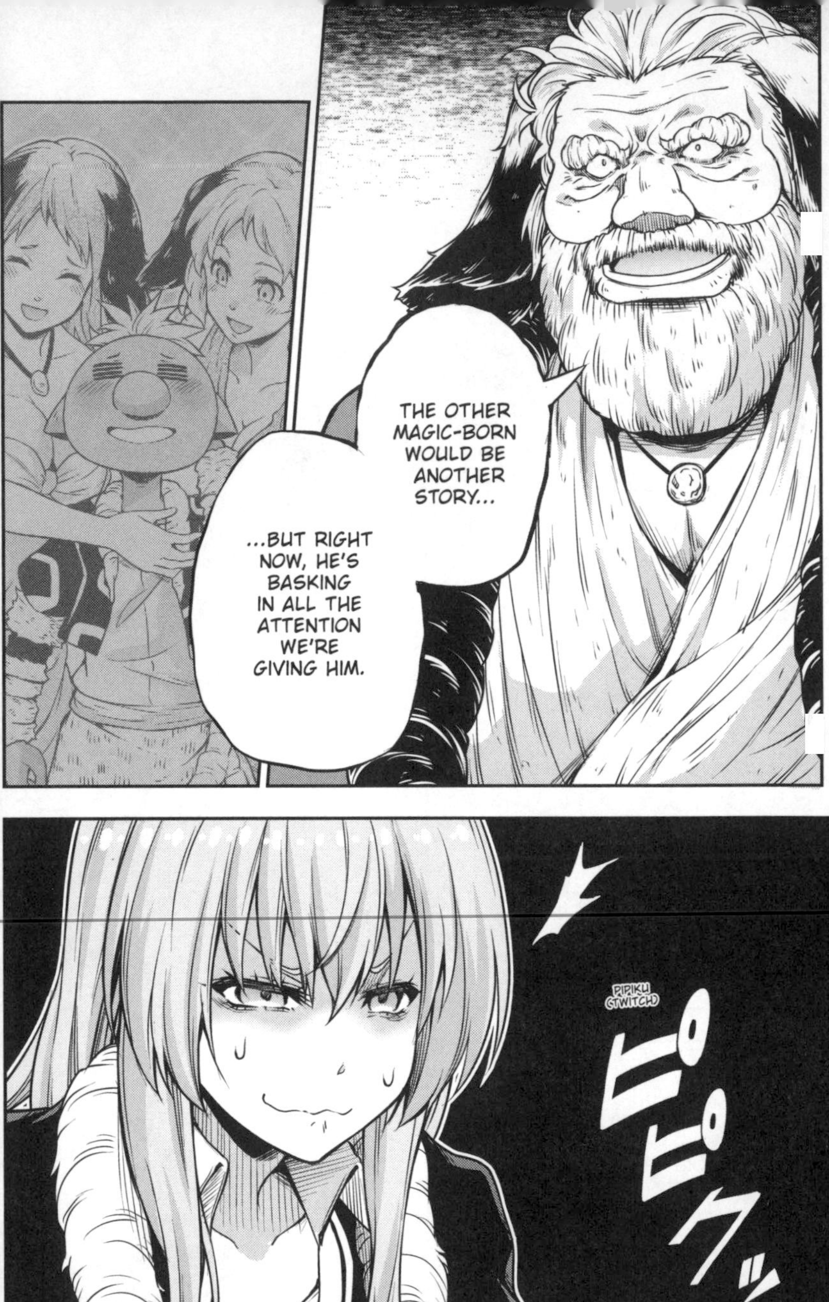
THE OTHER MAGIC-BORN WOULD BE ANOTHER STORY...
...BUT RIGHT NOW, HE'S BASKING IN ALL THE ATTENTION WE'RE GIVING HIM.
PIPIKU (TWITCH)

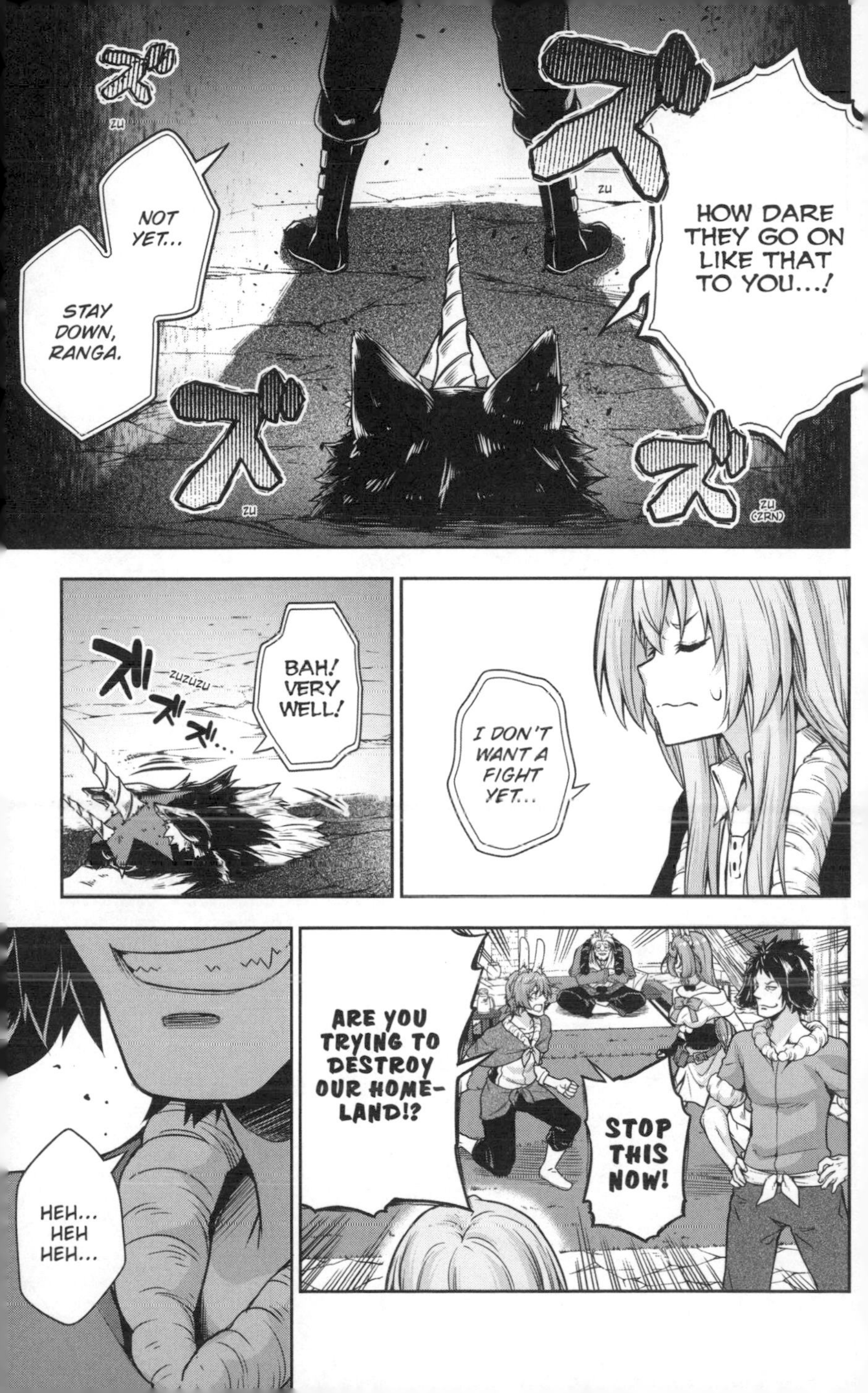
zu
HOW DARE THEY GO ON LIKE THAT TO YOU...!
zu (ZRN)
zu
NOT YET...
STAY DOWN, RANGA.
zu
I DON'T WANT A FIGHT YET...
BAH! VERY WELL!
zuzuzu
STOP THIS NOW!
ARE YOU TRYING TO DESTROY OUR HOME-LAND!?
HEH... HEH HEH...

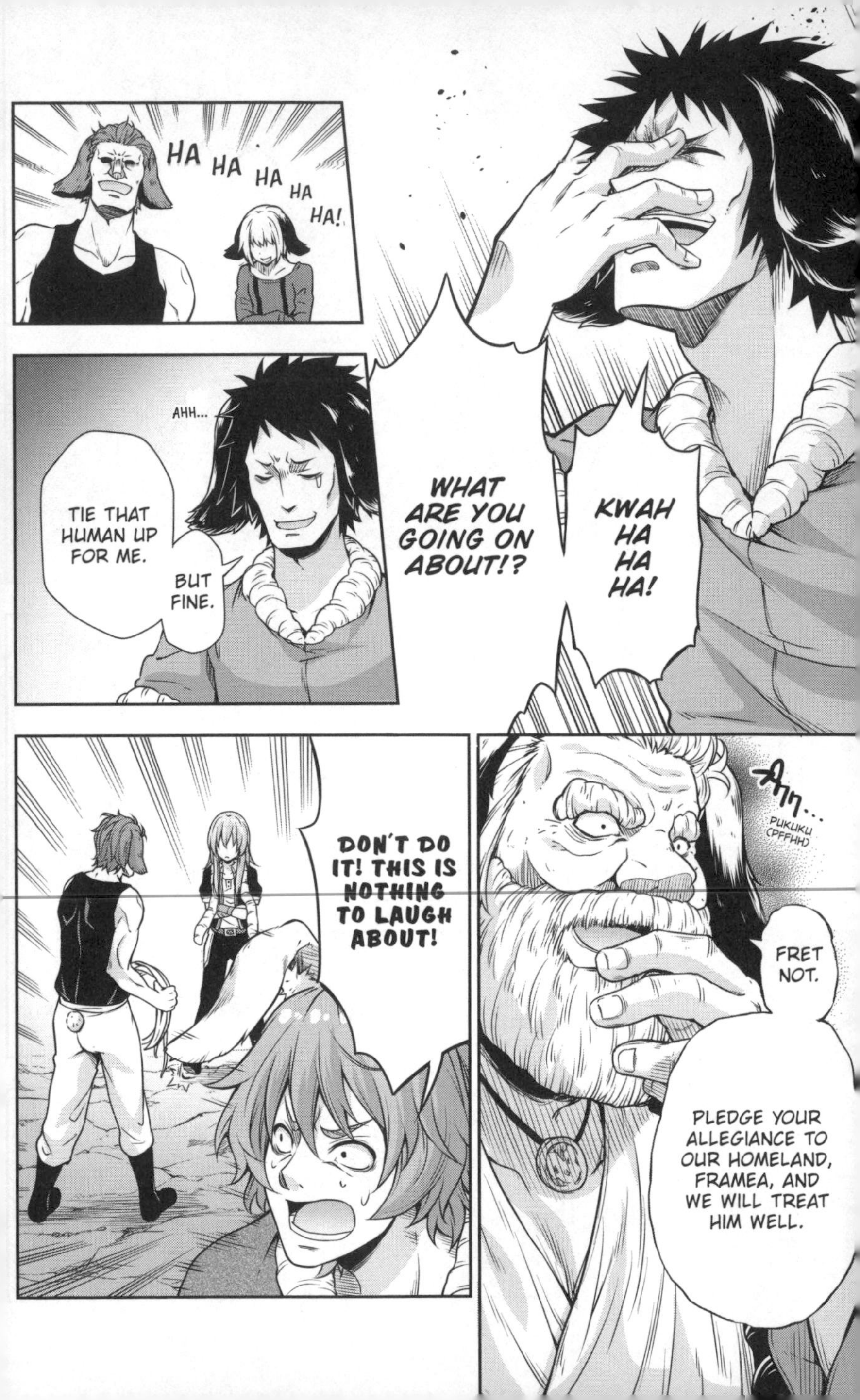
KWAH HA HA HA!
WHAT ARE YOU GOING ON ABOUT!?
HA HA HA HA HA!
AHH...
BUT FINE.
TIE THAT HUMAN UP FOR ME.
Am...
PUKUKU (PFFHH)
FRET NOT.
PLEDGE YOUR ALLEGIANCE TO OUR HOMELAND, FRAMEA, AND WE WILL TREAT HIM WELL.
DON'T DO IT! THIS IS NOTHING TO LAUGH ABOUT!

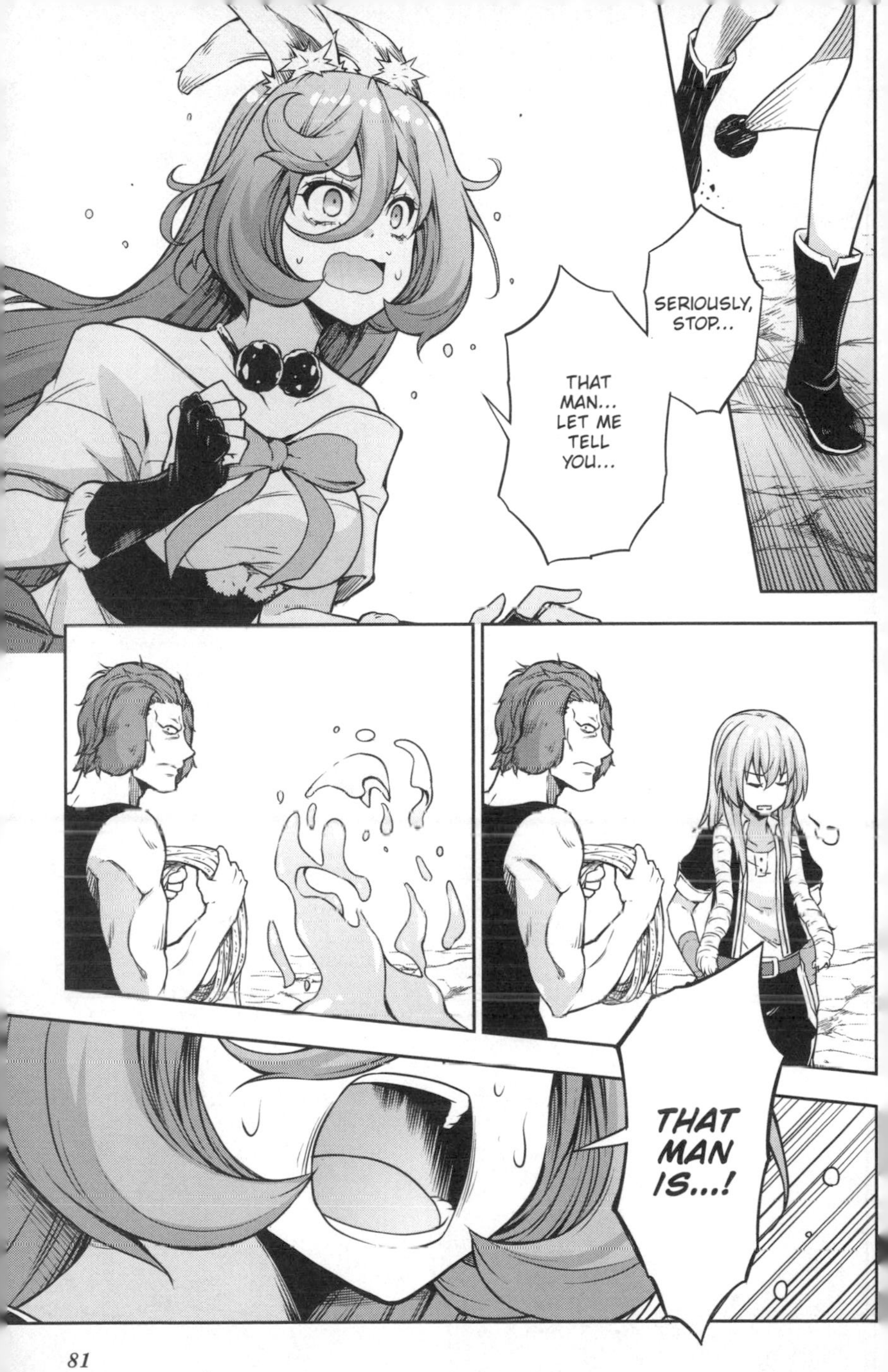
SERIOUSLY, STOP...
THAT MAN... LET ME TELL YOU...
THAT MAN IS...!

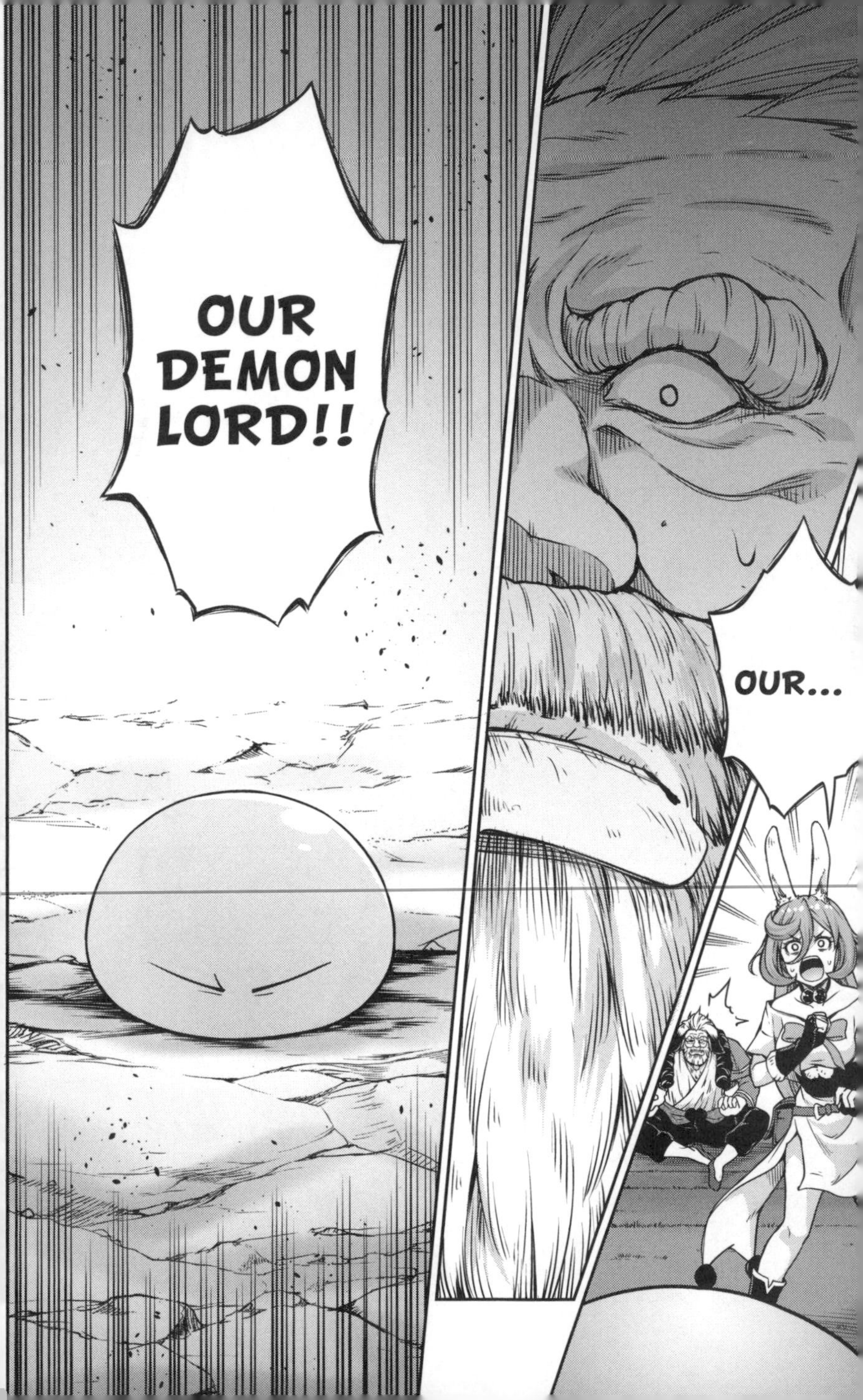
OUR...
OUR DEMON LORD!!

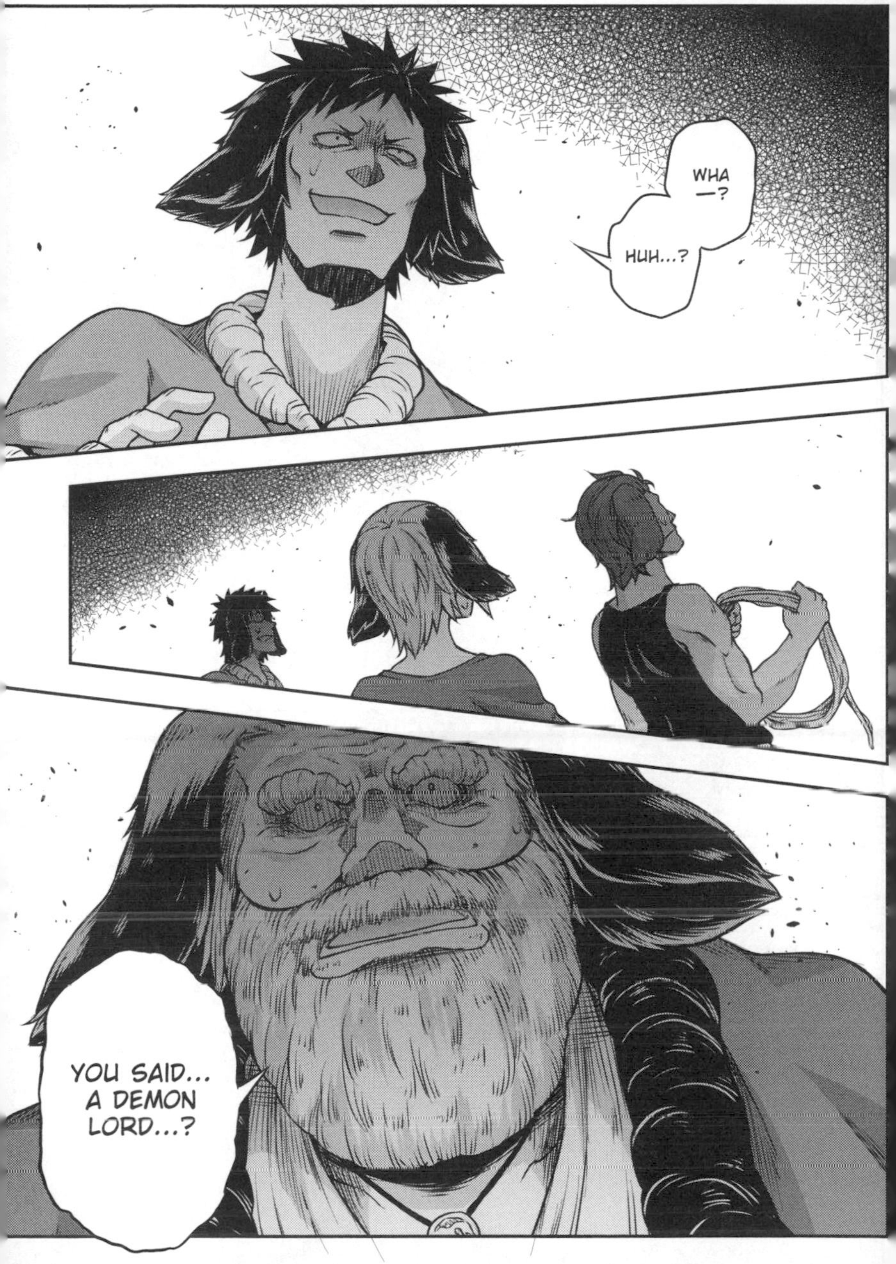
WHA—?
HUH...?
YOU SAID... A DEMON LORD...?

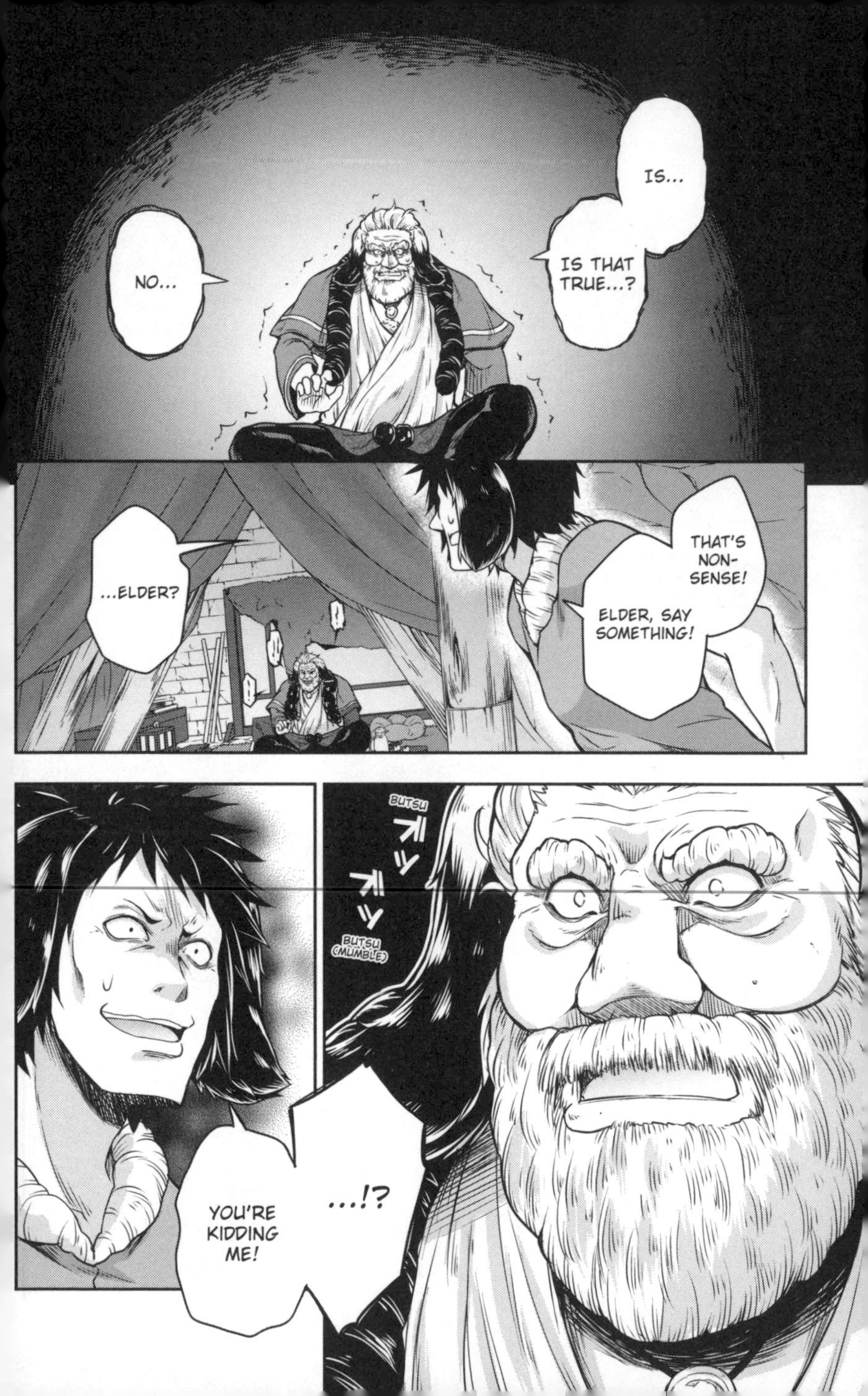
IS...
IS THAT TRUE...?
NO...
THAT'S NON-SENSE!
ELDER, SAY SOMETHING!
...ELDER?
BUTSU
BUTSU (MUMBLE)
...!?
YOU'RE KIDDING ME!

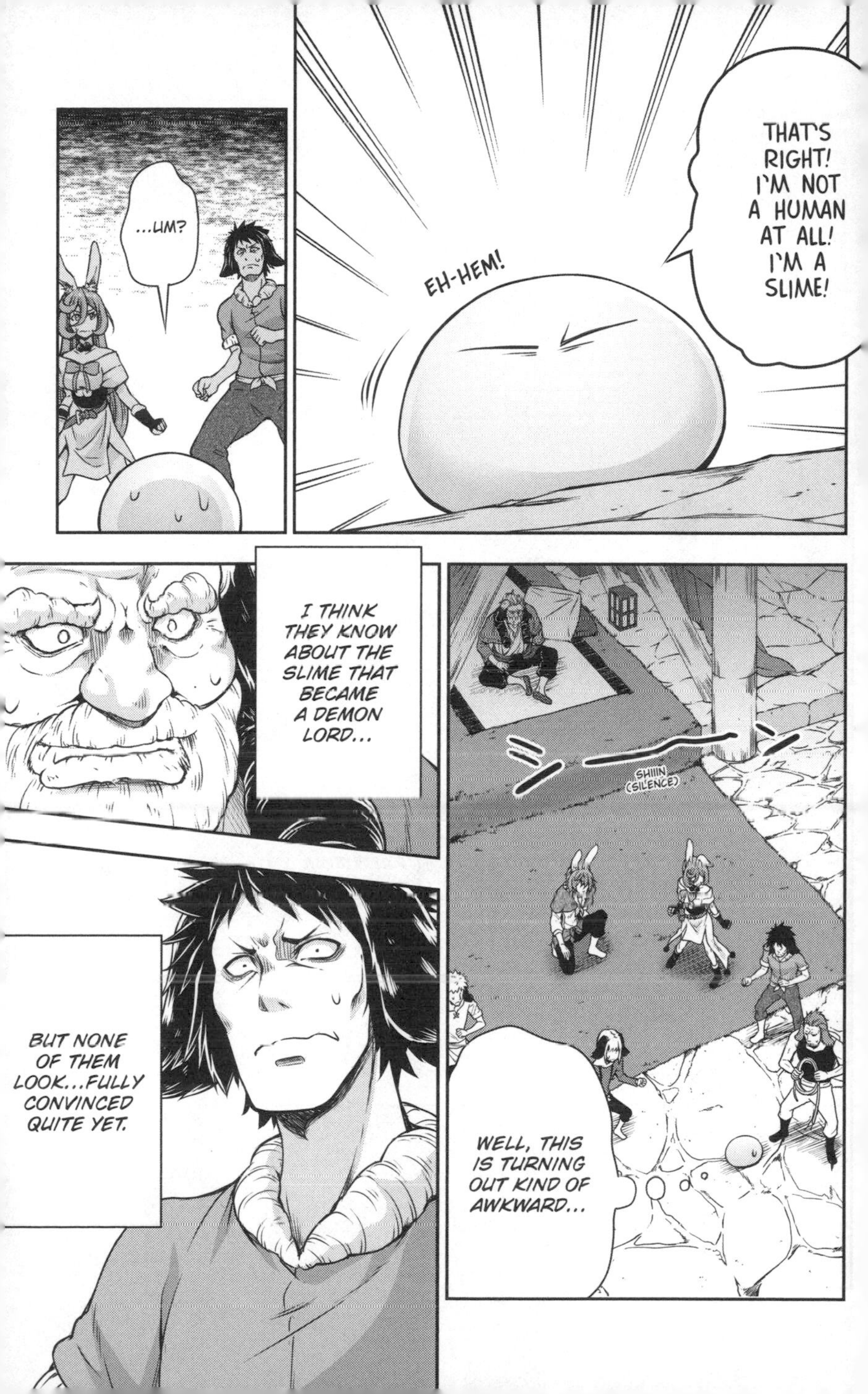
THAT'S RIGHT! I'M NOT A HUMAN AT ALL! I'M A SLIME!
EH-HEM!
...UM?
SHIIIN (SILENCE)
WELL, THIS IS TURNING OUT KIND OF AWKWARD...
I THINK THEY KNOW ABOUT THE SLIME THAT BECAME A DEMON LORD...
BUT NONE OF THEM LOOK...FULLY CONVINCED QUITE YET.

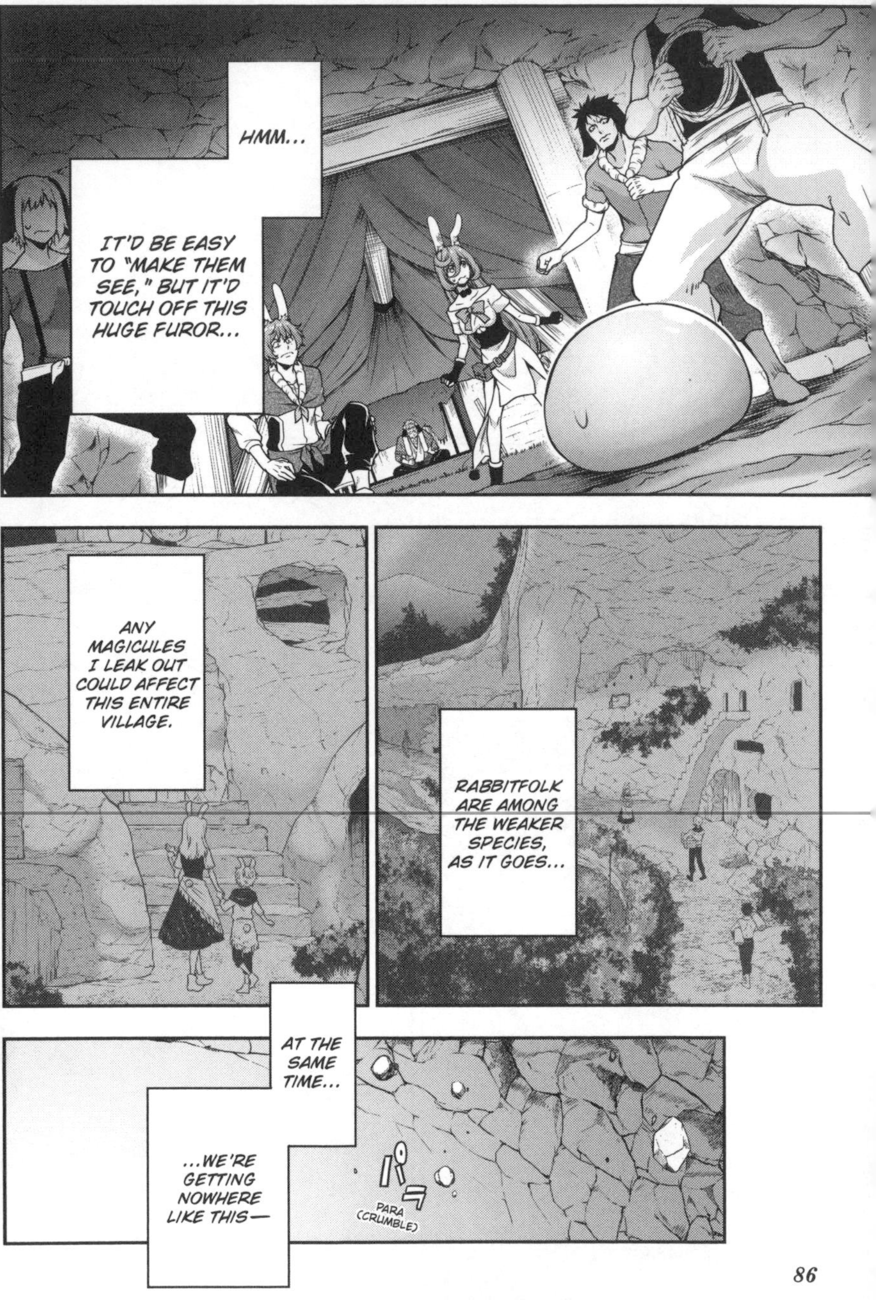
HMM…
IT'D BE EASY TO "MAKE THEM SEE," BUT IT'D TOUCH OFF THIS HUGE FUROR…
RABBITFOLK ARE AMONG THE WEAKER SPECIES, AS IT GOES…
ANY MAGICULES I LEAK OUT COULD AFFECT THIS ENTIRE VILLAGE.
AT THE SAME TIME…
…WE'RE GETTING NOWHERE LIKE THIS—
PARA (CRUMBLE)

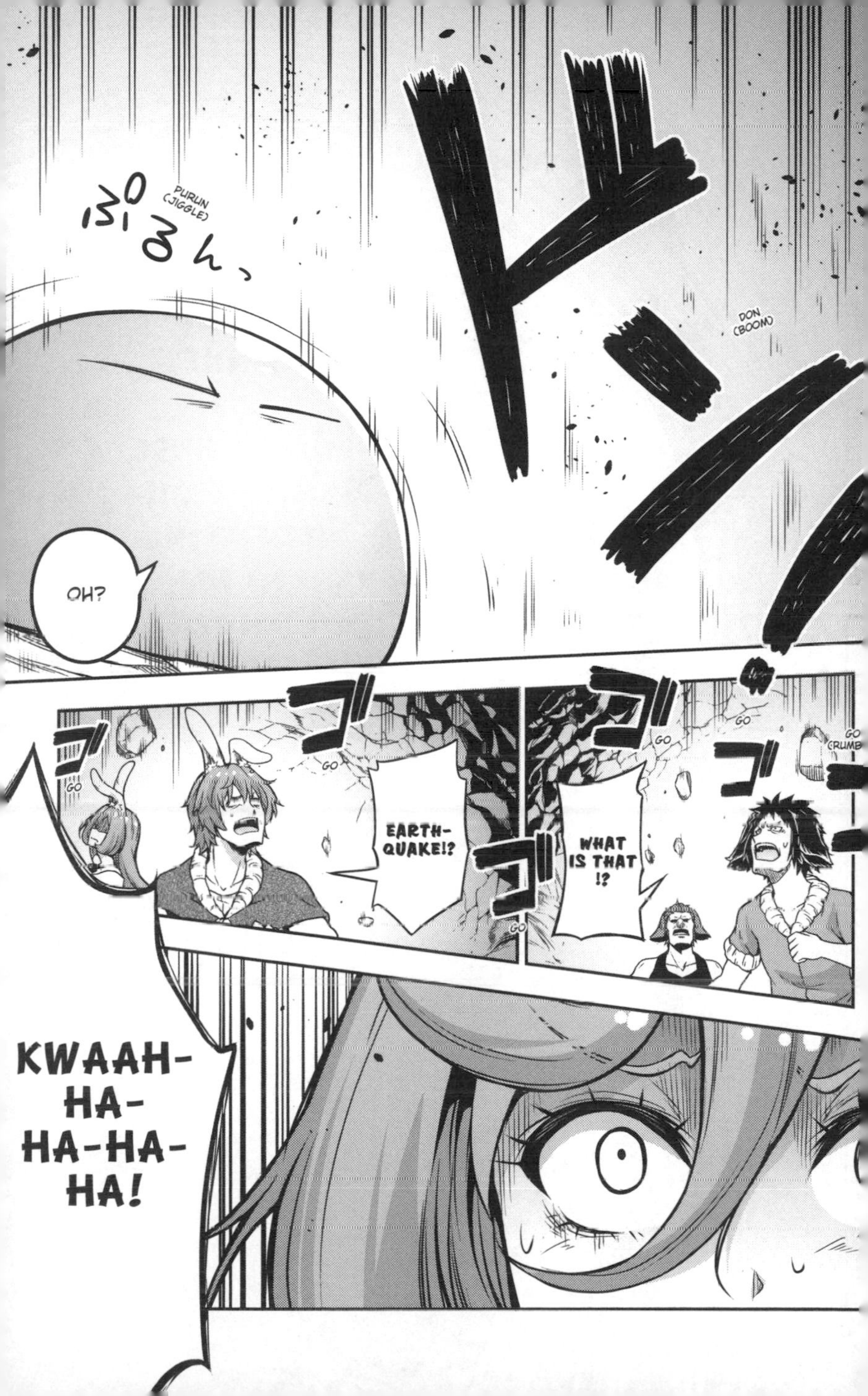
DON (BOOM)
PURUN (JIGGLE)
OH?
GO
GO
CRUMB
WHAT IS THAT !?
GO
GO
EARTH-QUAKE!?
GO
KWAAH-HA-HA-HA-HA!

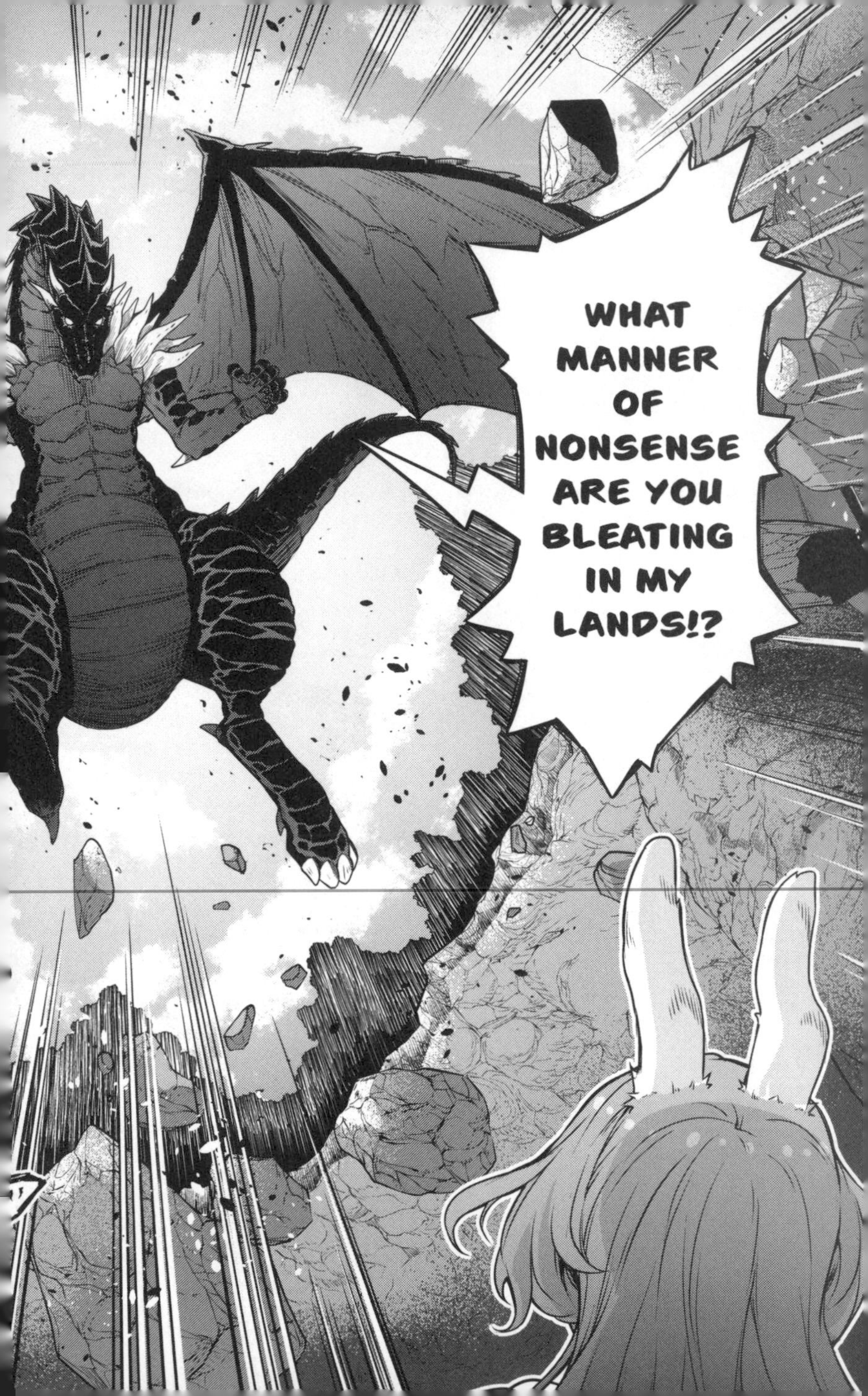
WHAT MANNER OF NONSENSE ARE YOU BLEATING IN MY LANDS!?

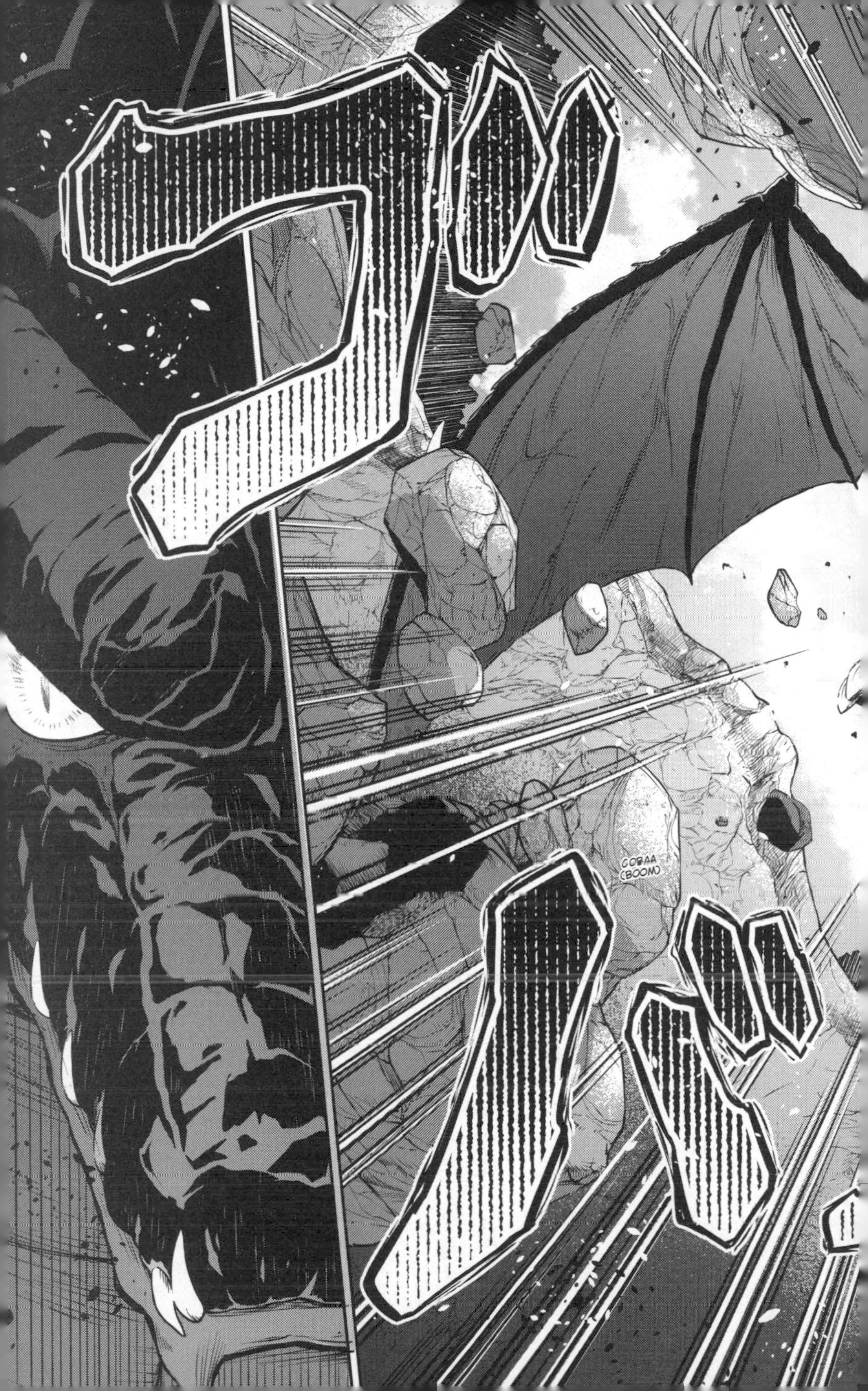
GOBAA (BOOM)

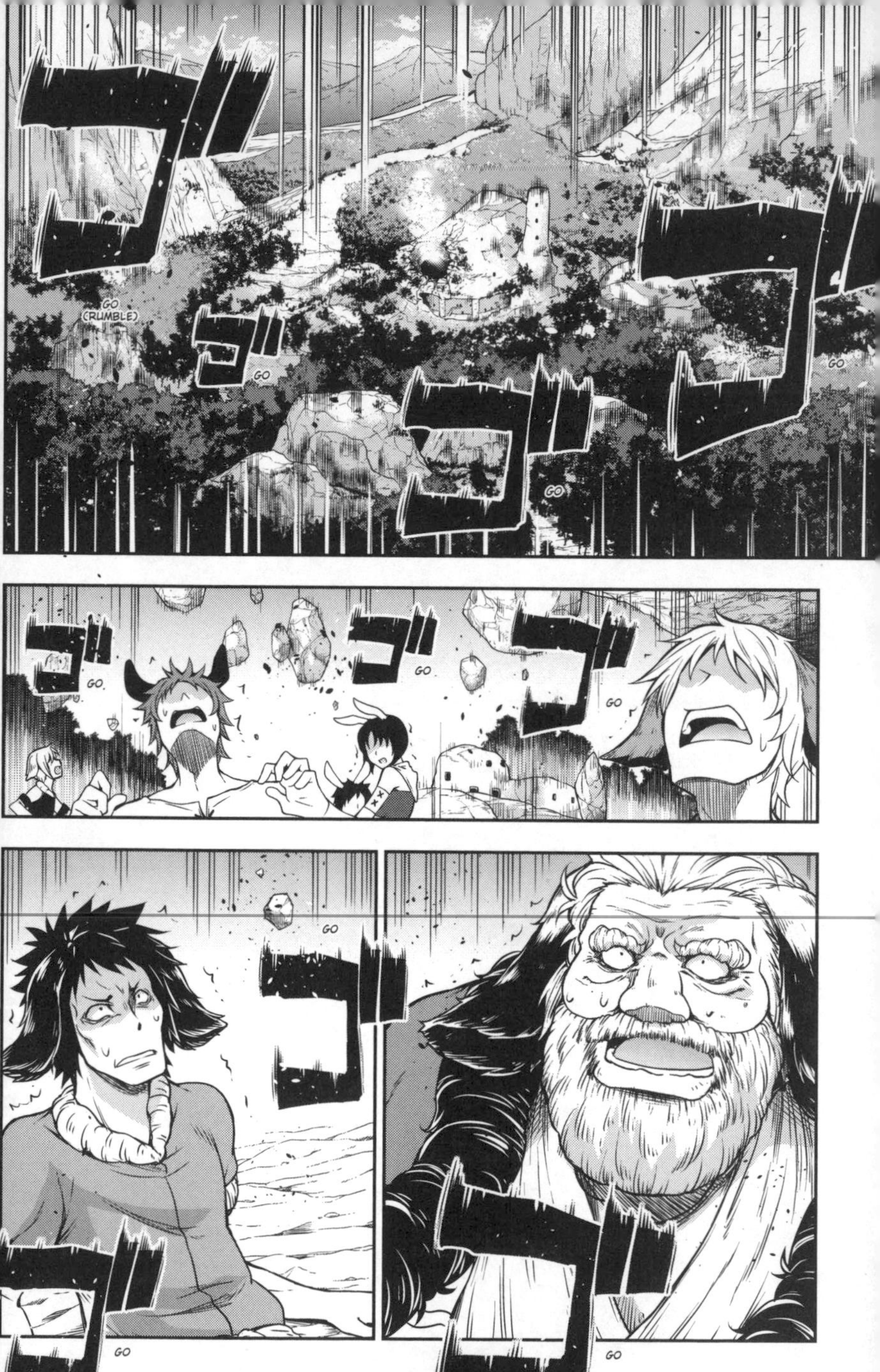
GO
GO
GO
GO
(RUMBLE)
GO
GO
GO
GO
GO
GO
GO

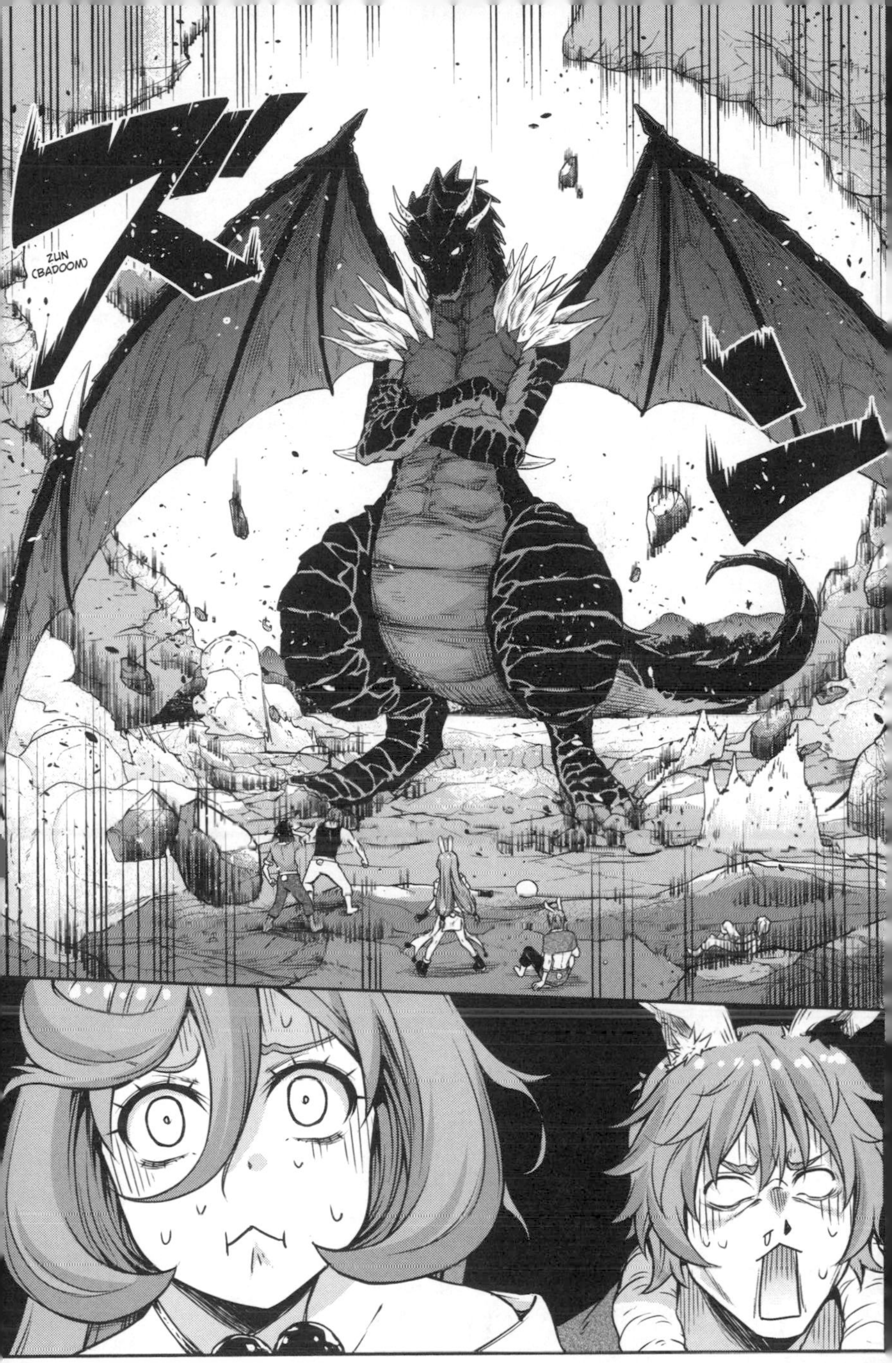
ZUN
(BADOOM)

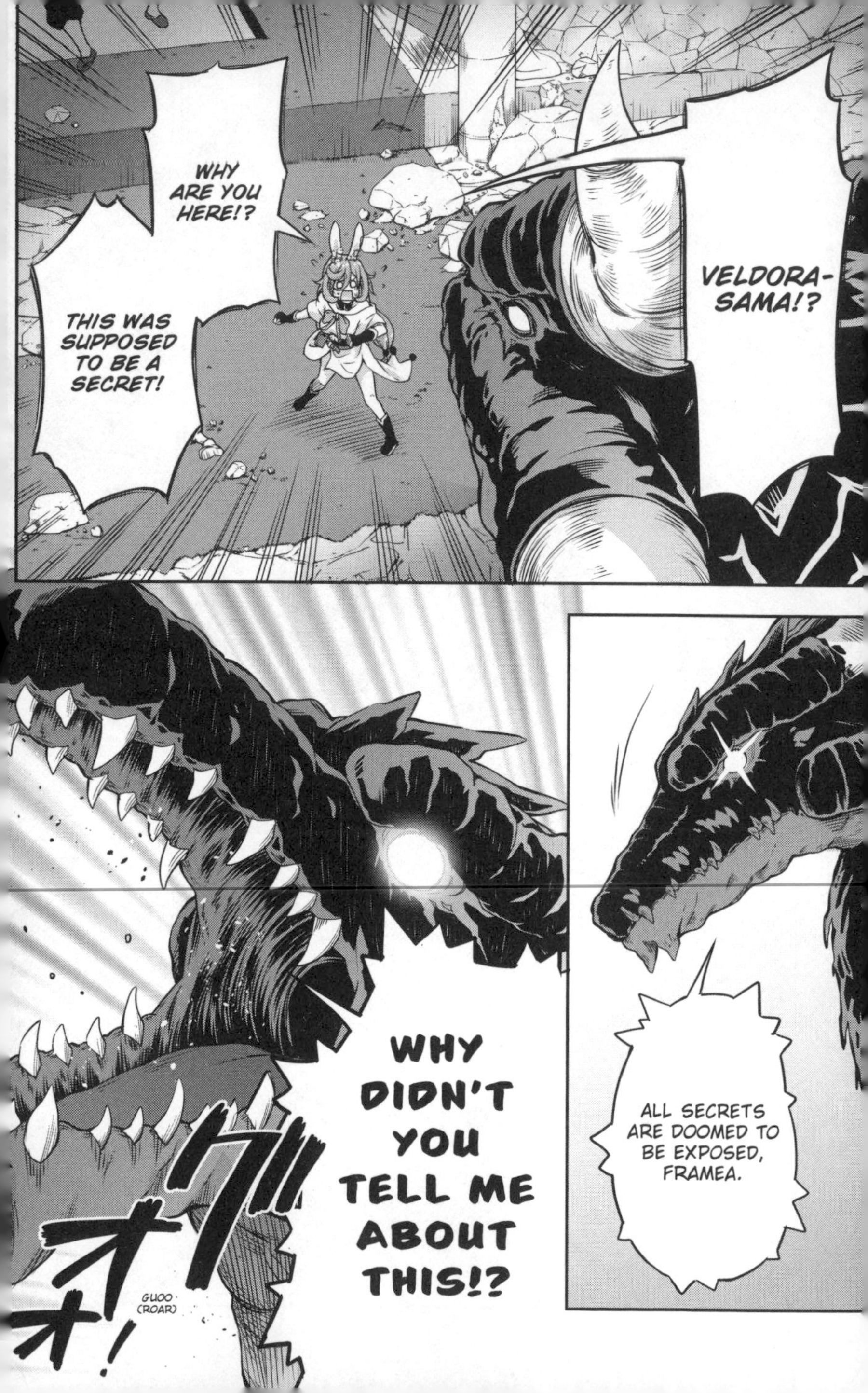
VELDORA-SAMA!?
WHY ARE YOU HERE!?
THIS WAS SUPPOSED TO BE A SECRET!
ALL SECRETS ARE DOOMED TO BE EXPOSED, FRAMEA.
WHY DIDN'T YOU TELL ME ABOUT THIS!?
GUOO (ROAR)

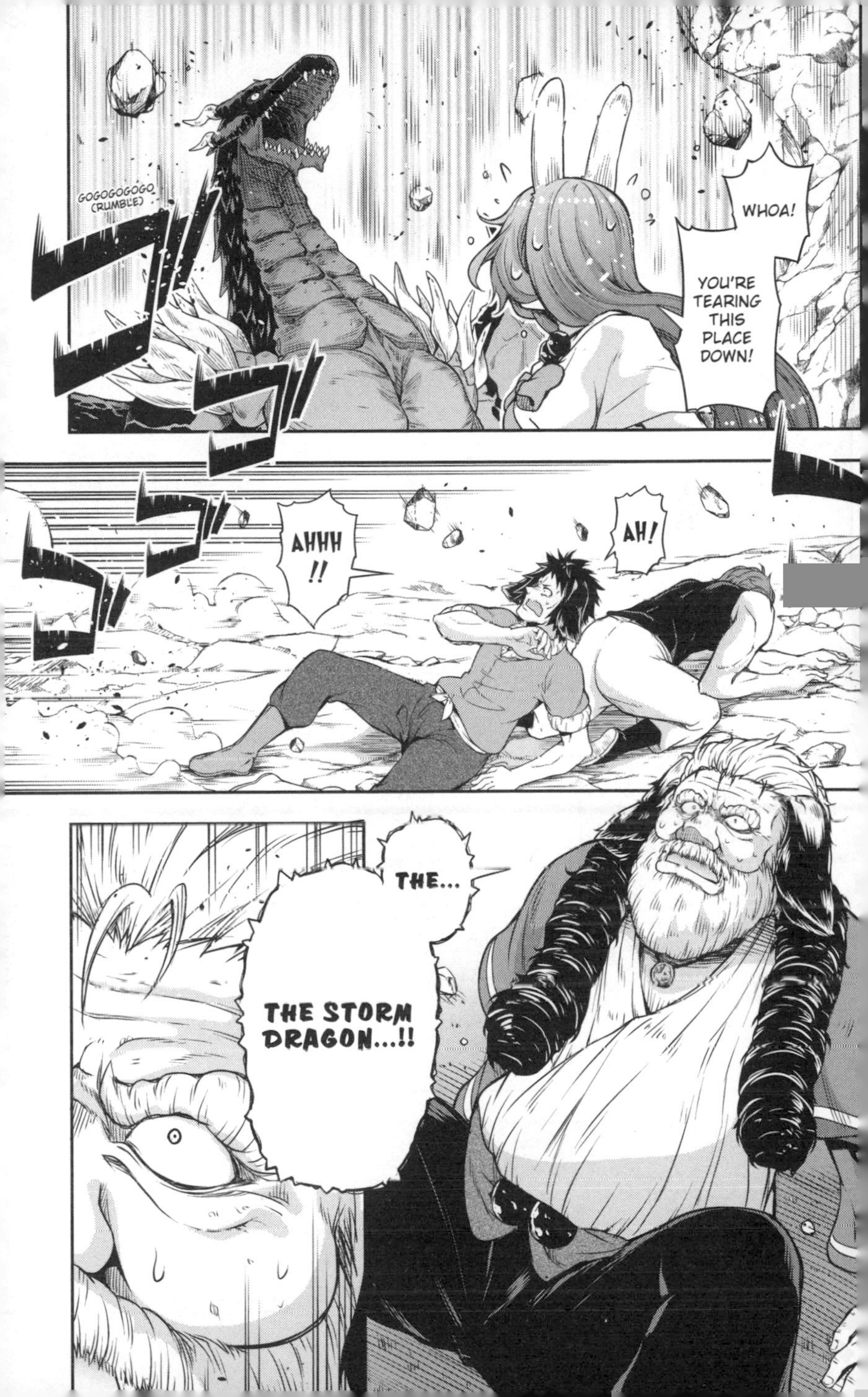
WHOA!
YOU'RE TEARING THIS PLACE DOWN!
GOGOGOGOGO (RUMBLE)
AH!
AHHH !!
THE...
THE STORM DRAGON...!!

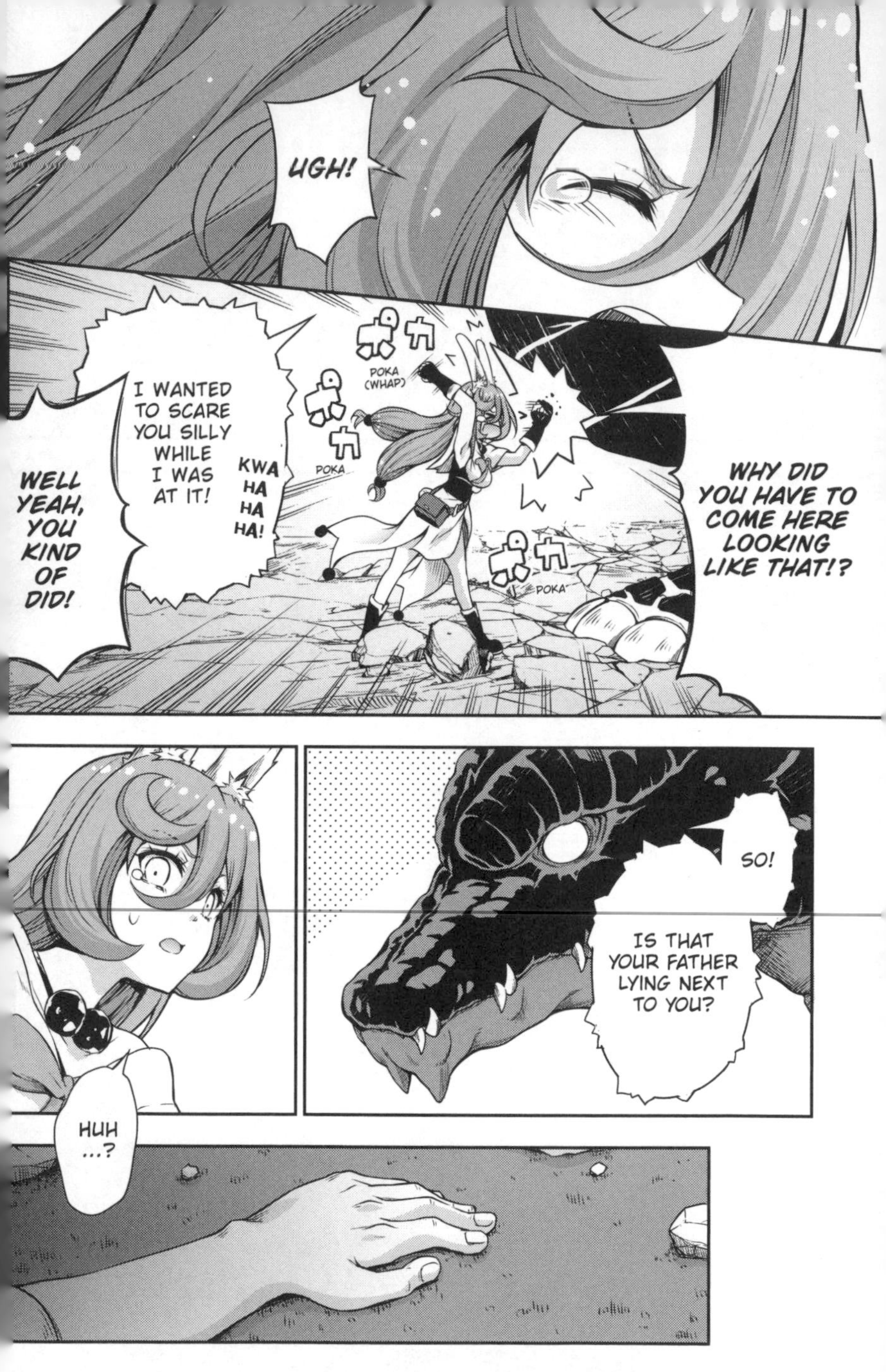
UGH!
WHY DID YOU HAVE TO COME HERE LOOKING LIKE THAT!?
POKA (WHAP)
POKA
POKA
I WANTED TO SCARE YOU SILLY WHILE I WAS AT IT!
KWA HA HA HA!
WELL YEAH, YOU KIND OF DID!
SO!
IS THAT YOUR FATHER LYING NEXT TO YOU?
HUH ...?

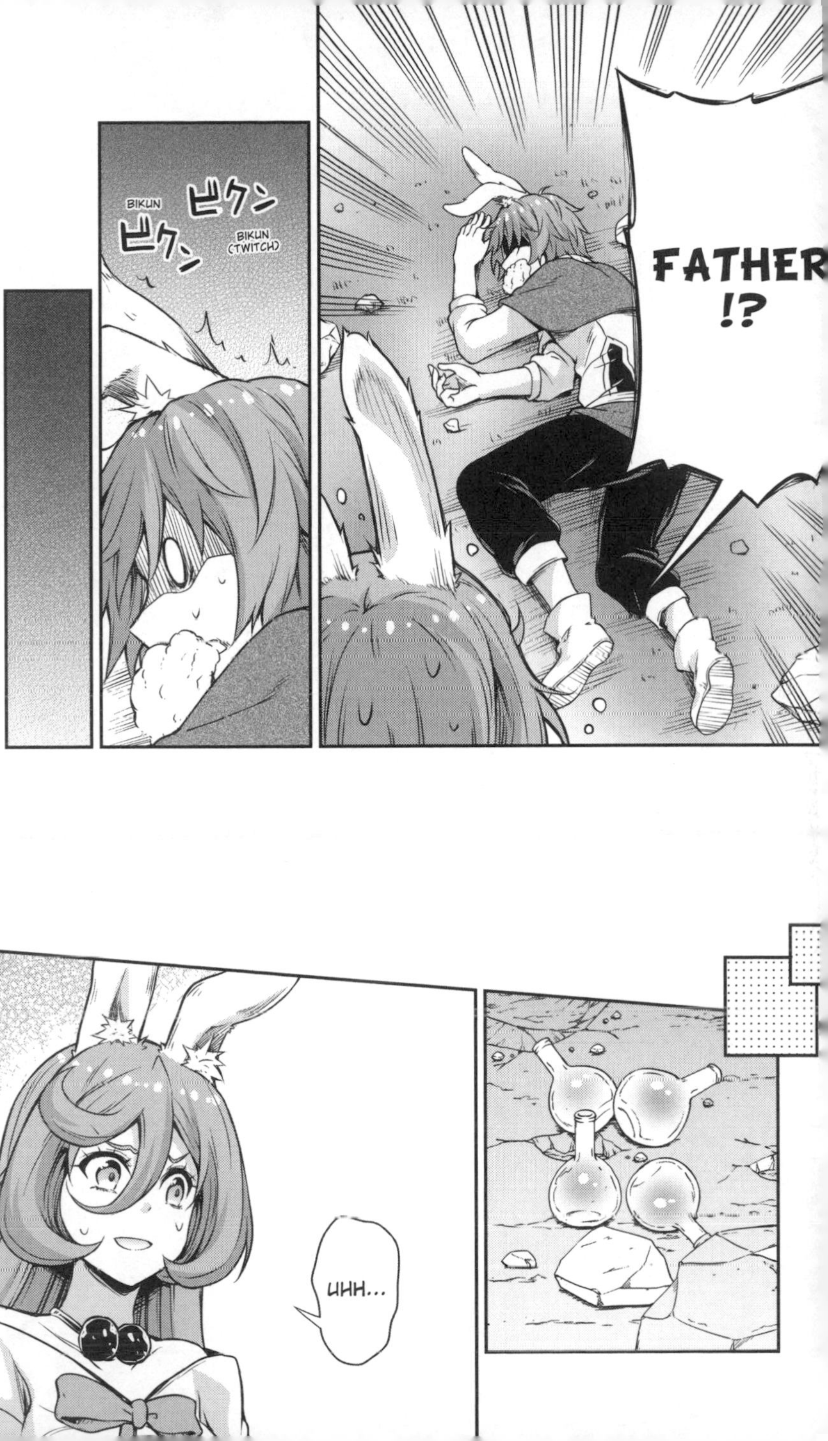
FATHER!?
ビクン
BIKUN
ビクン
BIKUN (TWITCH)
UHH...

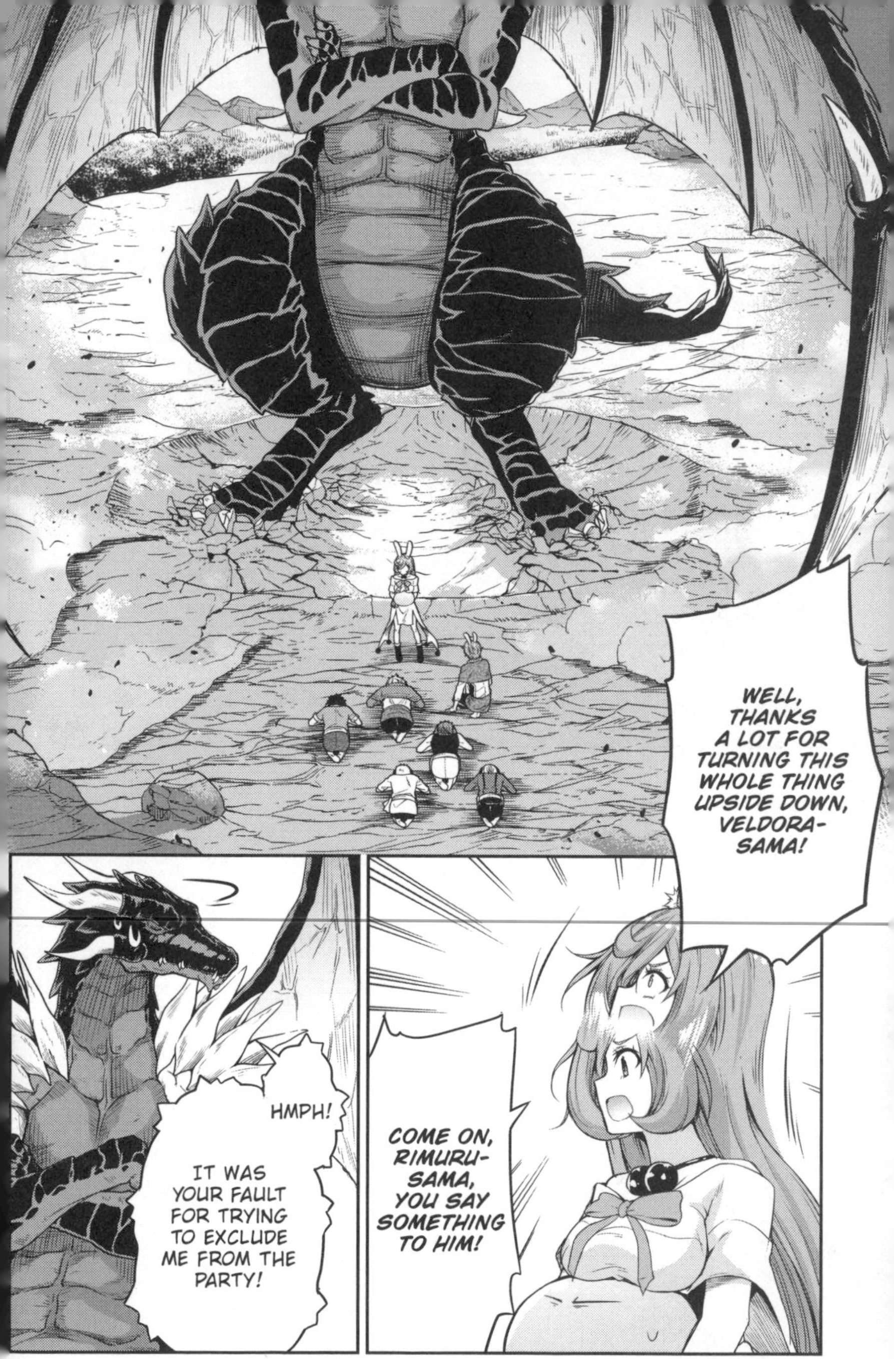

WELL, THANKS A LOT FOR TURNING THIS WHOLE THING UPSIDE DOWN, VELDORA-SAMA!
COME ON, RIMURU-SAMA, YOU SAY SOMETHING TO HIM!
HMPH!
IT WAS YOUR FAULT FOR TRYING TO EXCLUDE ME FROM THE PARTY!

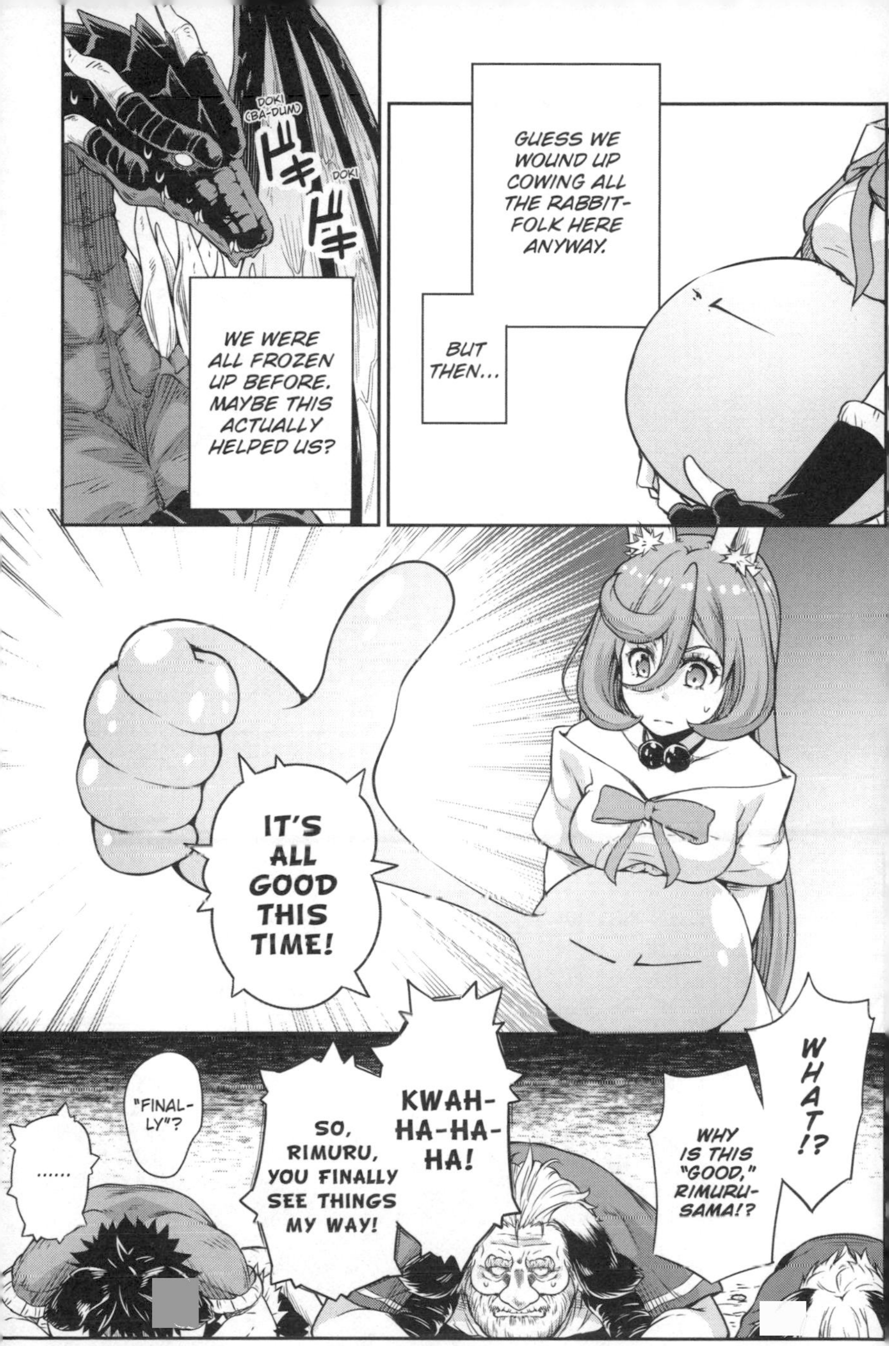
GUESS WE WOUND UP COWING ALL THE RABBIT-FOLK HERE ANYWAY.
BUT THEN...
ドキ
DOKI (BA-DUM)
ドキ
DOKI
WE WERE ALL FROZEN UP BEFORE. MAYBE THIS ACTUALLY HELPED US?
IT'S ALL GOOD THIS TIME!
WHAT!?
WHY IS THIS "GOOD," RIMURU-SAMA!?
KWAH-HA-HA-HA!
SO, RIMURU, YOU FINALLY SEE THINGS MY WAY!
"FINAL-LY"?
......

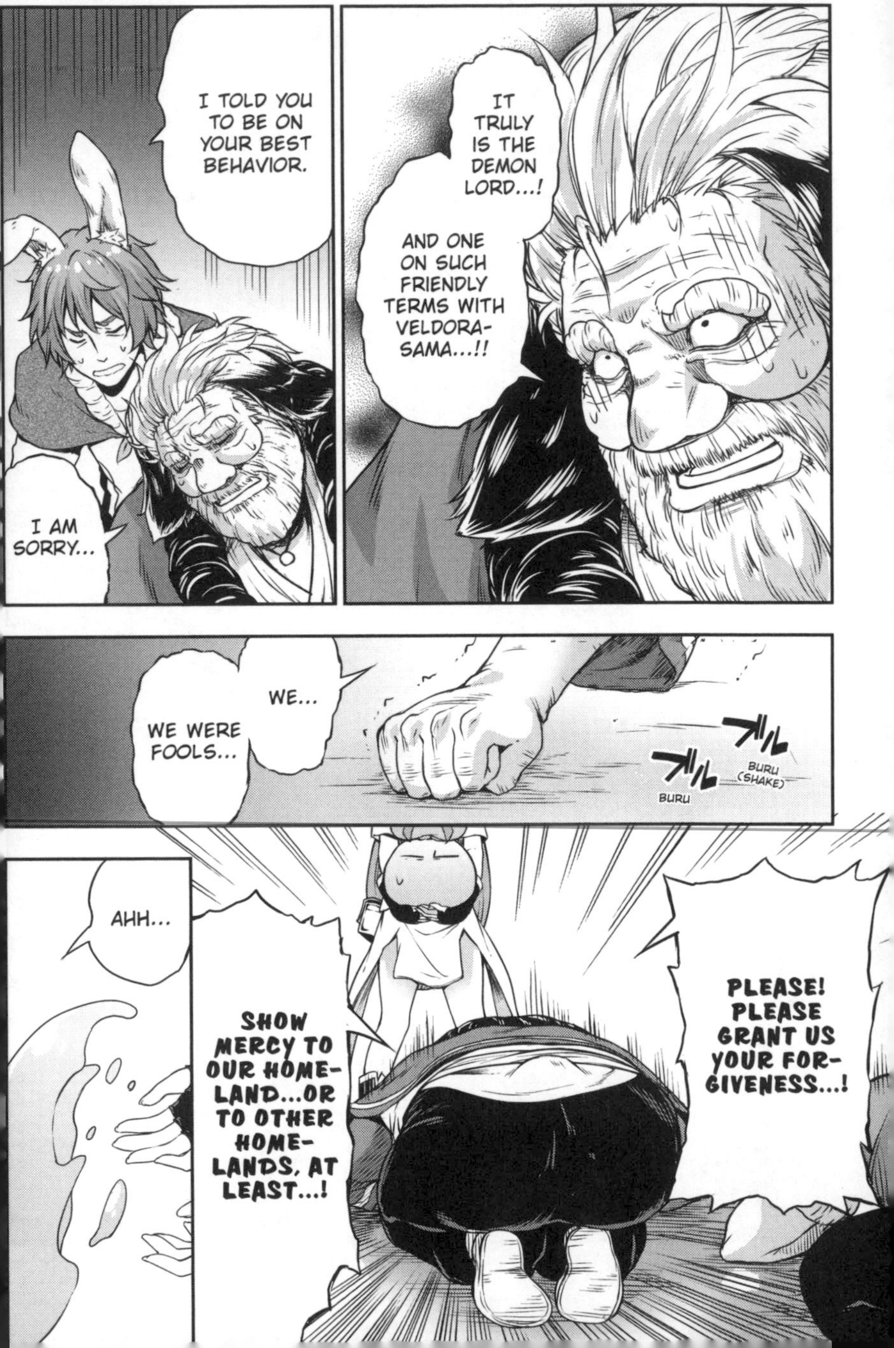
IT TRULY IS THE DEMON LORD...!
AND ONE ON SUCH FRIENDLY TERMS WITH VELDORA-SAMA...!!
I TOLD YOU TO BE ON YOUR BEST BEHAVIOR.
I AM SORRY...
ブル
BURU (SHAKE)
ブル
BURU
WE...
WE WERE FOOLS...
PLEASE! PLEASE GRANT US YOUR FOR-GIVENESS...!
SHOW MERCY TO OUR HOME-LAND...OR TO OTHER HOME-LANDS, AT LEAST...!
AHH...

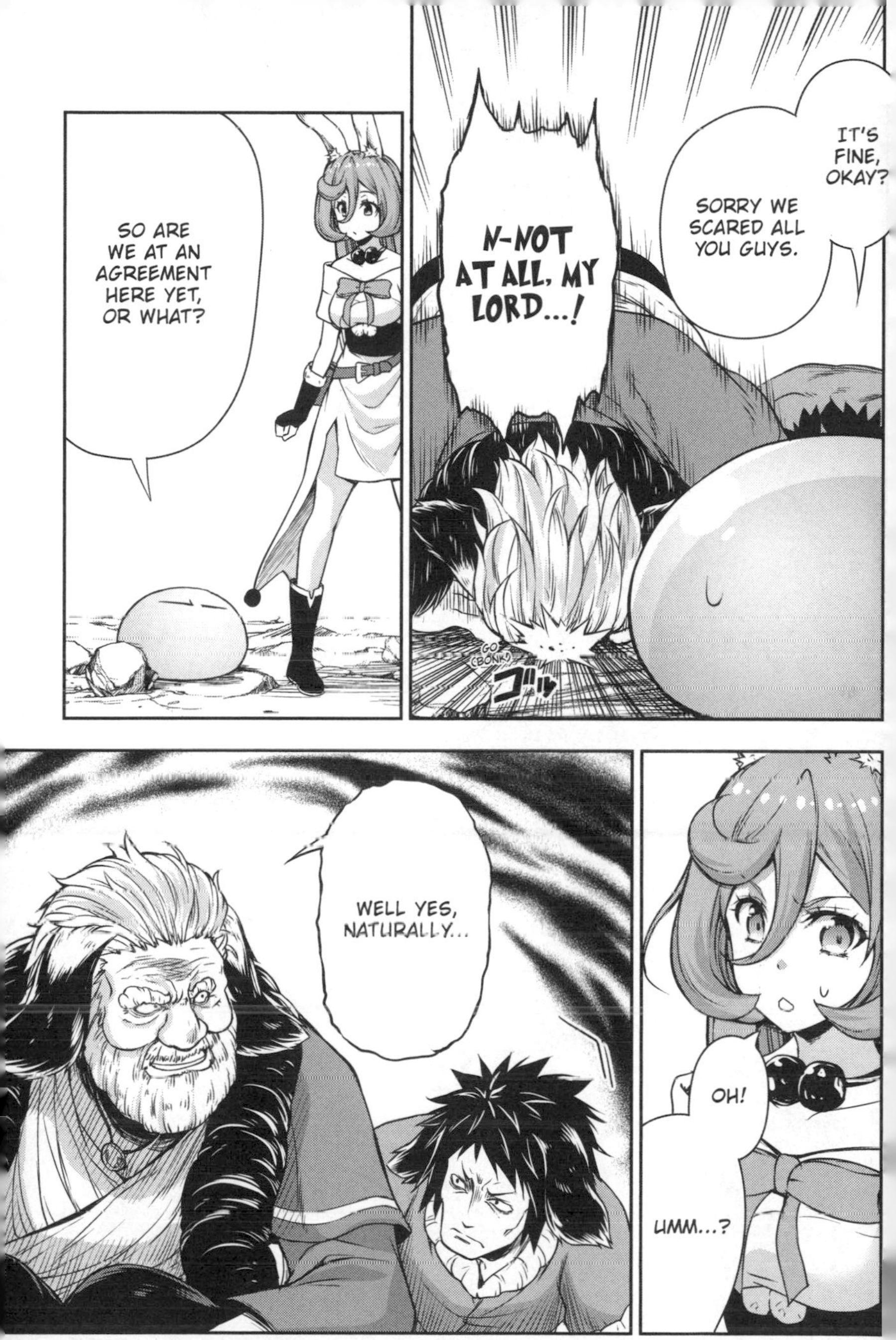
IT'S FINE, OKAY?
SORRY WE SCARED ALL YOU GUYS.
N-NOT AT ALL, MY LORD...!
GO (BONK!)
SO ARE WE AT AN AGREEMENT HERE YET, OR WHAT?
OH!
UMM...?
WELL YES, NATURALLY...

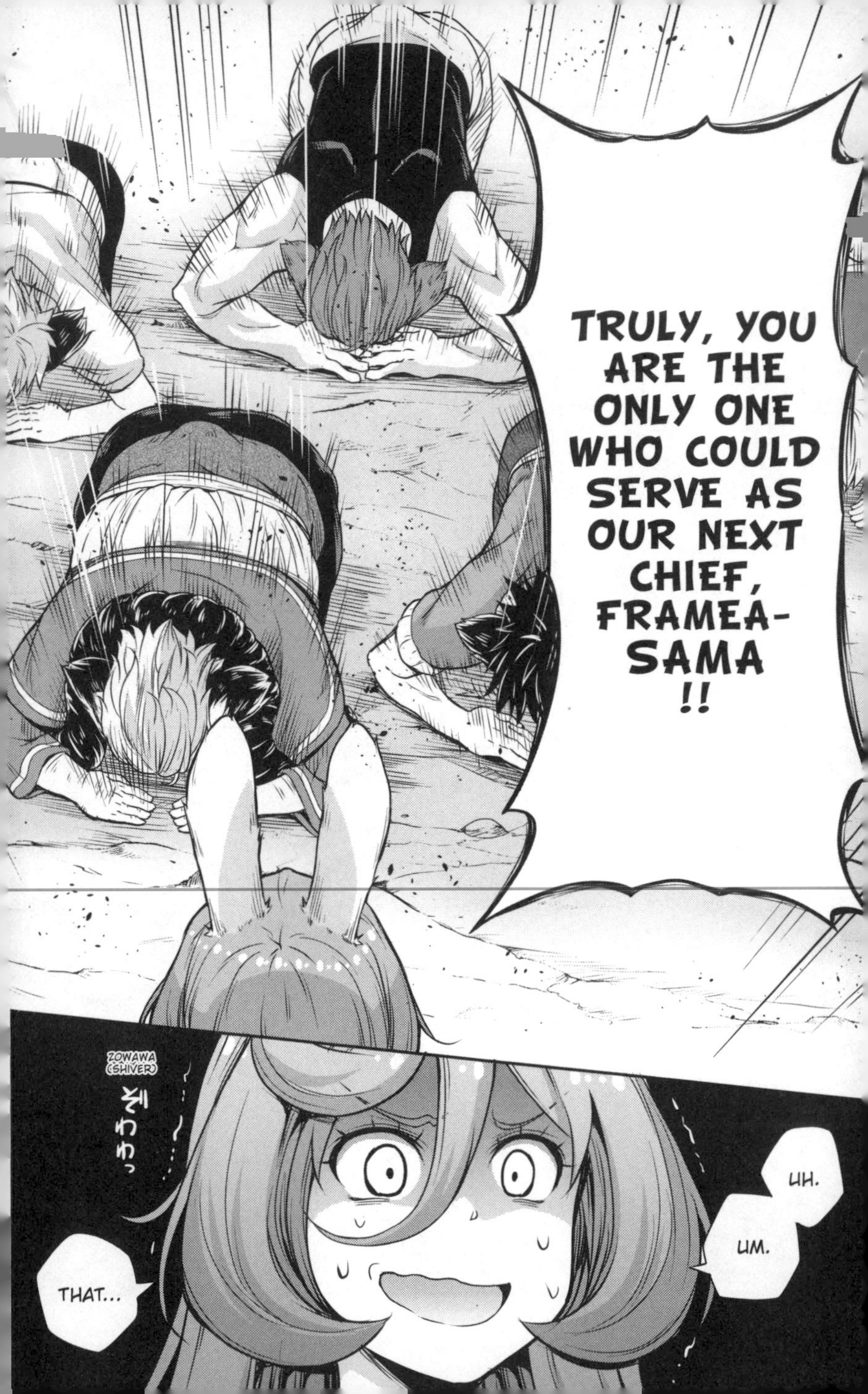
TRULY, YOU ARE THE ONLY ONE WHO COULD SERVE AS OUR NEXT CHIEF, FRAMEA-SAMA !!
ZOWAWA (SHIVER)
ぞわわっ
UH.
UM.
THAT...

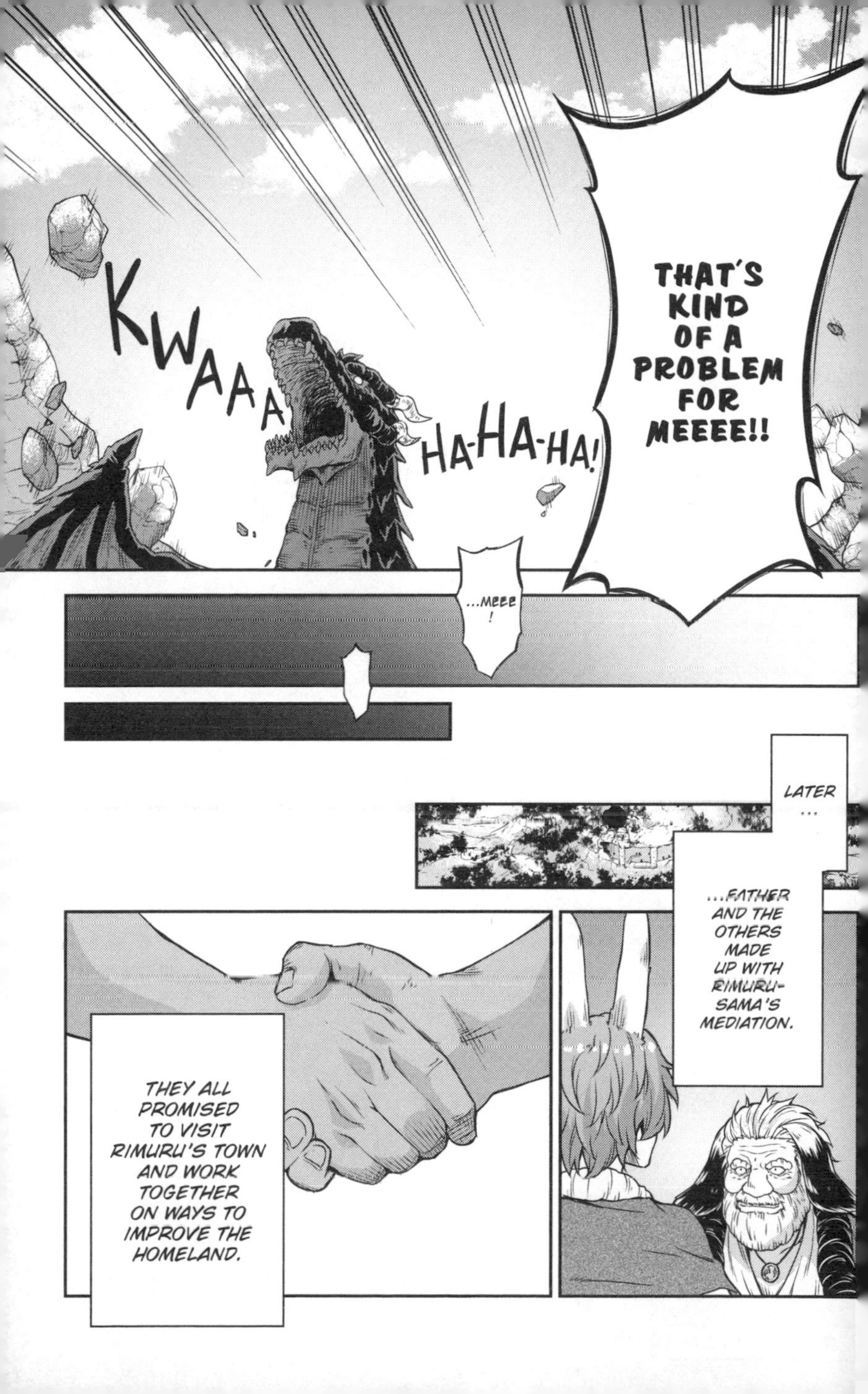
THAT'S KIND OF A PROBLEM FOR MEEEE!!
KWAAAAHA-HA-HA!
...MEEE!
LATER...
...FATHER AND THE OTHERS MADE UP WITH RIMURU-SAMA'S MEDIATION.
THEY ALL PROMISED TO VISIT RIMURU'S TOWN AND WORK TOGETHER ON WAYS TO IMPROVE THE HOMELAND.

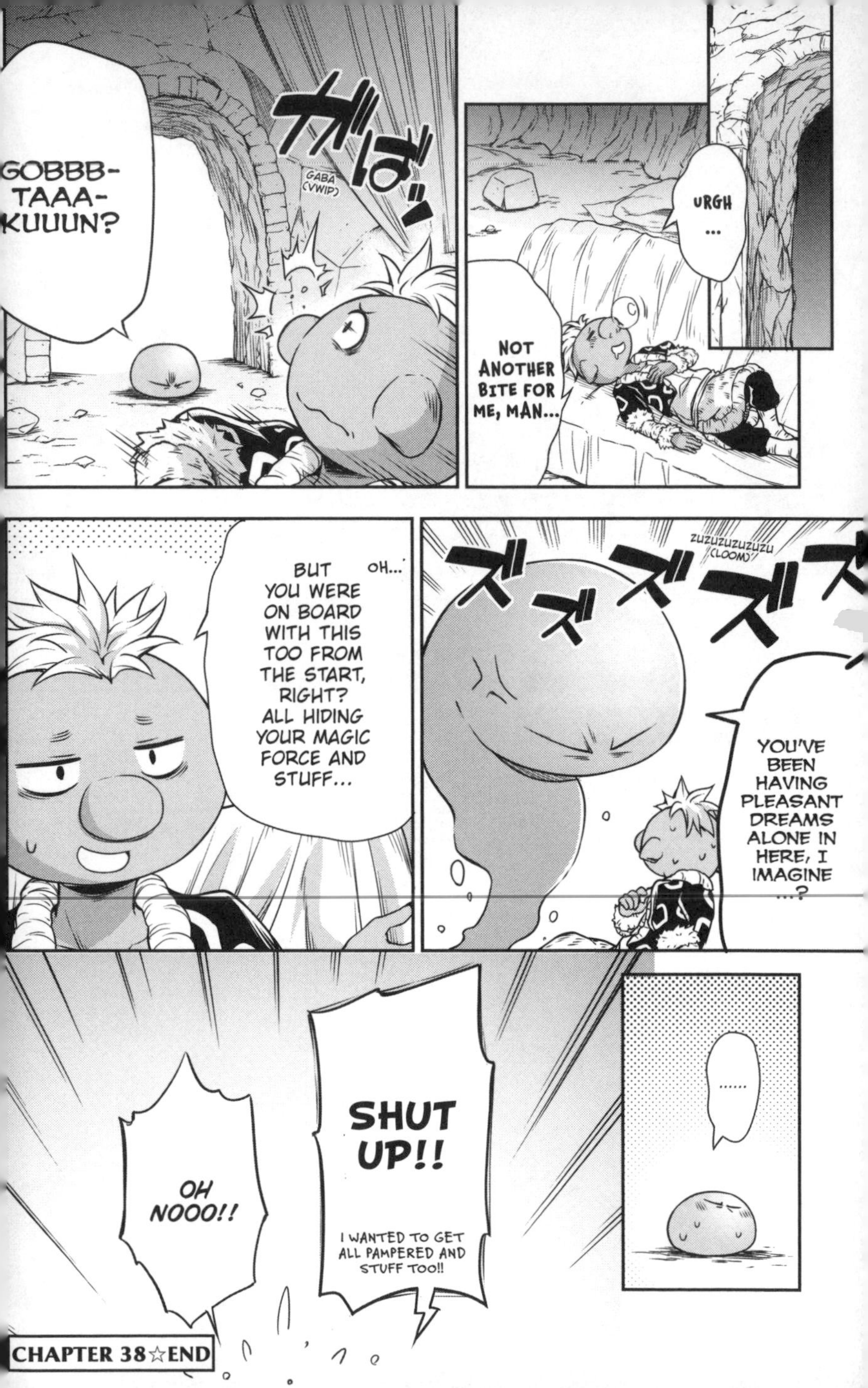
URGH ...
NOT ANOTHER BITE FOR ME, MAN...
GABA (VWIP)
GOBBB-TAAA-KUUUN?
ZUZUZUZUZUZU (LOOM)
YOU'VE BEEN HAVING PLEASANT DREAMS ALONE IN HERE, I IMAGINE ...?
OH...
BUT YOU WERE ON BOARD WITH THIS TOO FROM THE START, RIGHT? ALL HIDING YOUR MAGIC FORCE AND STUFF...
......
SHUT UP!!
I WANTED TO GET ALL PAMPERED AND STUFF TOO!!
OH NOOO!!

CHAPTER 38☆END

That **Time I Got**
Rèincarnated
as SLIME
a
The Ways of the Monster Nation

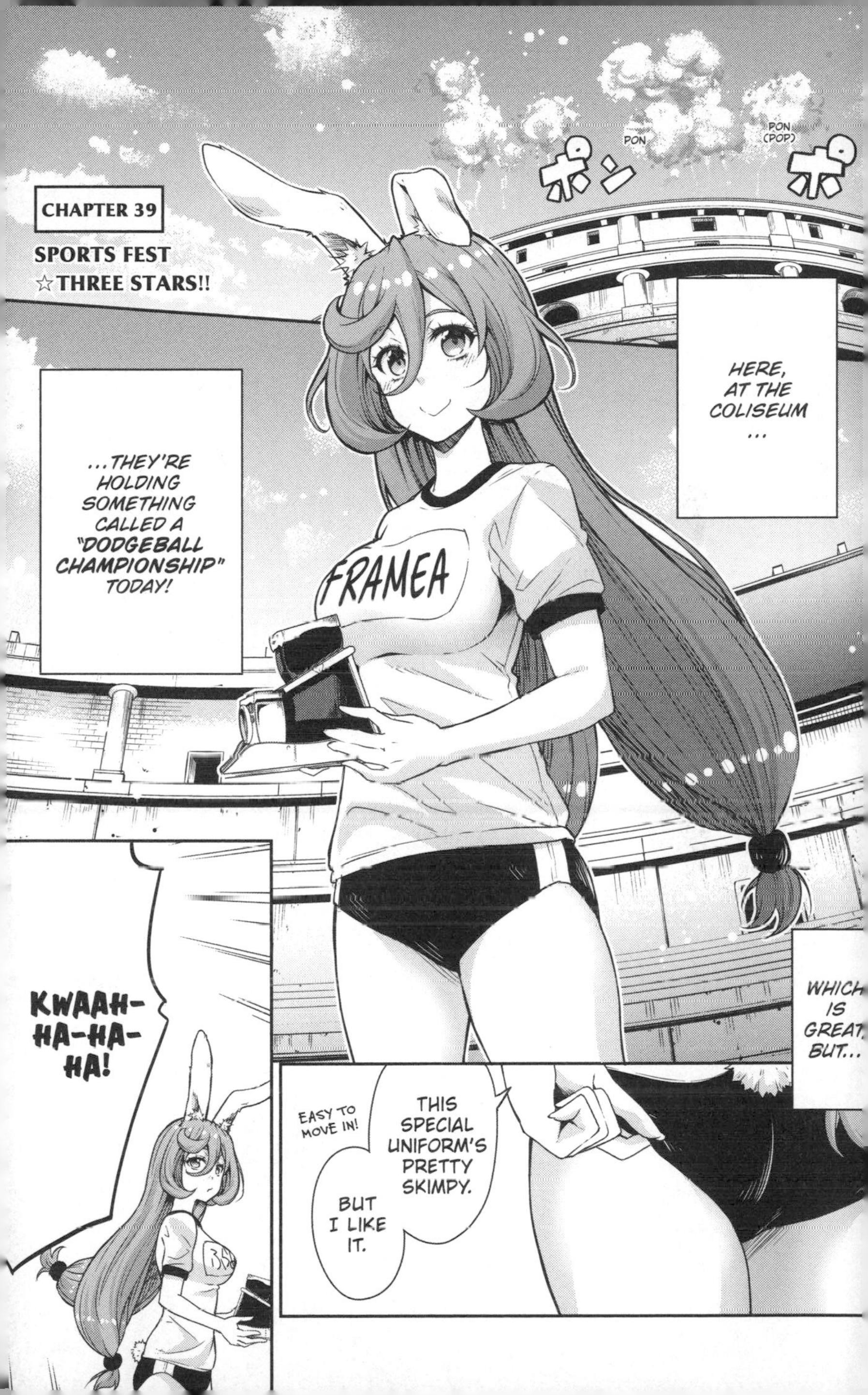
PON (POP)
PON
CHAPTER 39
SPORTS FEST ☆THREE STARS!!
HERE, AT THE COLISEUM…
…THEY'RE HOLDING SOMETHING CALLED A "DODGEBALL CHAMPIONSHIP" TODAY!
WHICH IS GREAT, BUT…
THIS SPECIAL UNIFORM'S PRETTY SKIMPY.
EASY TO MOVE IN!
BUT I LIKE IT.
KWAAH-HA-HA-HA!

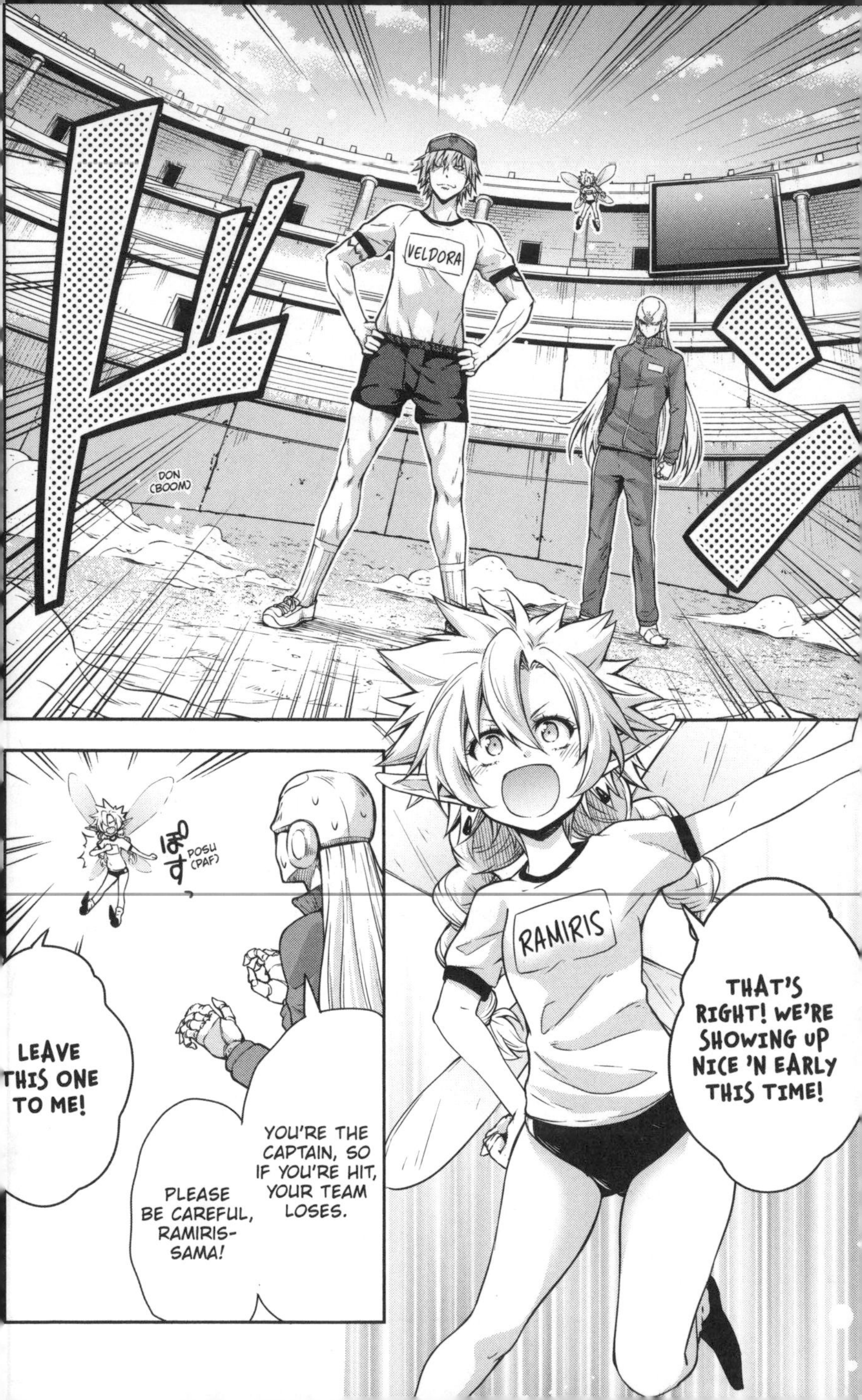
DON (BOOM)
VELDORA
THAT'S RIGHT! WE'RE SHOWING UP NICE 'N EARLY THIS TIME!
RAMIRIS
ぽす
POSU (PAF)
YOU'RE THE CAPTAIN, SO IF YOU'RE HIT, YOUR TEAM LOSES.
PLEASE BE CAREFUL, RAMIRIS-SAMA!
LEAVE THIS ONE TO ME!

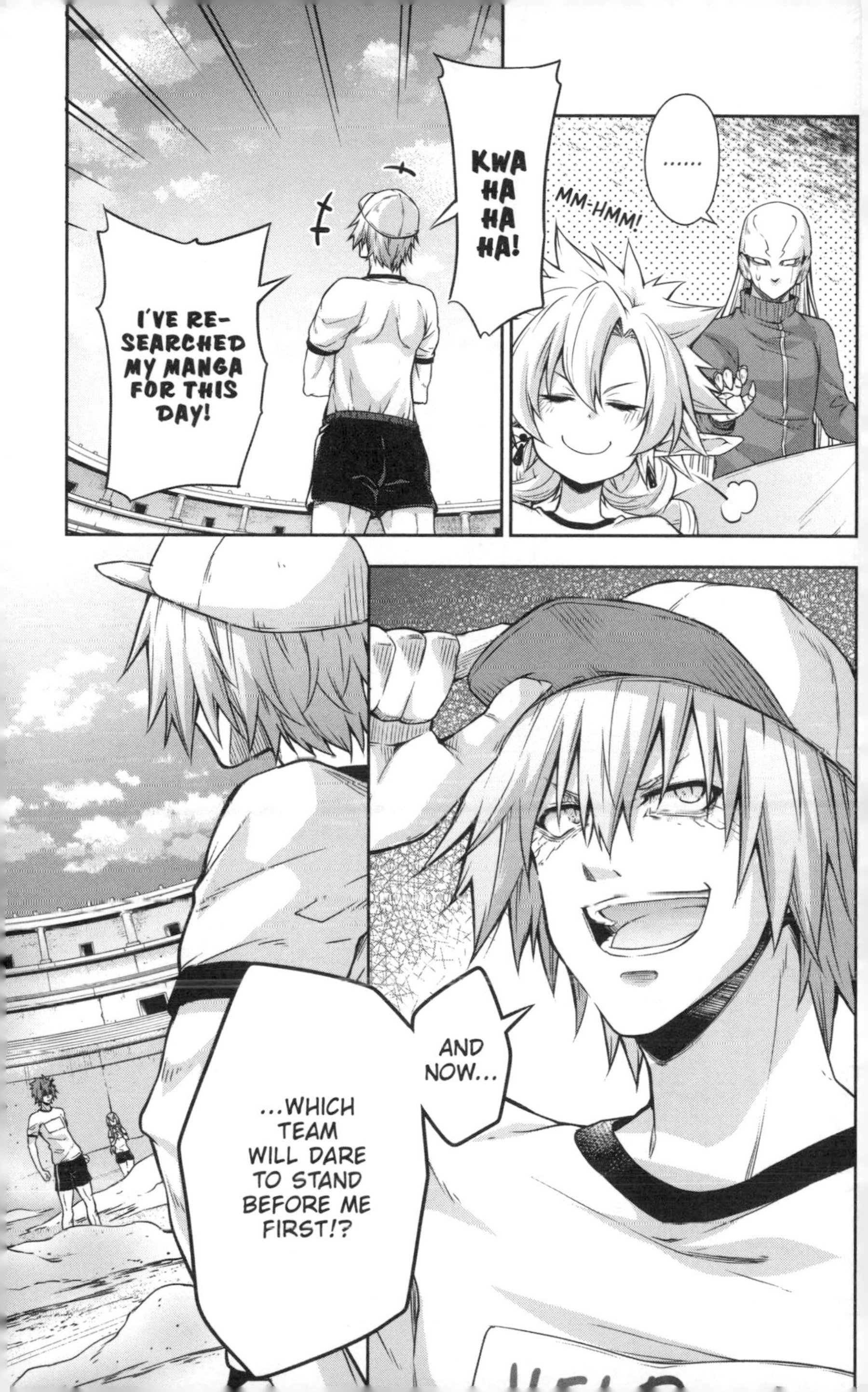
......
MM-HMM!
KWA HA HA HA HA!
I'VE RE-SEARCHED MY MANGA FOR THIS DAY!
AND NOW...
...WHICH TEAM WILL DARE TO STAND BEFORE ME FIRST!?

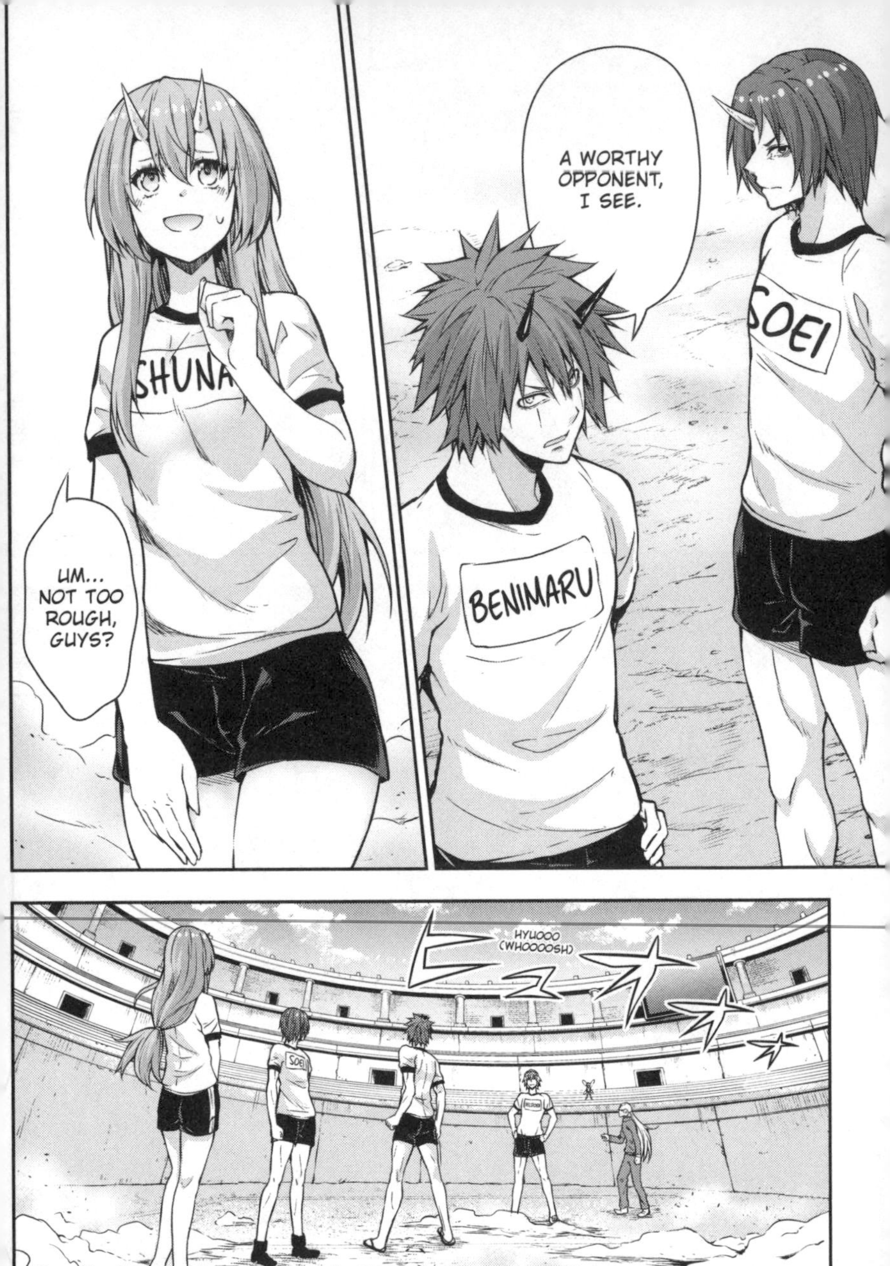
A WORTHY OPPONENT, I SEE.
SOEI
BENIMARU
SHUNA
UM... NOT TOO ROUGH, GUYS?
HYUOOO (WHOOOOSH)
SOEI

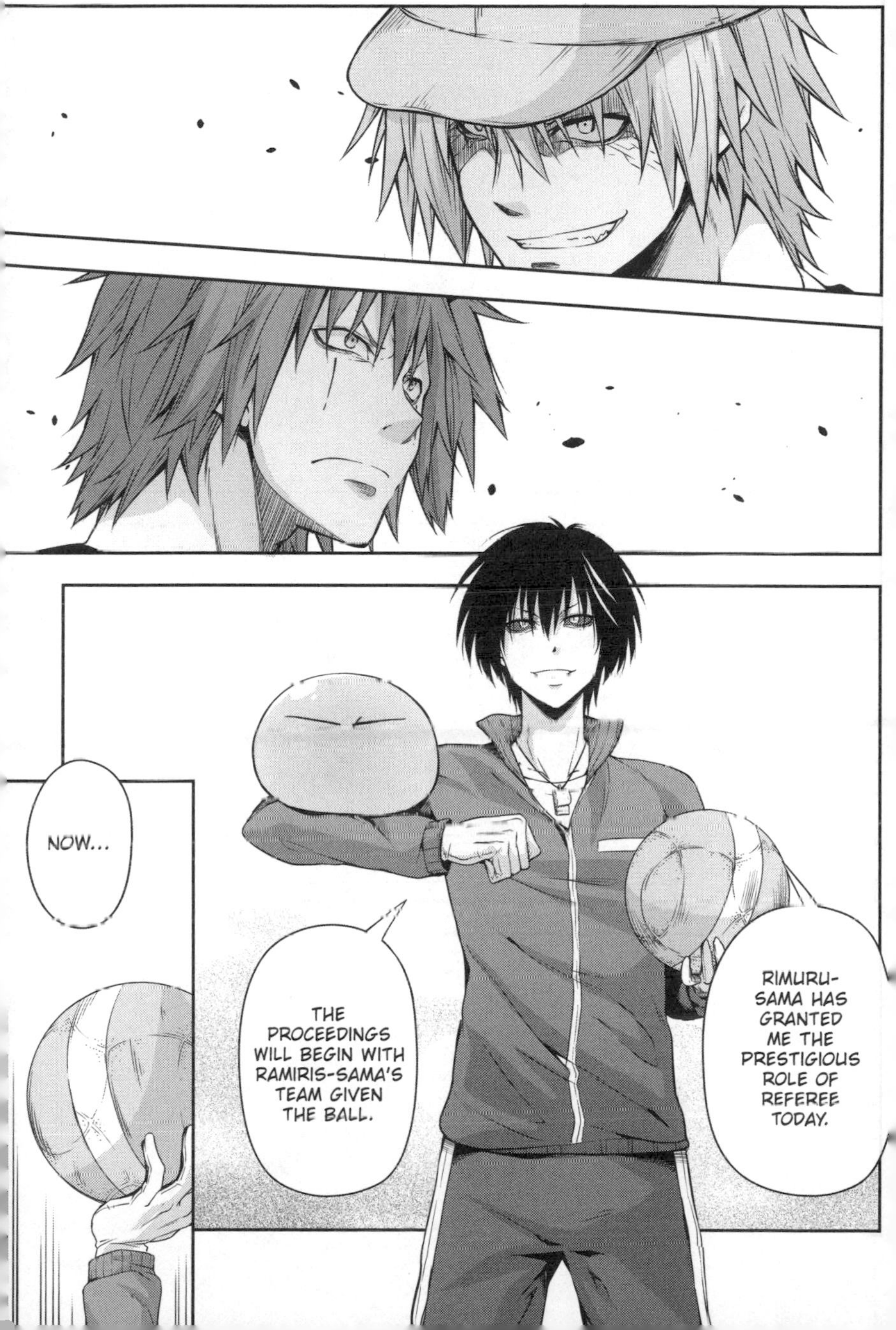
RIMURU-SAMA HAS GRANTED ME THE PRESTIGIOUS ROLE OF REFEREE TODAY.
THE PROCEEDINGS WILL BEGIN WITH RAMIRIS-SAMA'S TEAM GIVEN THE BALL.
NOW...

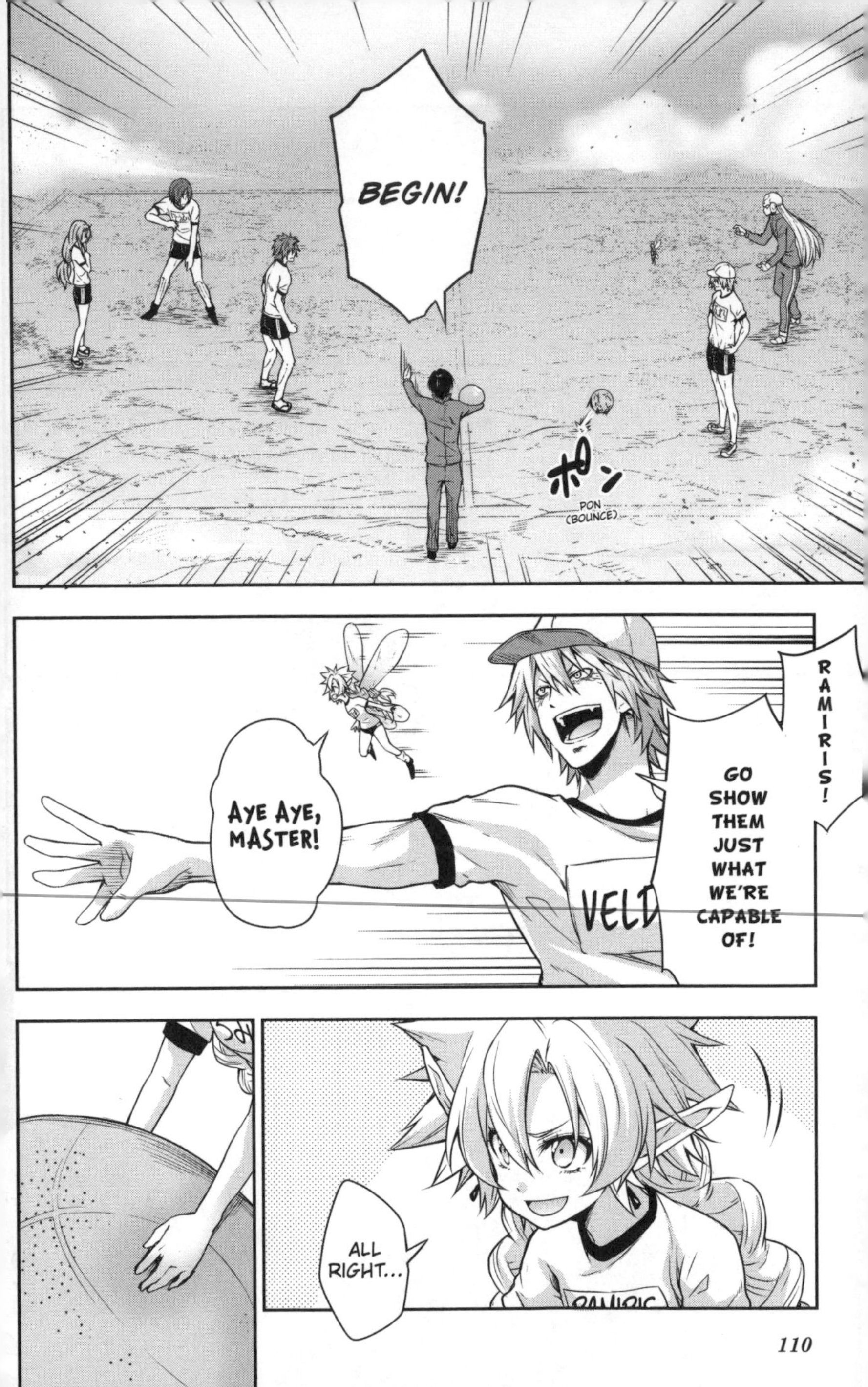
BEGIN!
ポン
PON (BOUNCE)
RAMIRIS!
GO SHOW THEM JUST WHAT WE'RE CAPABLE OF!
AYE AYE, MASTER!
ALL RIGHT...

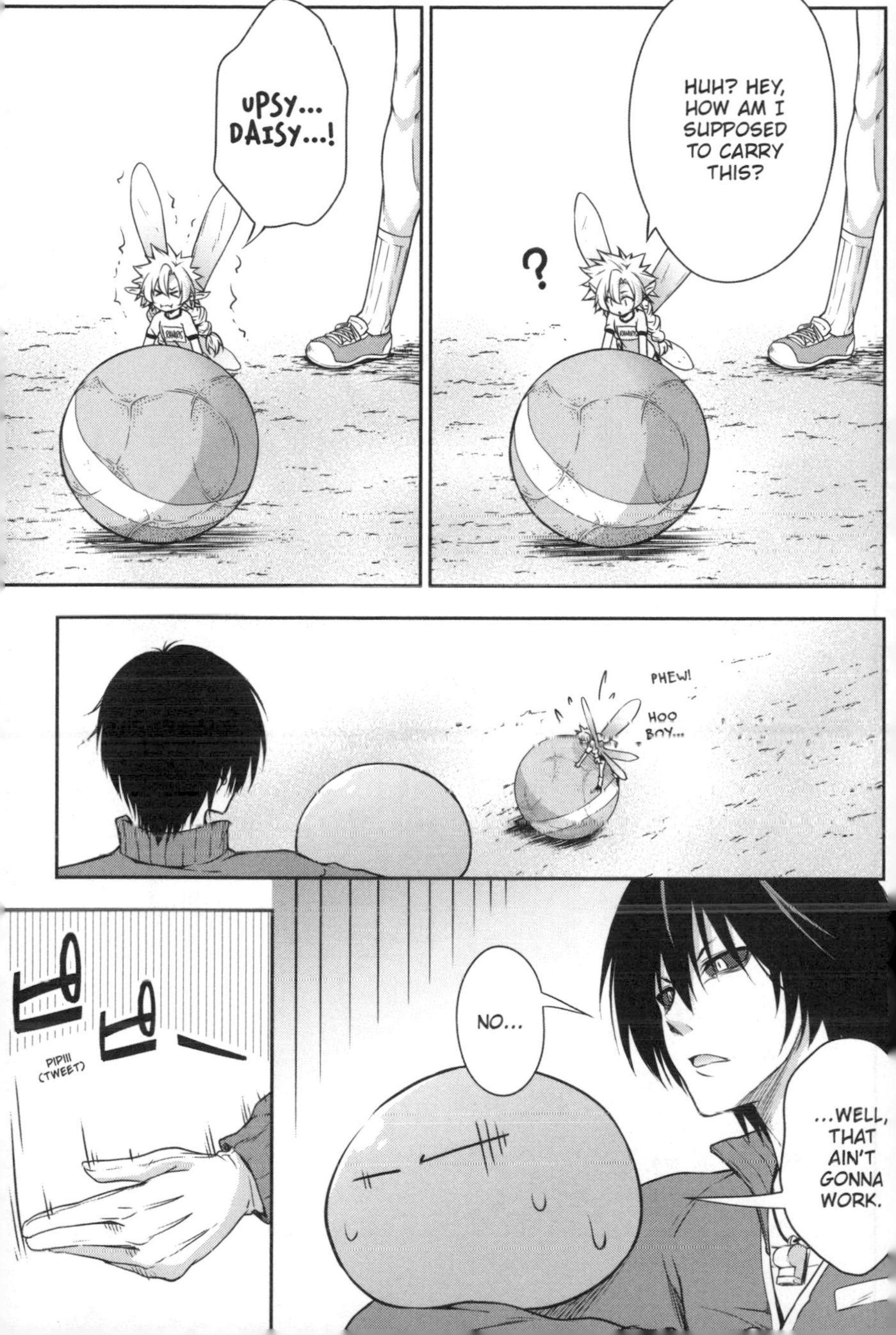
HUH? HEY, HOW AM I SUPPOSED TO CARRY THIS?
?
UPSY... DAISY...!
PHEW!
HOO BOY...
NO...
...WELL, THAT AIN'T GONNA WORK.
PIPIII (TWEET)

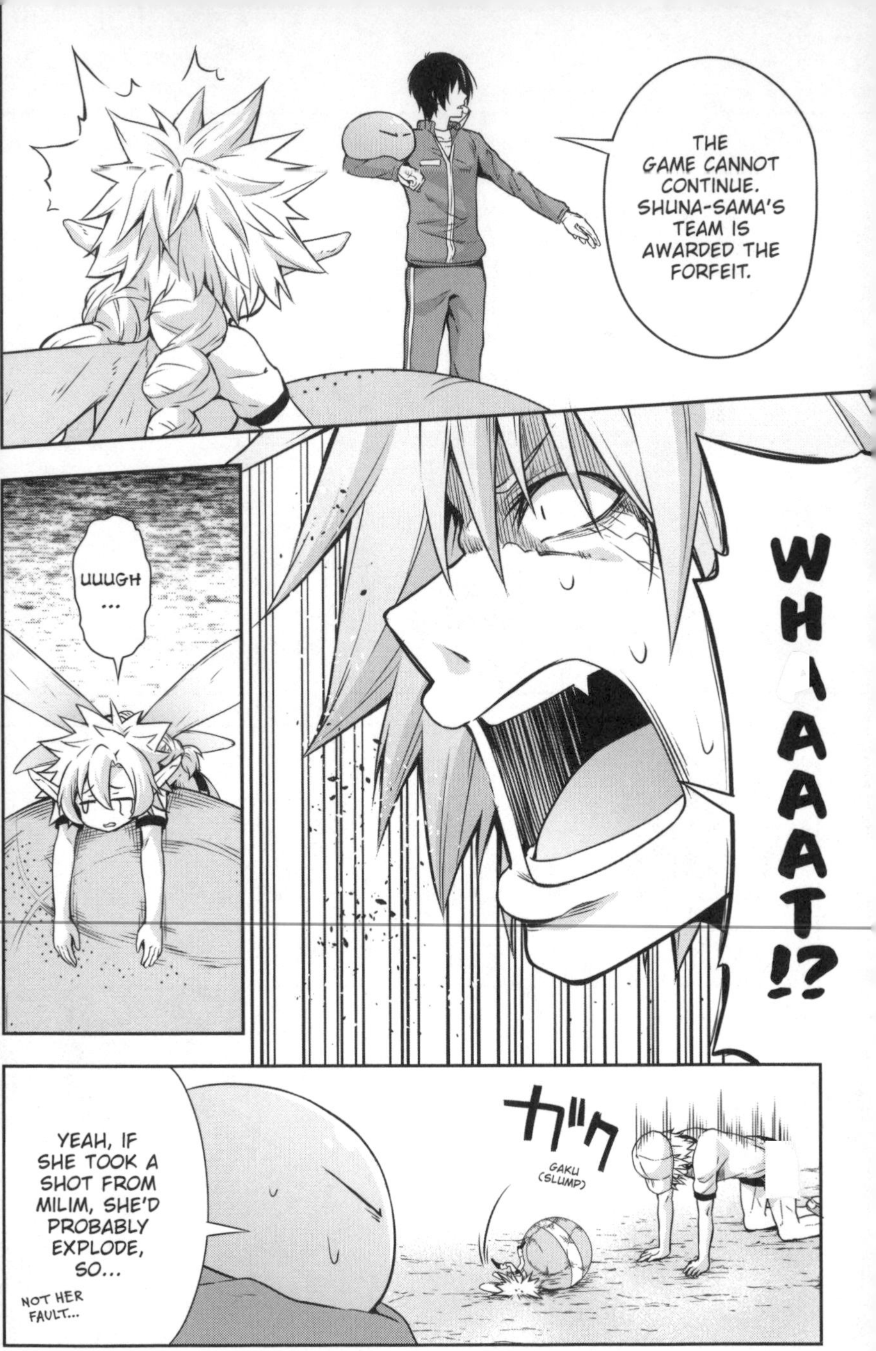
THE GAME CANNOT CONTINUE. SHUNA-SAMA'S TEAM IS AWARDED THE FORFEIT.
WHAAAAT!?
UUUGH...
ガク
GAKU (SLUMP)
YEAH, IF SHE TOOK A SHOT FROM MILIM, SHE'D PROBABLY EXPLODE, SO...
NOT HER FAULT...

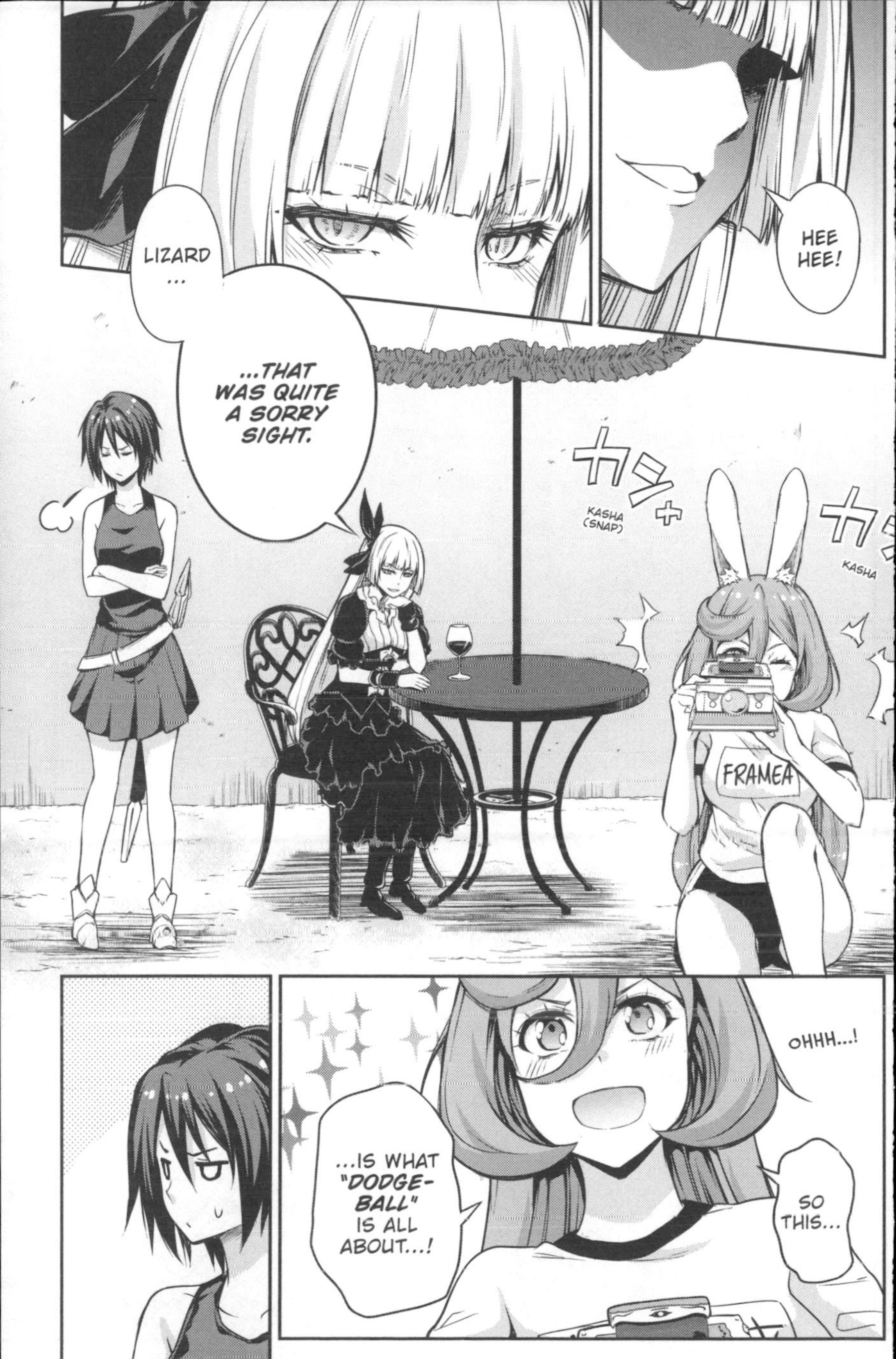
HEE HEE!
LIZARD ...
...THAT WAS QUITE A SORRY SIGHT.
カシャ
KASHA (SNAP)
カシャ
KASHA
FRAMEA
OHHH...!
SO THIS...
...IS WHAT "DODGE-BALL" IS ALL ABOUT...!

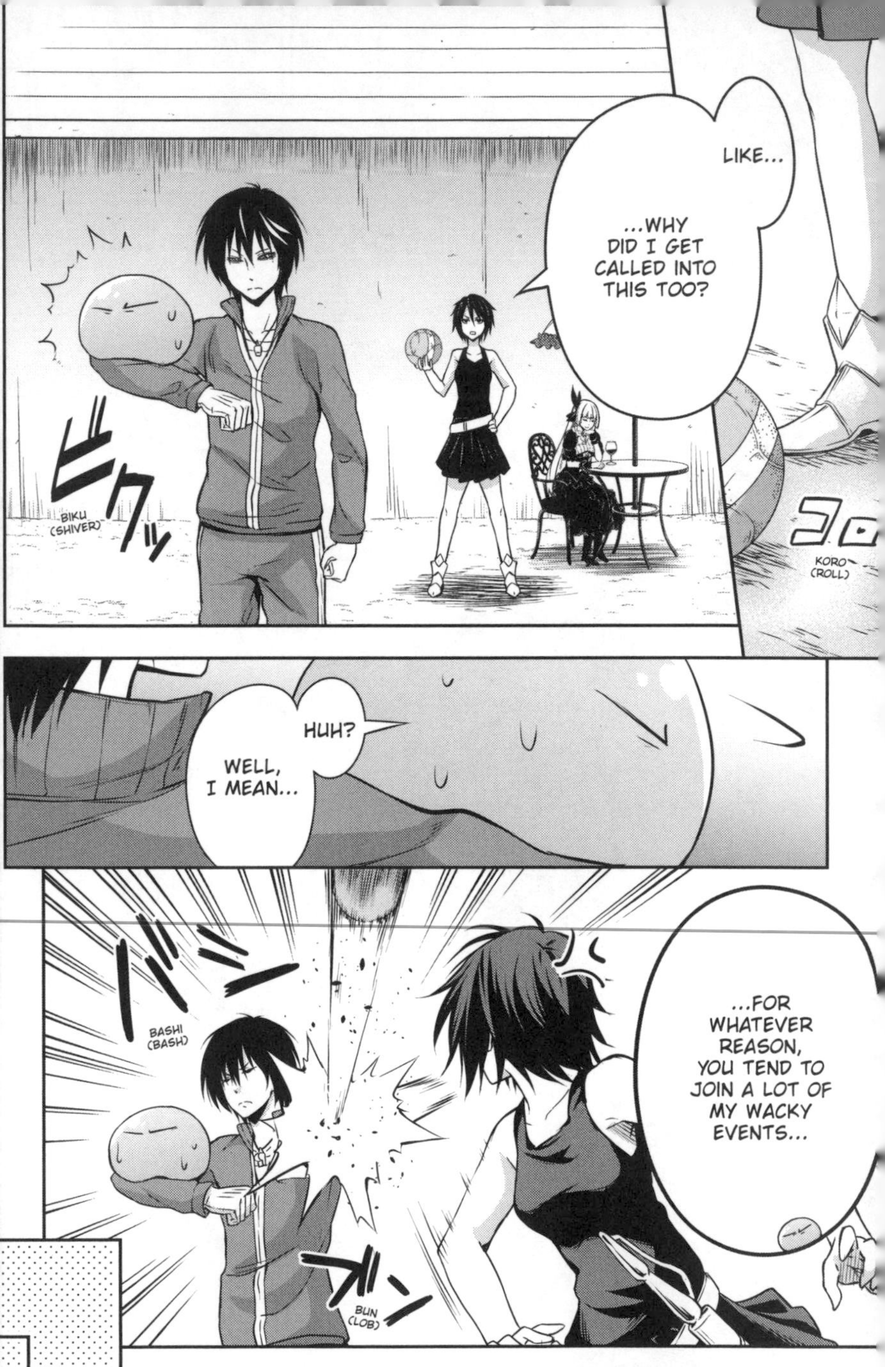
LIKE...
...WHY DID I GET CALLED INTO THIS TOO?
KORO (ROLL)
BIKU (SHIVER)
HUH?
WELL, I MEAN...
...FOR WHATEVER REASON, YOU TEND TO JOIN A LOT OF MY WACKY EVENTS...
BASHI (BASH)
BUN (LOB)

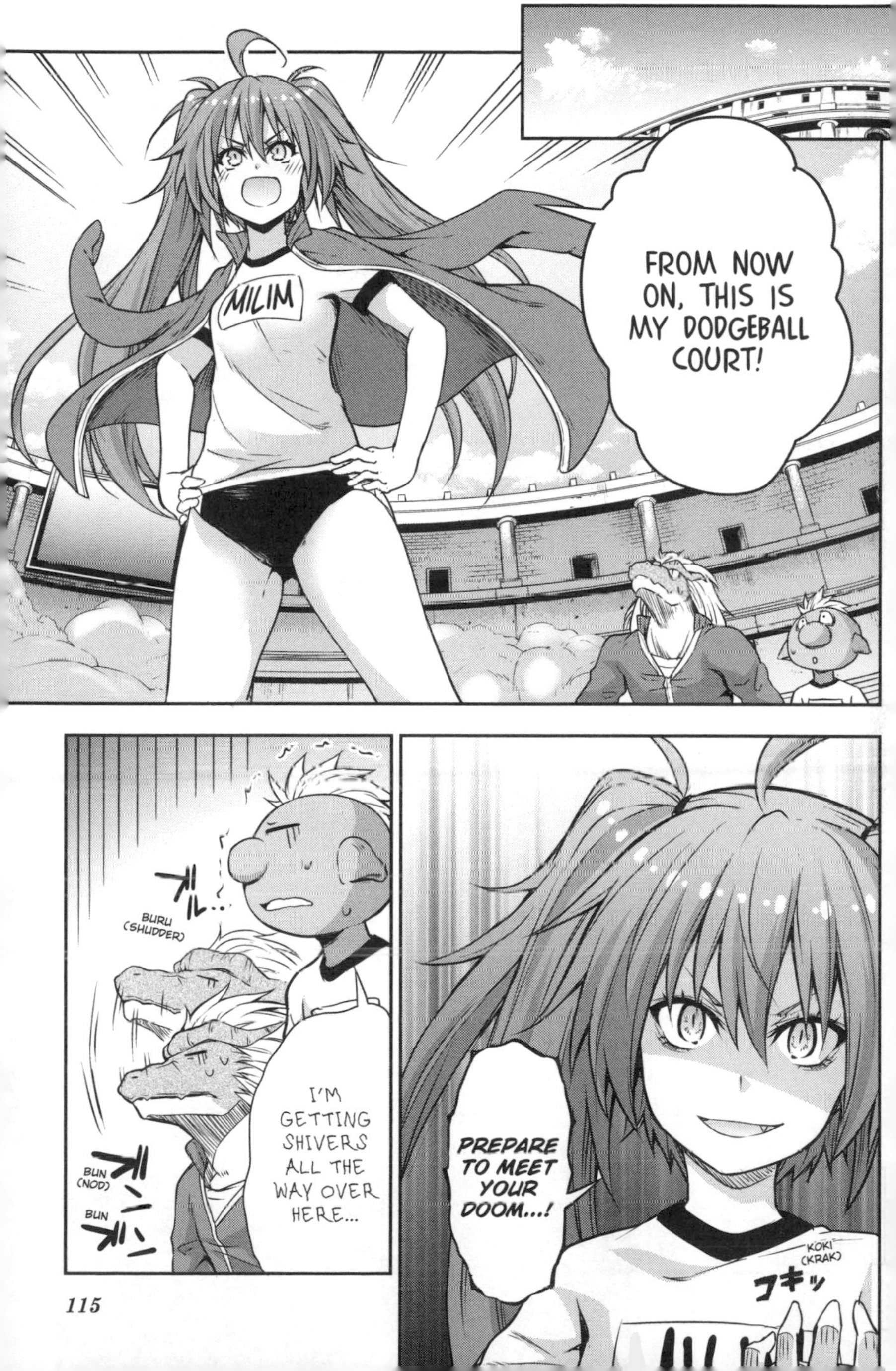
FROM NOW ON, THIS IS MY DODGEBALL COURT!
MILIM
PREPARE TO MEET YOUR DOOM...!
KOKI (KRAK)
コキッ
BURU (SHUDDER)
ブル…
I'M GETTING SHIVERS ALL THE WAY OVER HERE...
BUN (NOD)
BUN
ブンブン

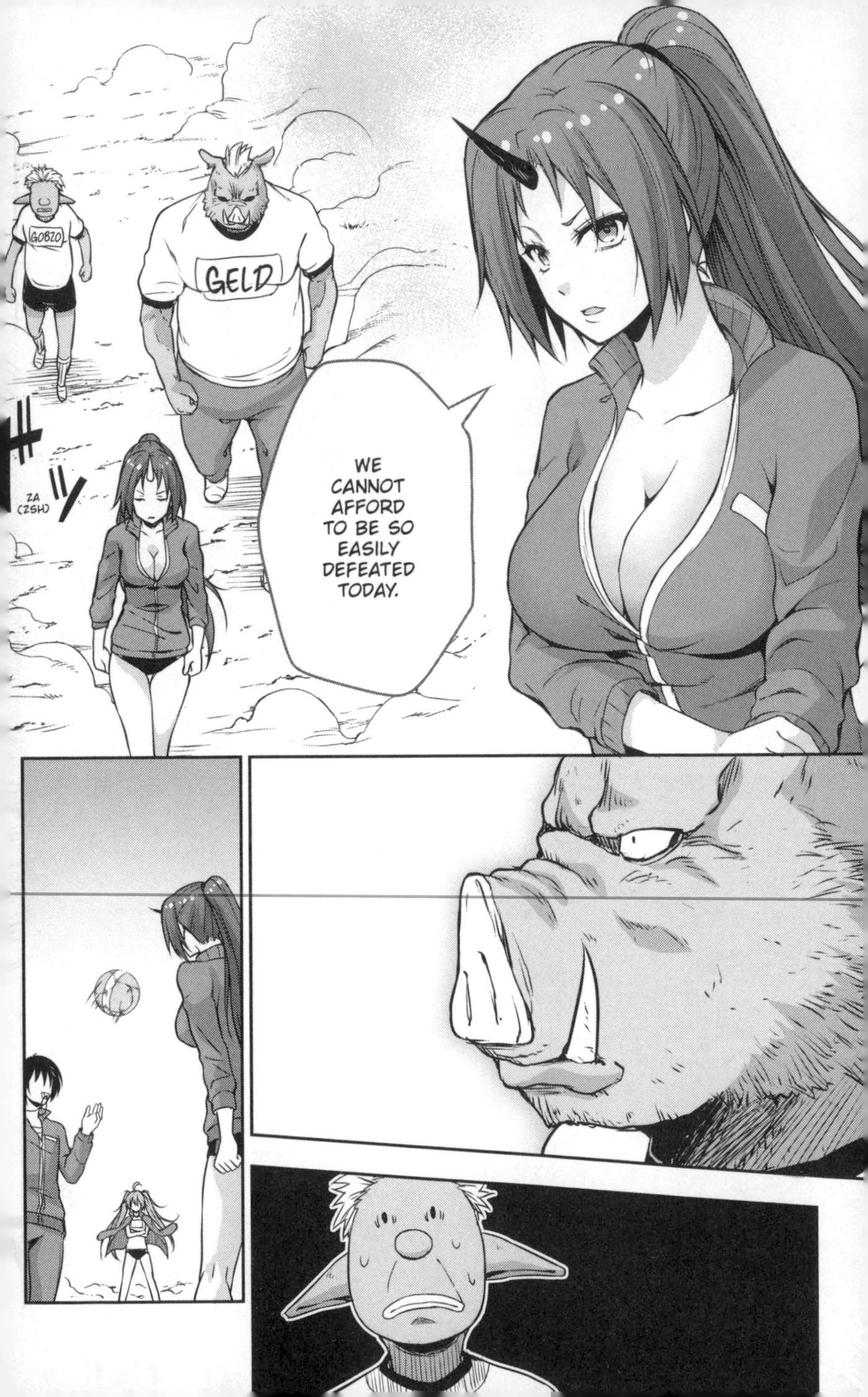
GELD
GOBZO
WE CANNOT AFFORD TO BE SO EASILY DEFEATED TODAY.
ZA (ZSH)

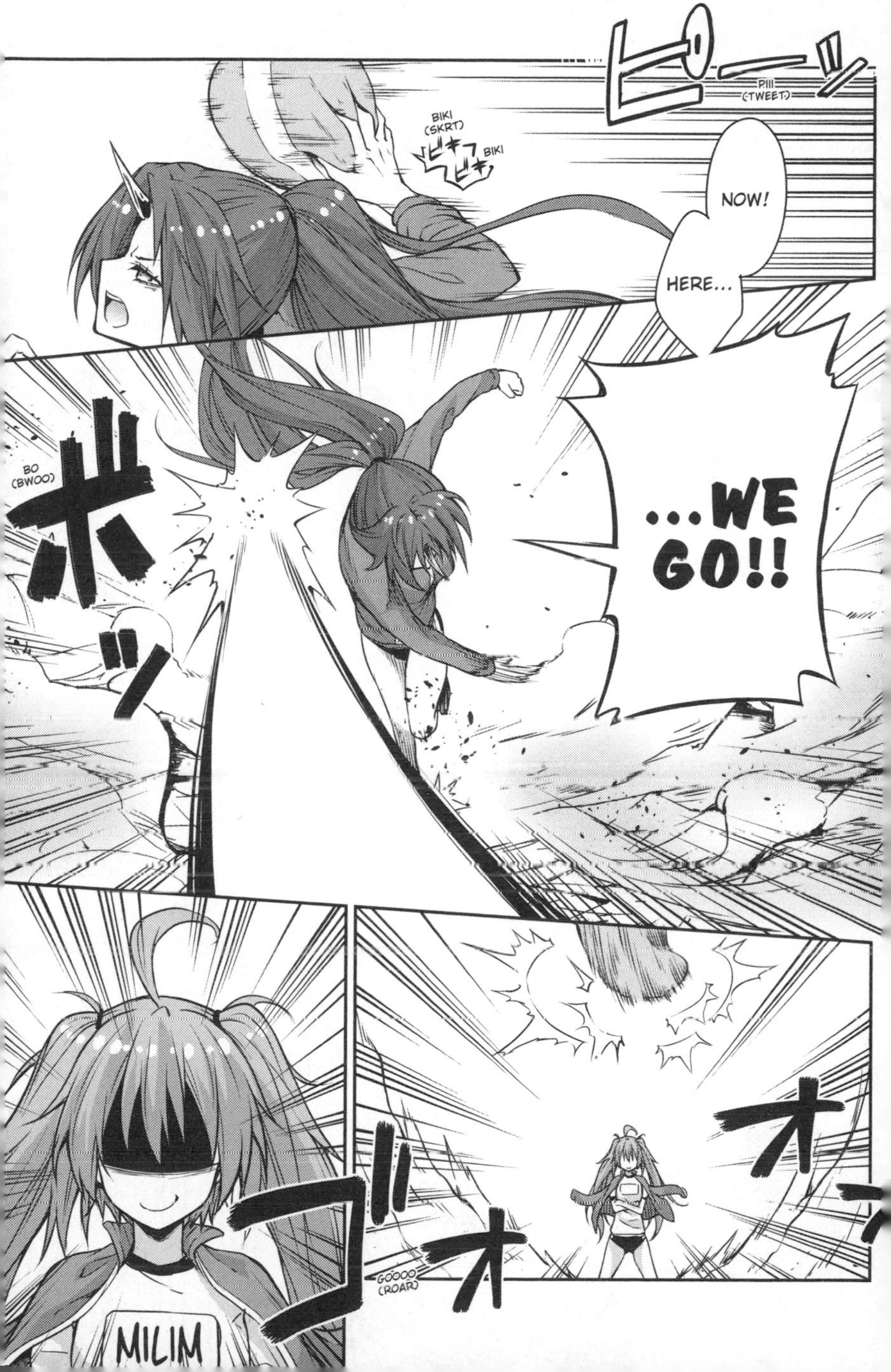
PIII
(TWEET)
BIKI
(SKRT)
BIKI
NOW!
HERE...
...WE GO!!
BO
(BWOO)
GOOOO
(ROAR)
MILIM

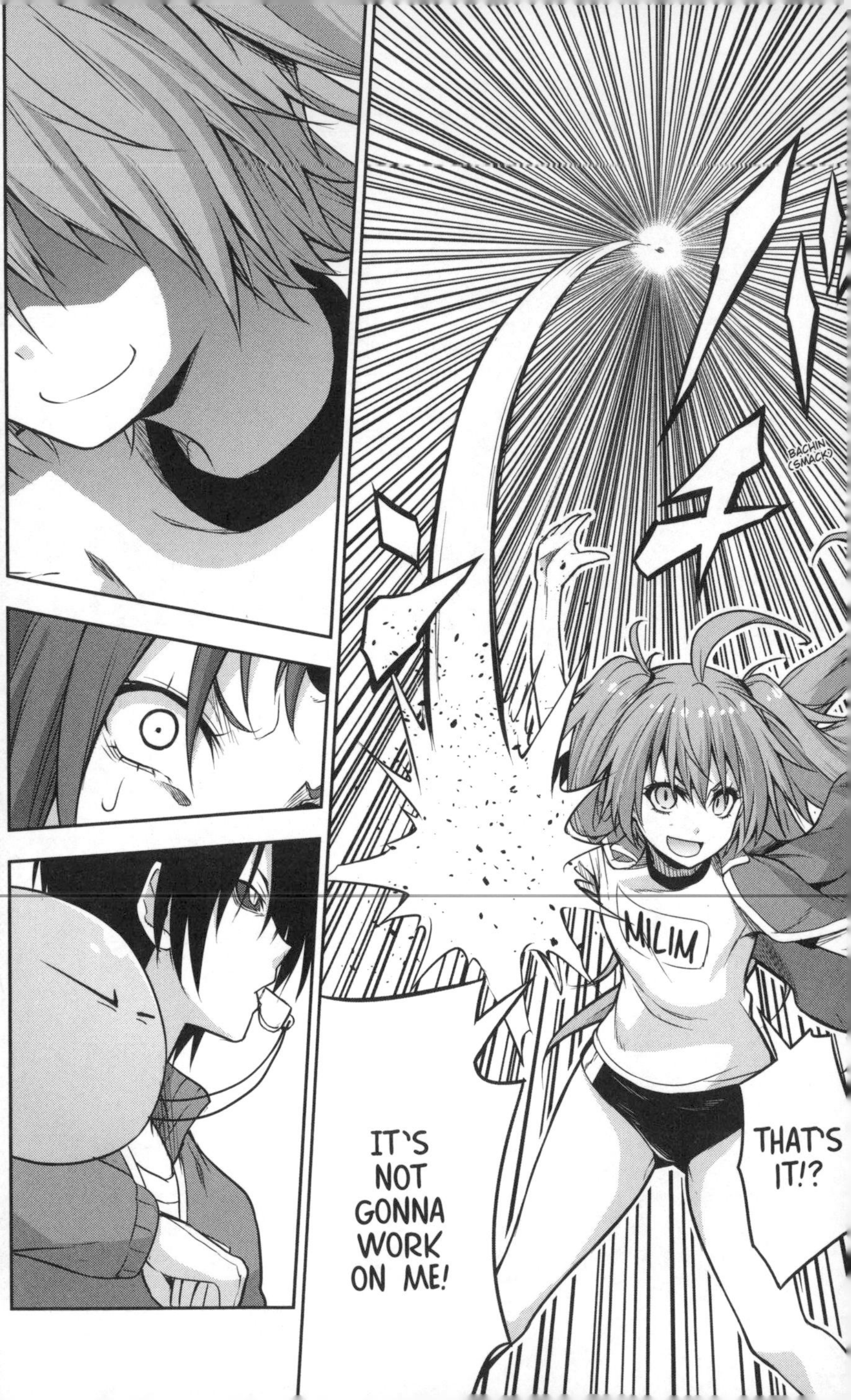
BACHIN (SMACK)
MILIM
THAT'S IT!?
IT'S NOT GONNA WORK ON ME!

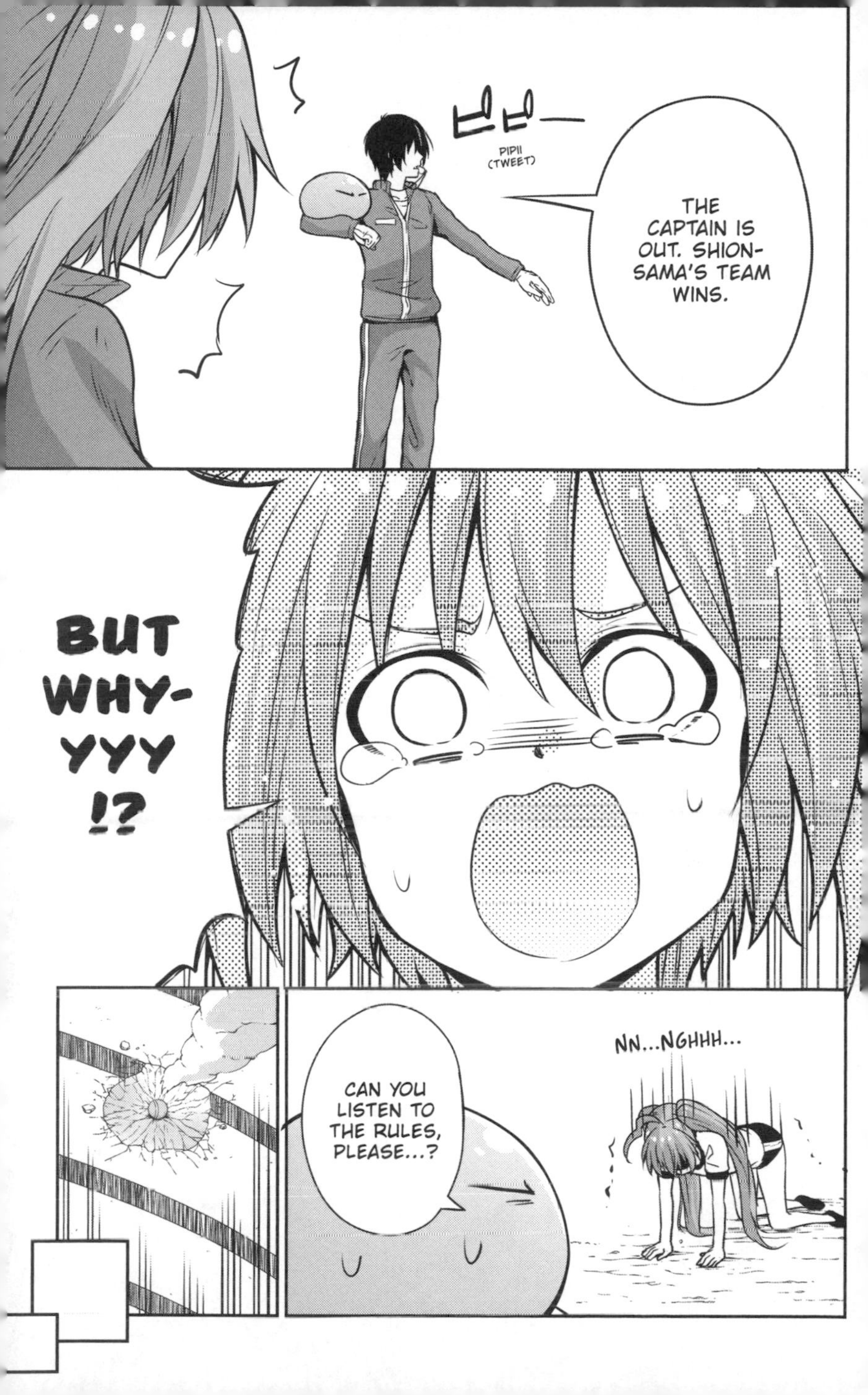
ピピー
PIPII (TWEET)
THE CAPTAIN IS OUT. SHION-SAMA'S TEAM WINS.
BUT WHY-YYY !?
NN...NGHHH...
CAN YOU LISTEN TO THE RULES, PLEASE...?

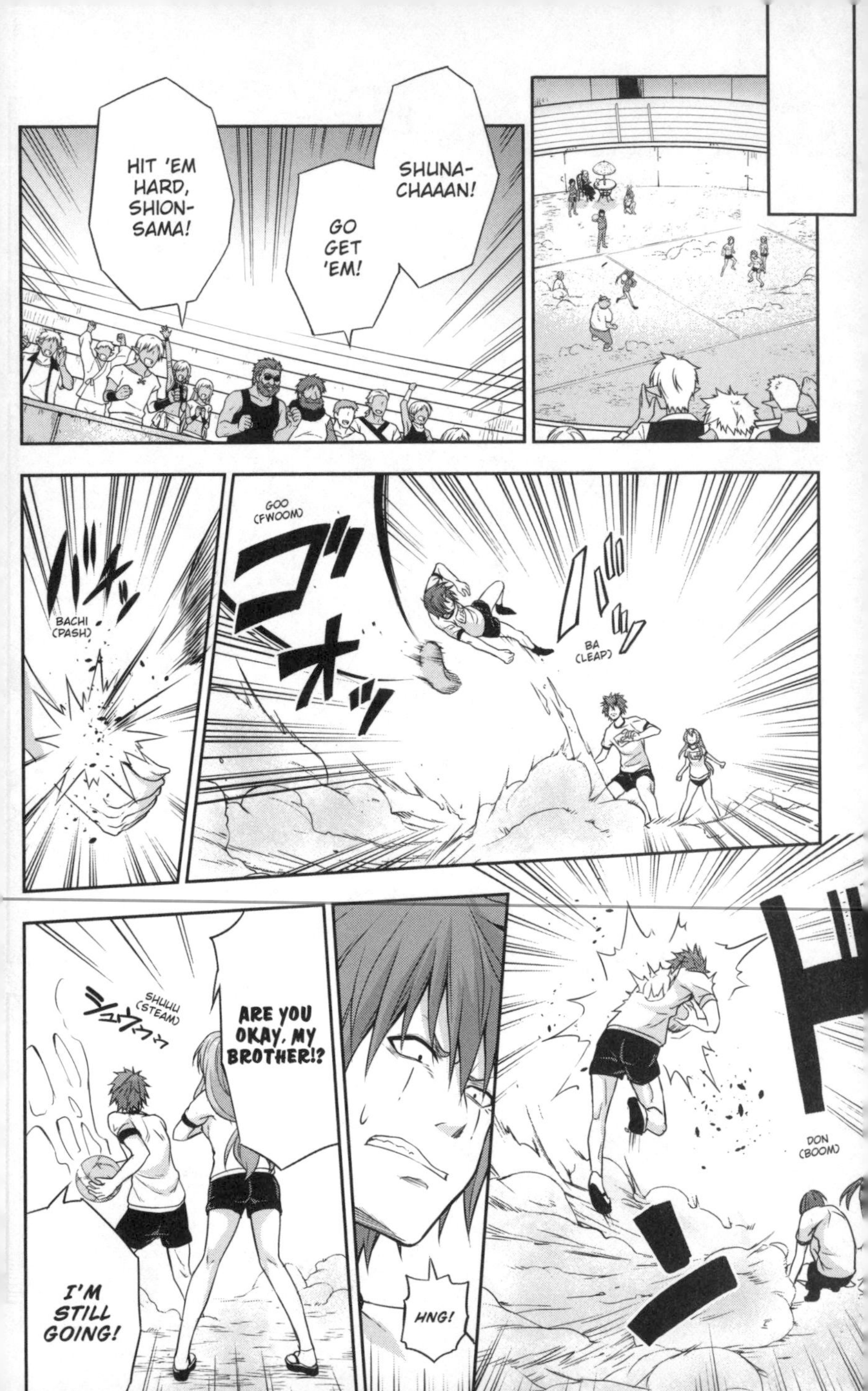
SHUNA-CHAAAN!
GO GET 'EM!
HIT 'EM HARD, SHION-SAMA!
GOO (FWOOM)
BA (LEAP)
BACHI (PASH)
DON (BOOM)
HNG!
ARE YOU OKAY, MY BROTHER!?
SHUUU (STEAM)
I'M STILL GOING!

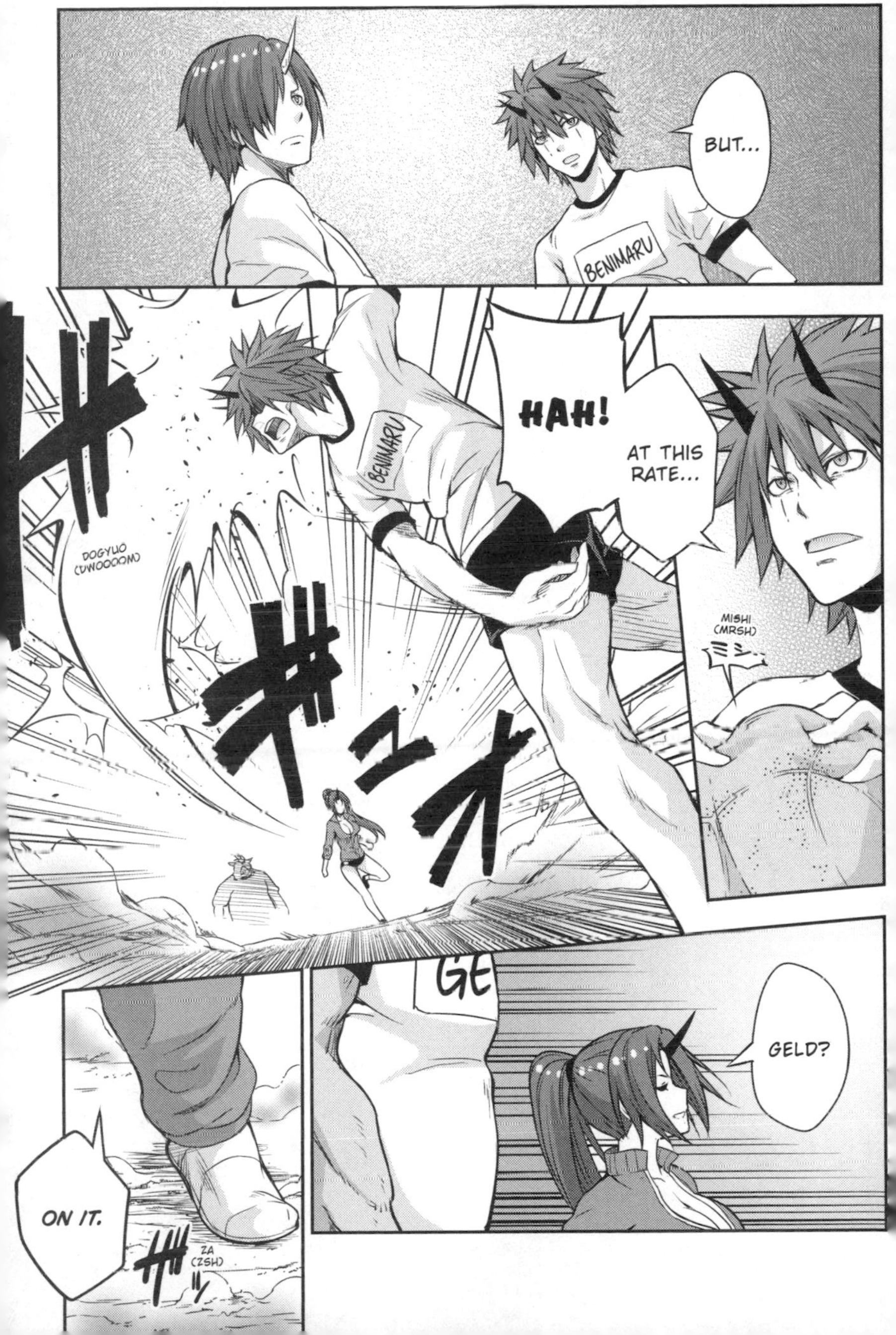
BUT...
AT THIS RATE...
MISHI (MRSH)
HAH!
DOGYUO (DWOOOOM)
GE
GELD?
ON IT.
ZA (ZSH)

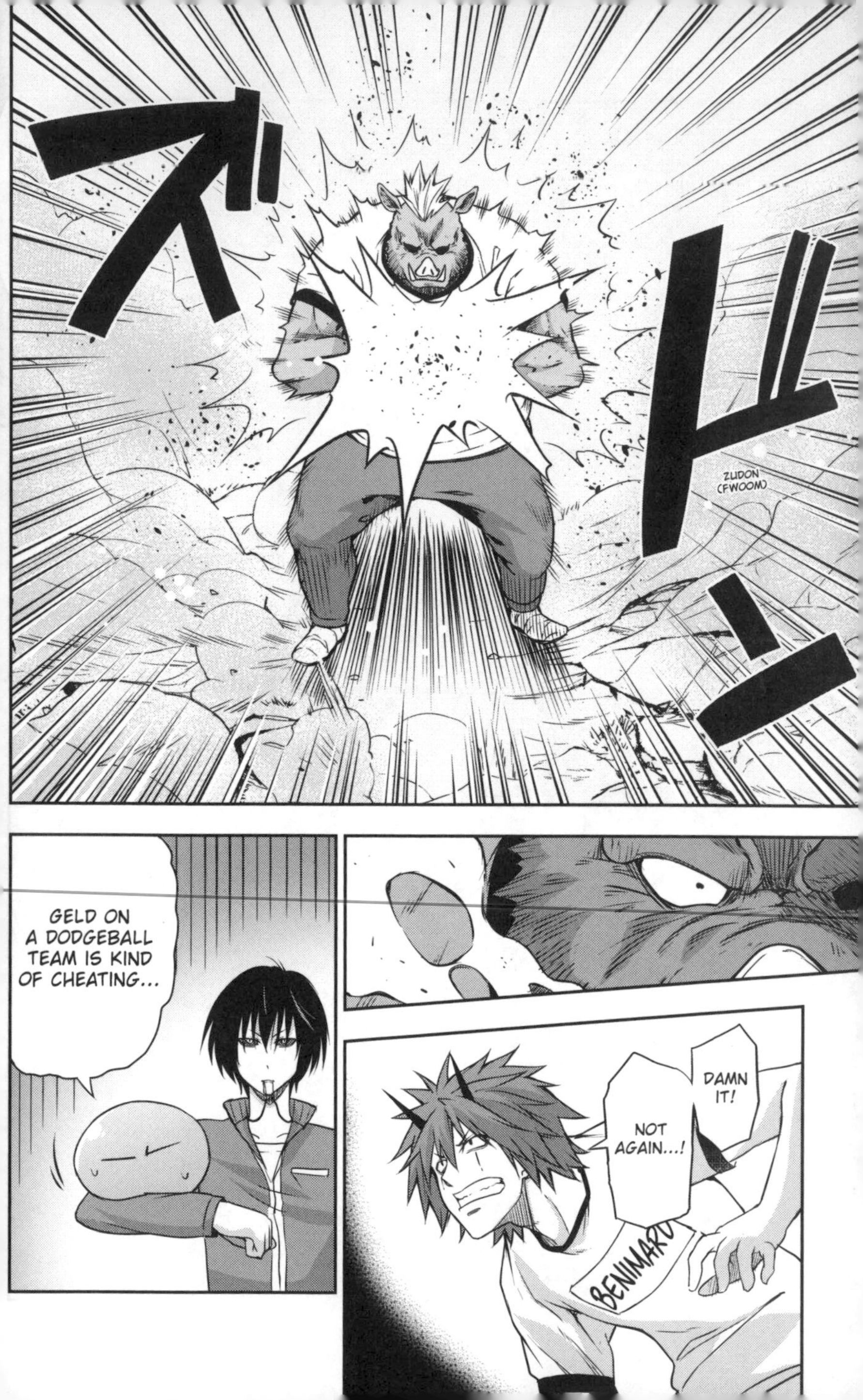

ズドンッ
ZUDON (FWOOM)
DAMN IT!
NOT AGAIN...!
BENIMARU
GELD ON A DODGEBALL TEAM IS KIND OF CHEATING...

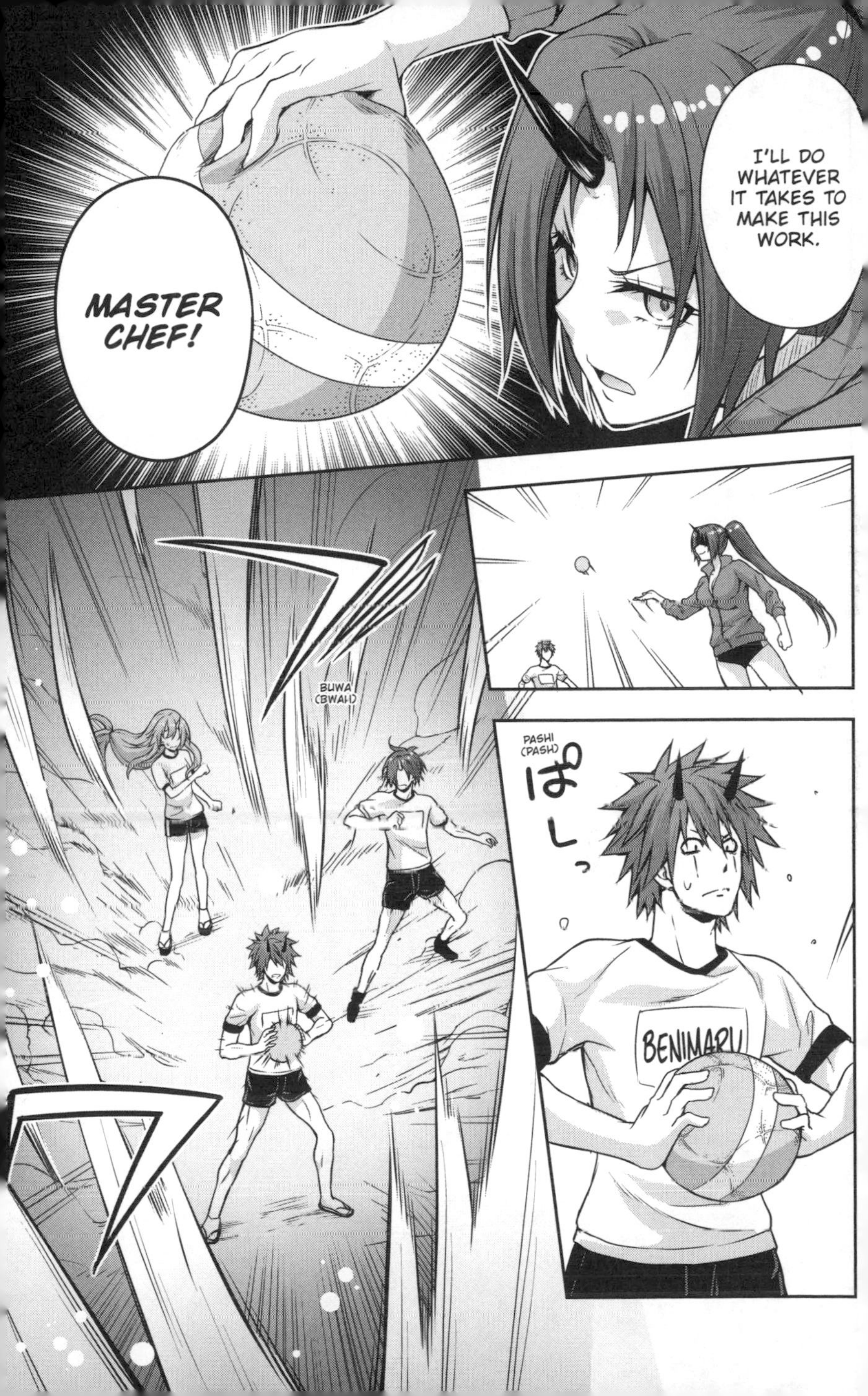
I'LL DO WHATEVER IT TAKES TO MAKE THIS WORK.
MASTER CHEF!
PASHI (PASH)
ぱしっ
BUWA (BWAH)

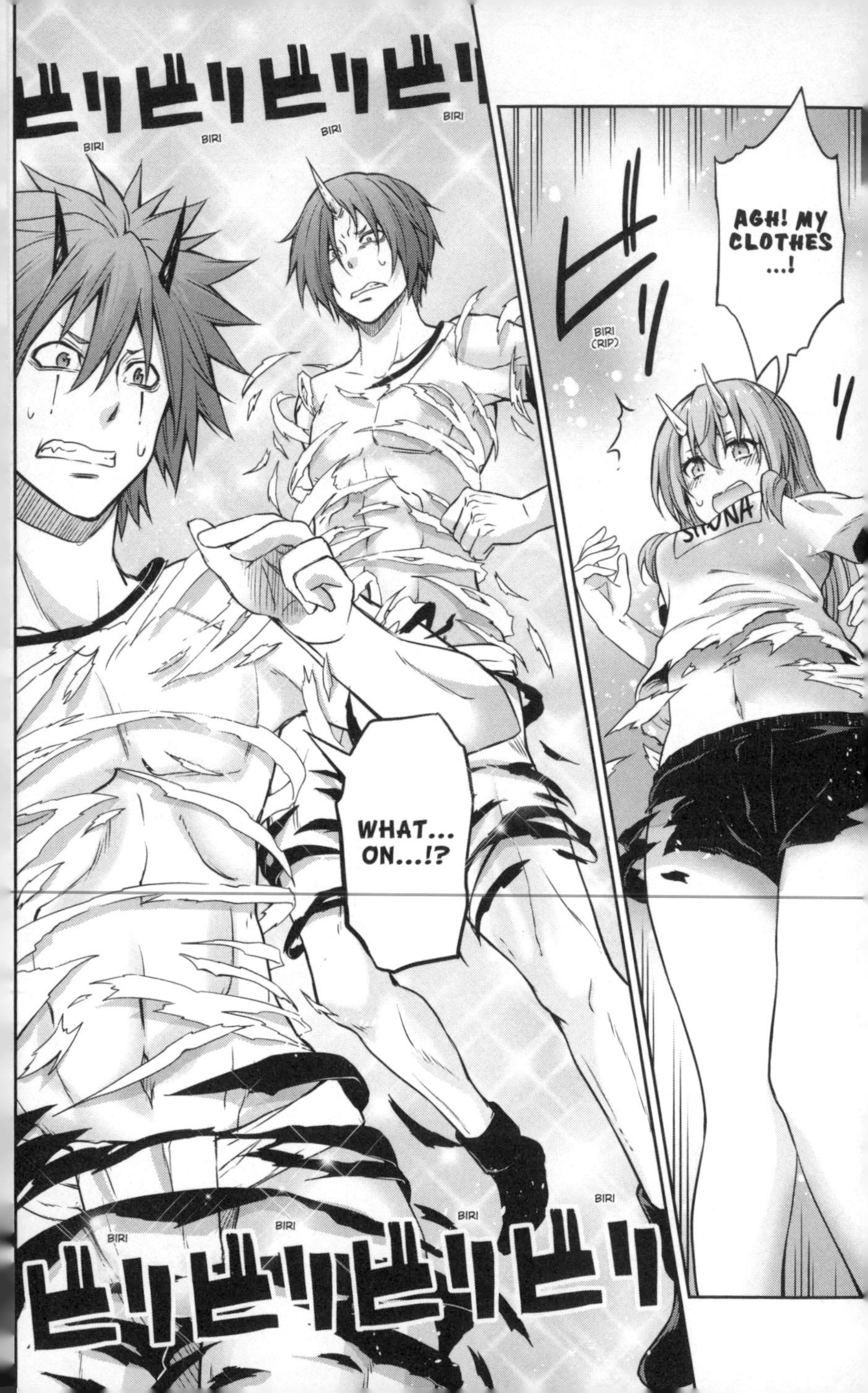
ビリ
BIRI (RIP)
AGH! MY CLOTHES ...!
ビリビリビリビリ
BIRI BIRI BIRI BIRI
WHAT... ON...!?
ビリビリビリビリ
BIRI BIRI BIRI BIRI

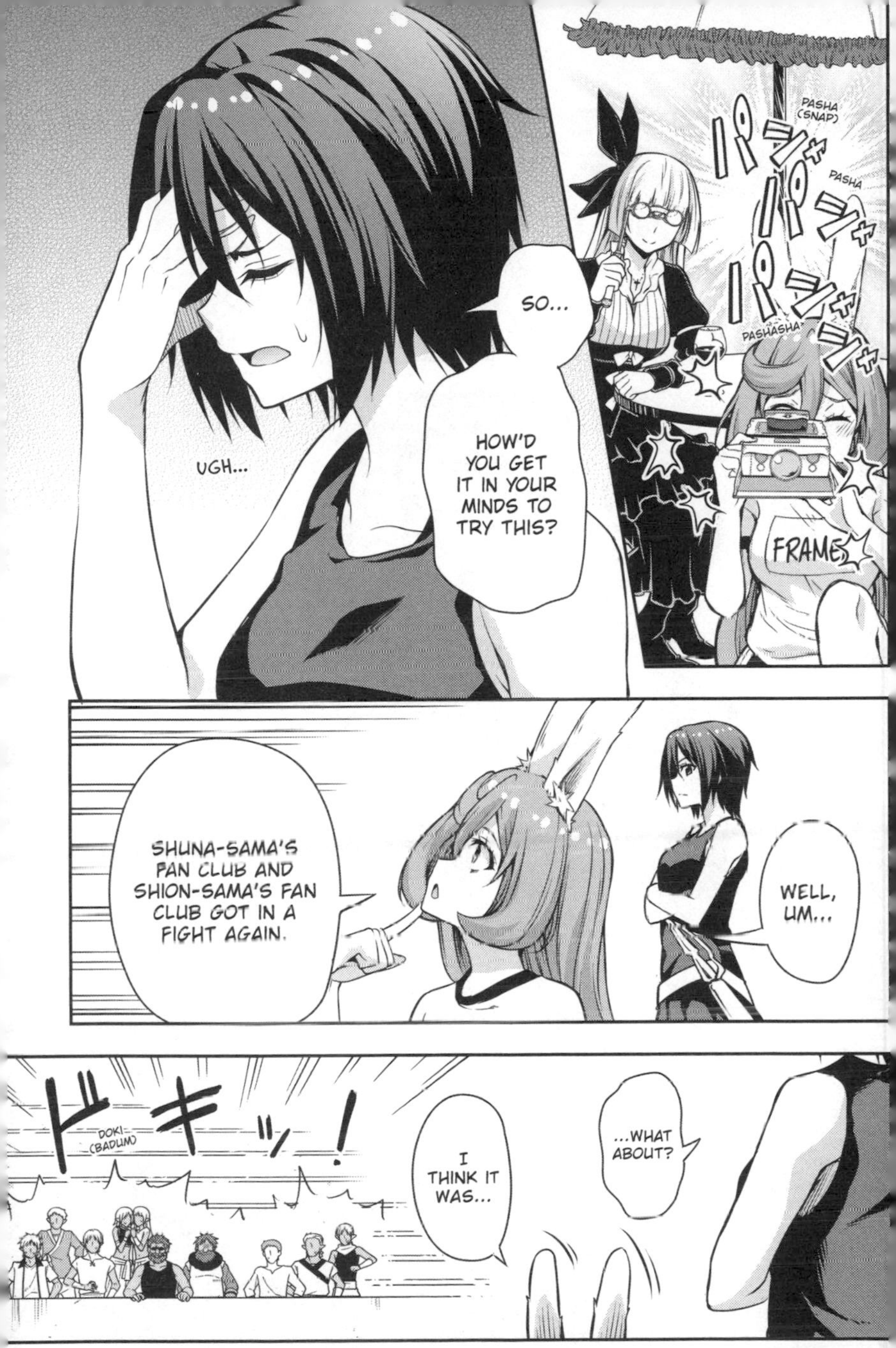
PASHA (SNAP)
PASHA
PASHASHA
FRAME
SO...
HOW'D YOU GET IT IN YOUR MINDS TO TRY THIS?
UGH...
WELL, UM...
SHUNA-SAMA'S FAN CLUB AND SHION-SAMA'S FAN CLUB GOT IN A FIGHT AGAIN.
...WHAT ABOUT?
I THINK IT WAS...
DOKI (BADUM)

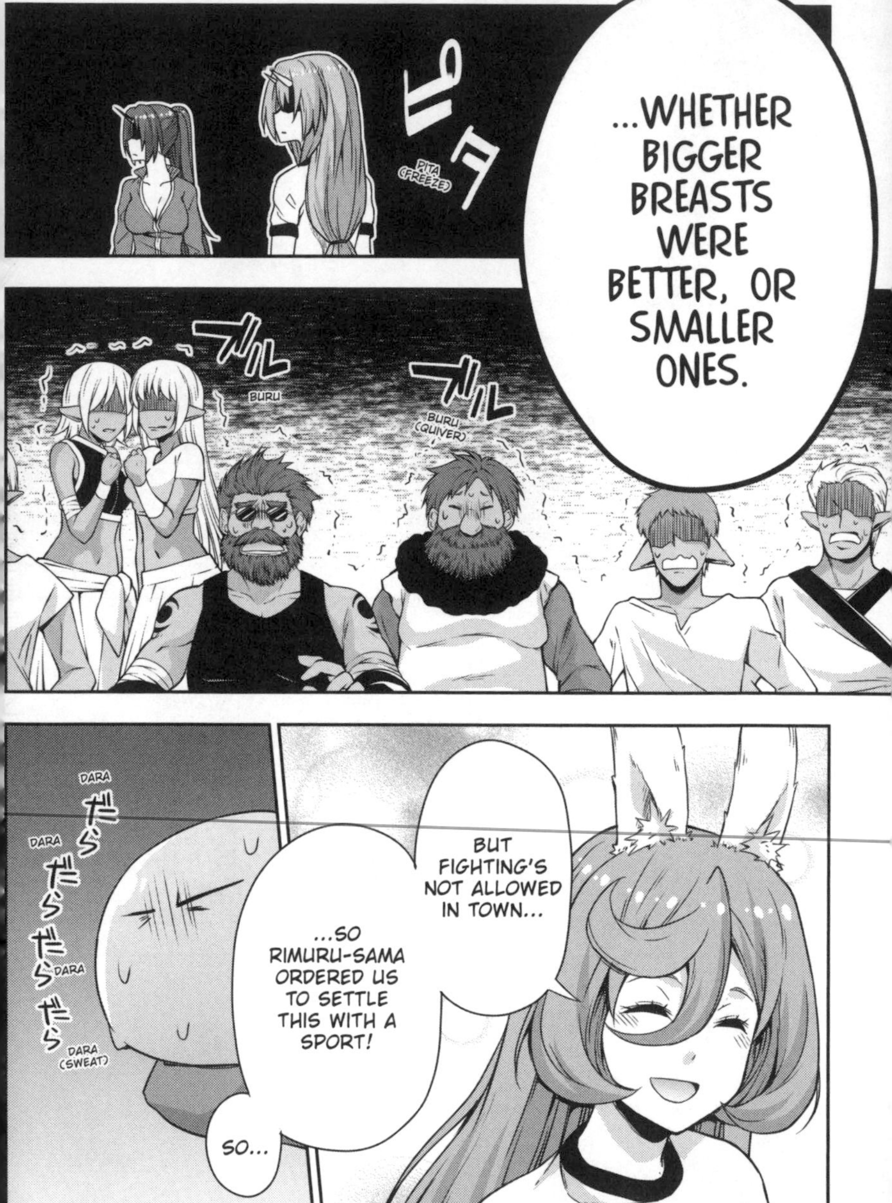
...WHETHER BIGGER BREASTS WERE BETTER, OR SMALLER ONES.
PITA (FREEZE)
BURU (QUIVER)
BURU
BUT FIGHTING'S NOT ALLOWED IN TOWN...
...SO RIMURU-SAMA ORDERED US TO SETTLE THIS WITH A SPORT!
SO...
DARA
だら
DARA
だら
だら
DARA
だら
DARA (SWEAT)

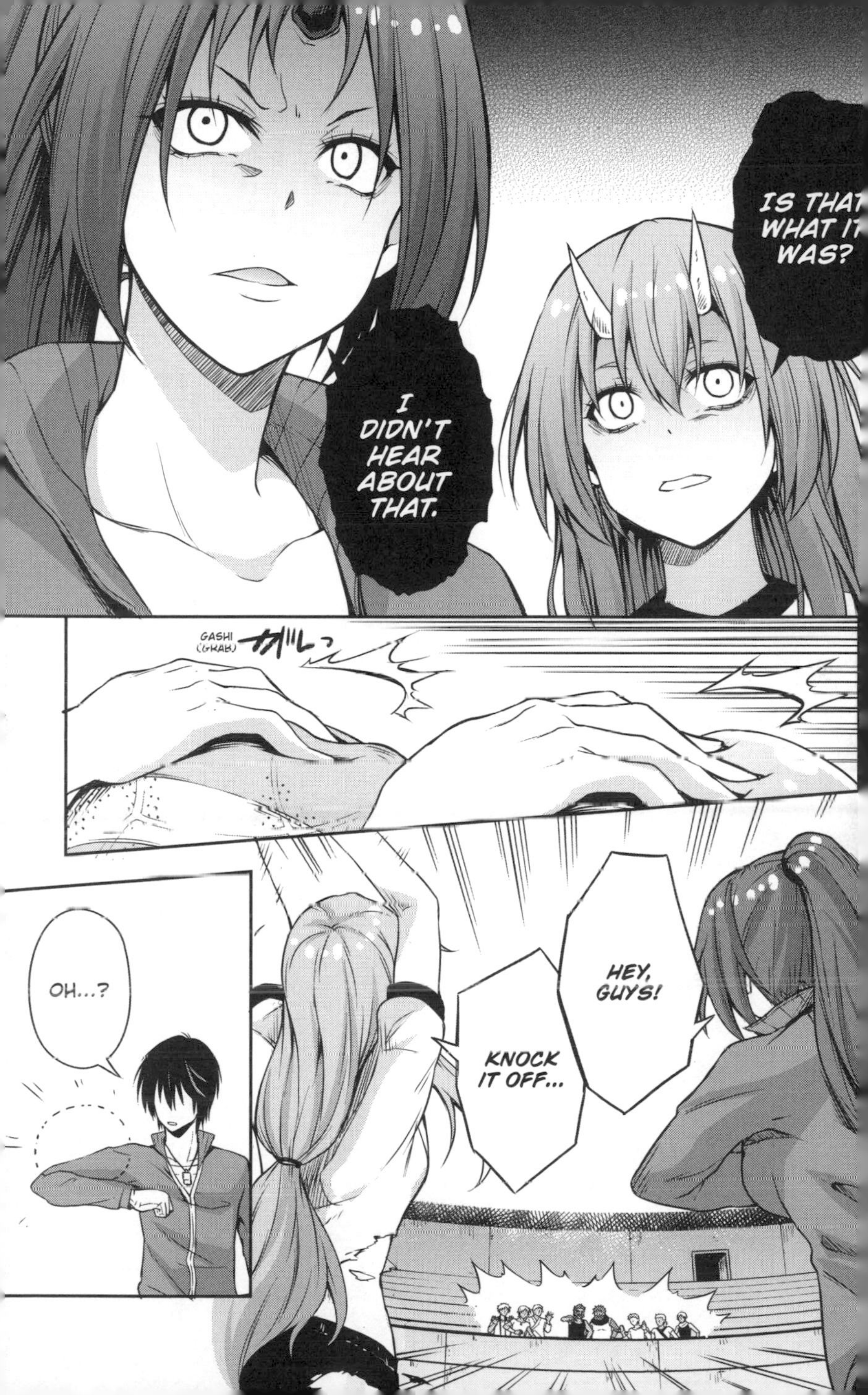
IS THAT WHAT IT WAS?
I DIDN'T HEAR ABOUT THAT.
GASHI (GRAB)
HEY, GUYS!
KNOCK IT OFF...
OH...?

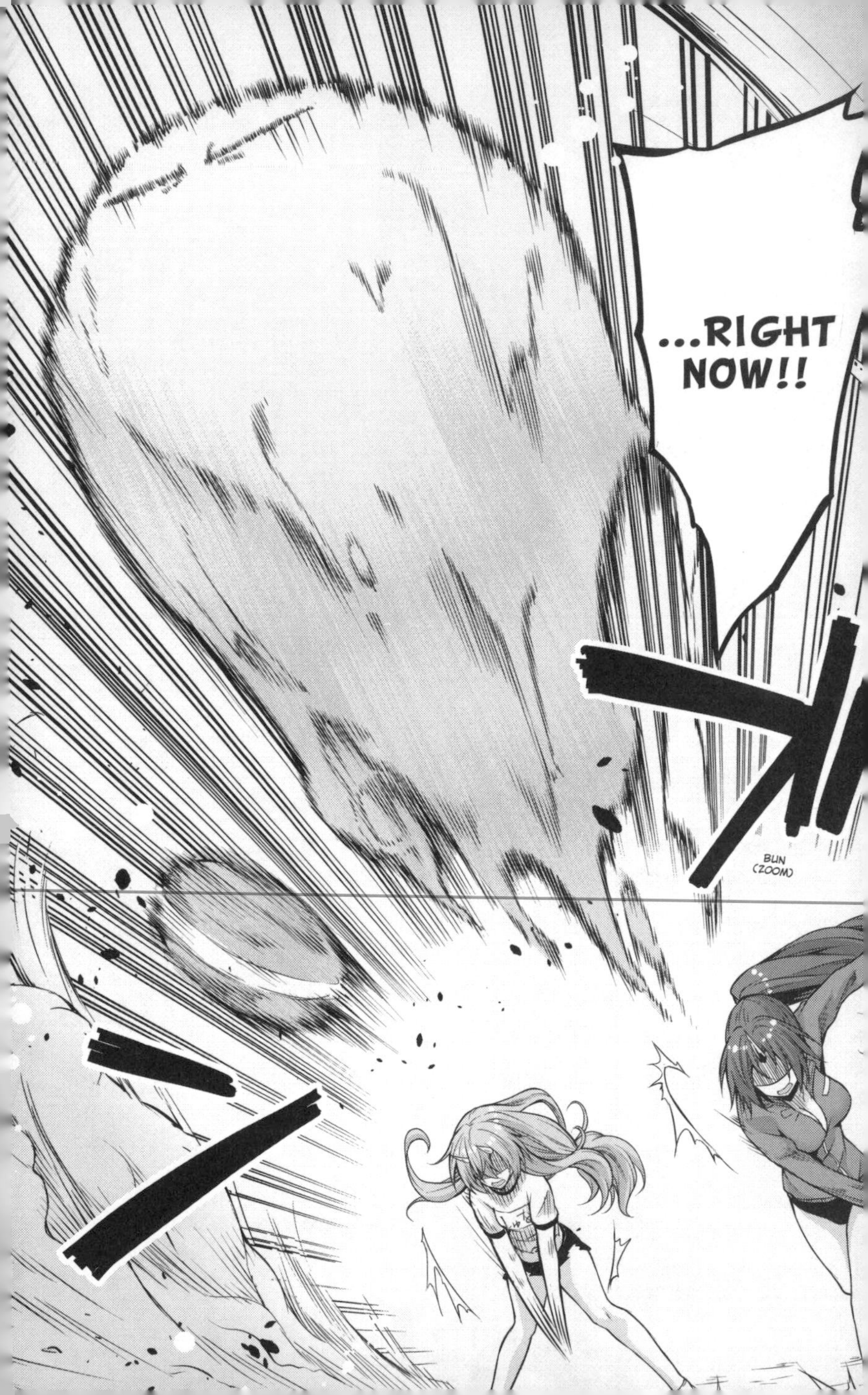
...RIGHT NOW!!
BUN (ZOOM)

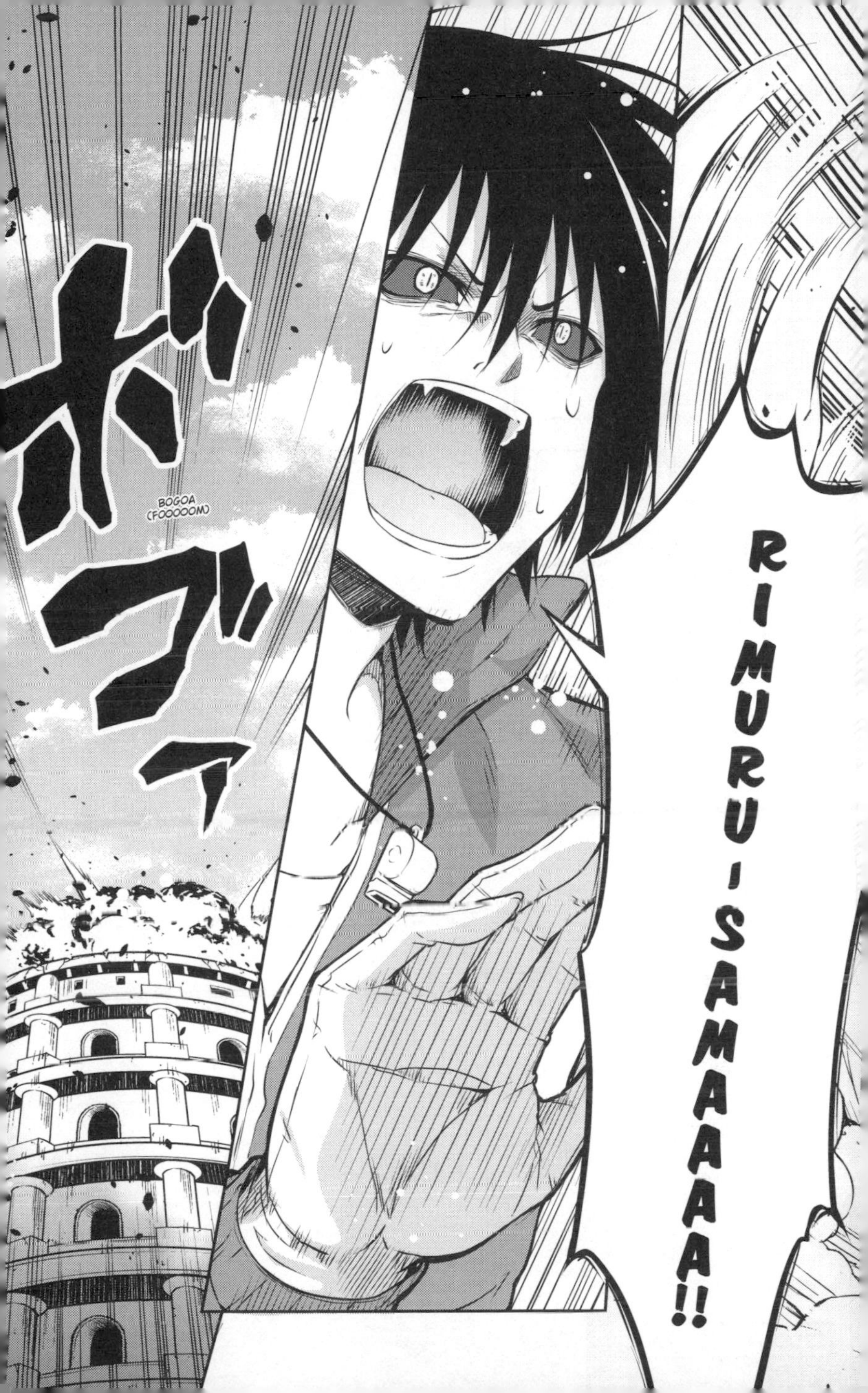
RIMURU-SAMAAAA!!
ボゴァ
BOGOA (FOOOOOM)

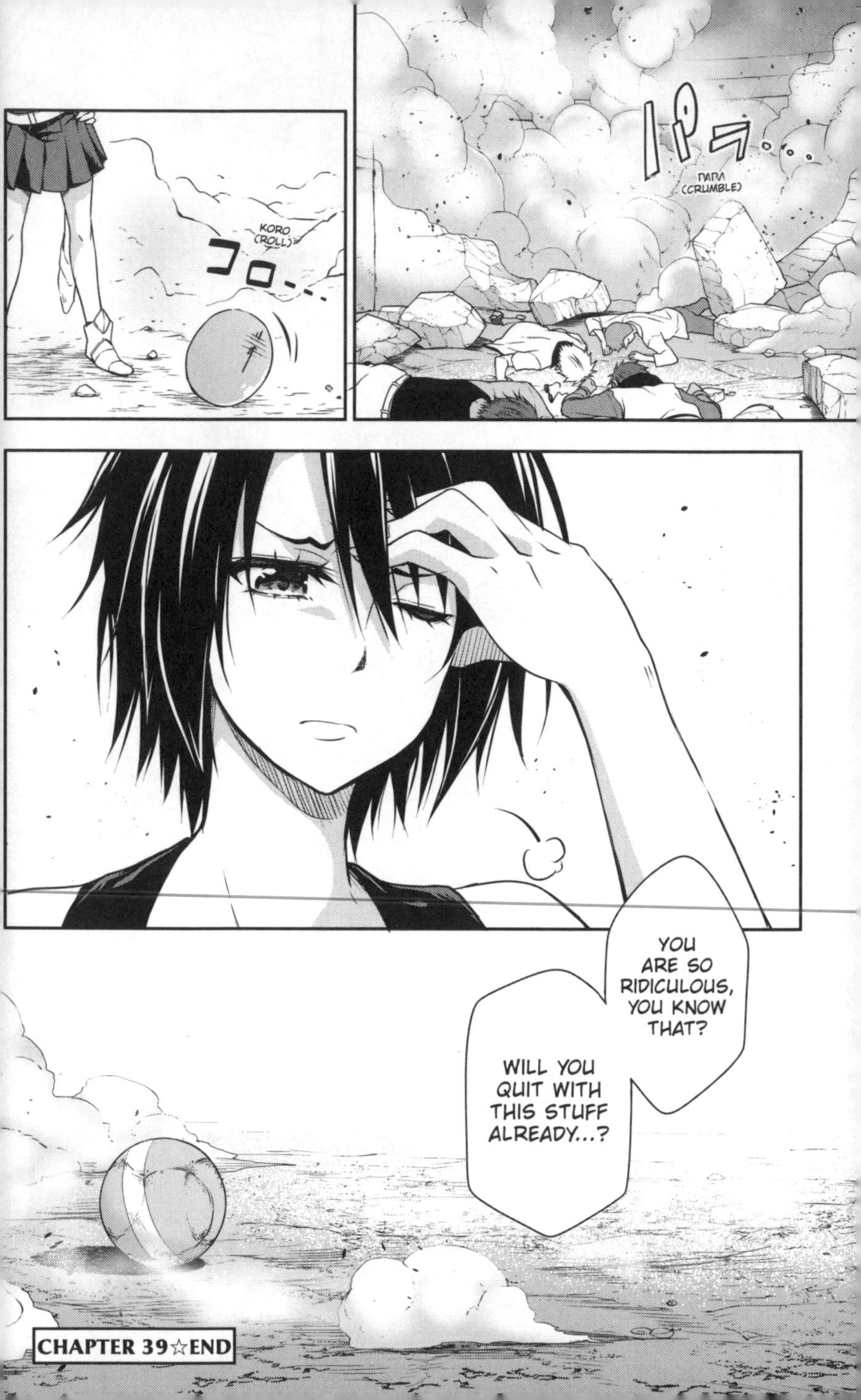
パラ...
PARA (CRUMBLE)
KORO (ROLL)
コロ...
YOU ARE SO RIDICULOUS, YOU KNOW THAT?
WILL YOU QUIT WITH THIS STUFF ALREADY...?
CHAPTER 39☆END

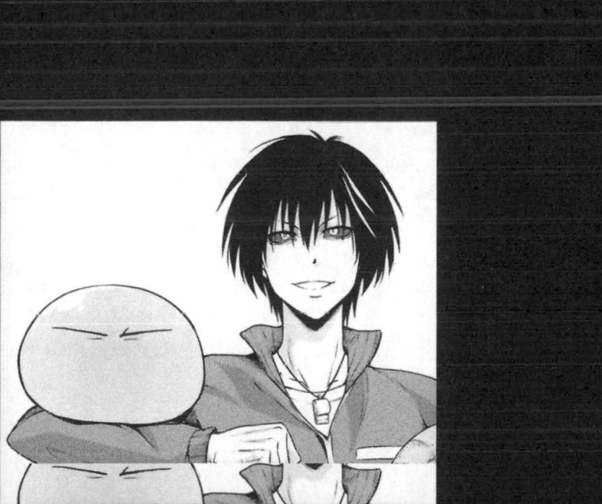

That Time I Got Reincarnated as a SLIME

The Ways of the Monster Nation

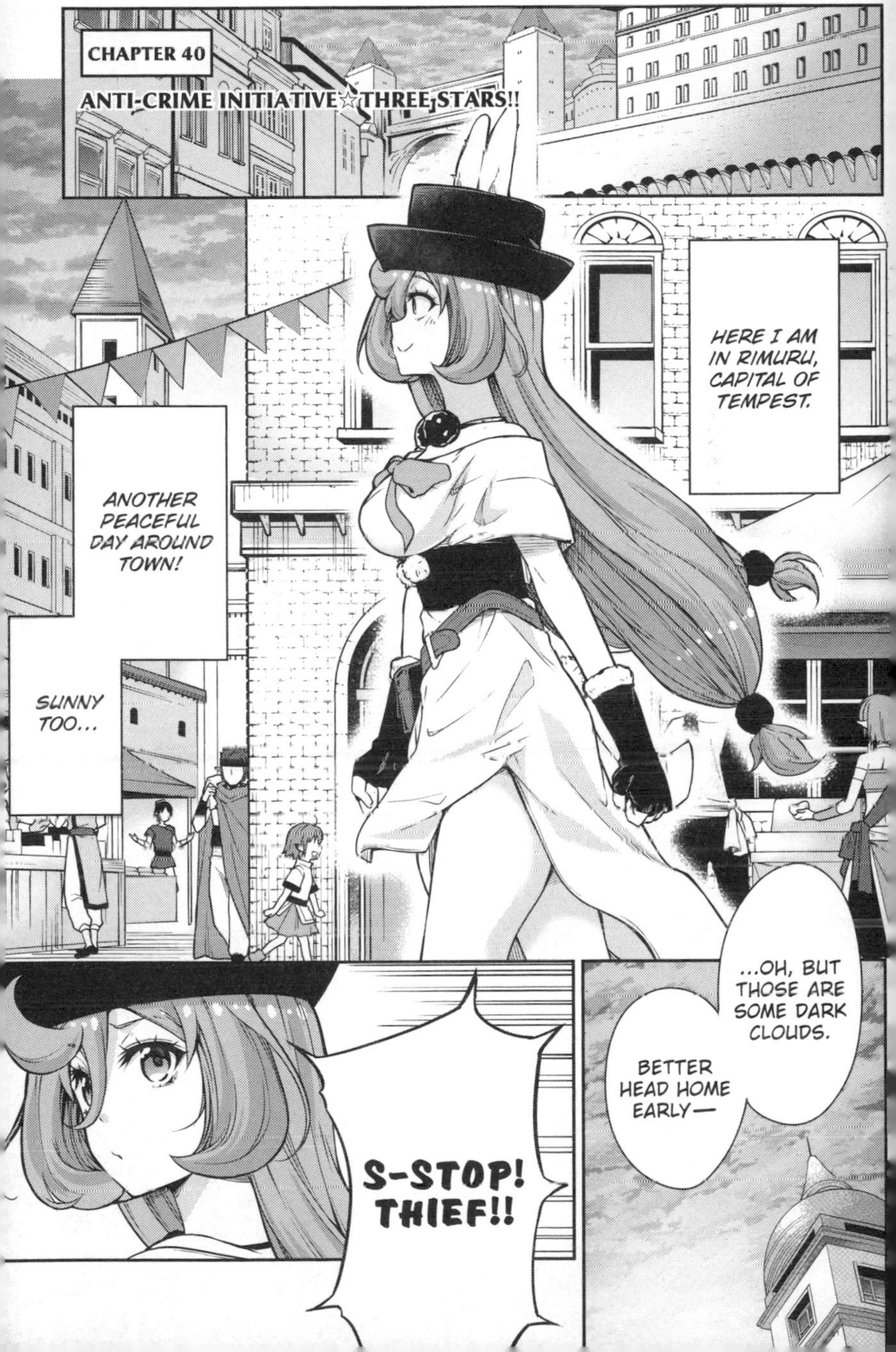
CHAPTER 40
ANTI-CRIME INITIATIVE☆THREE STARS!!
HERE I AM IN RIMURU, CAPITAL OF TEMPEST.
ANOTHER PEACEFUL DAY AROUND TOWN!
SUNNY TOO...
...OH, BUT THOSE ARE SOME DARK CLOUDS.
BETTER HEAD HOME EARLY—
S-STOP! THIEF!!

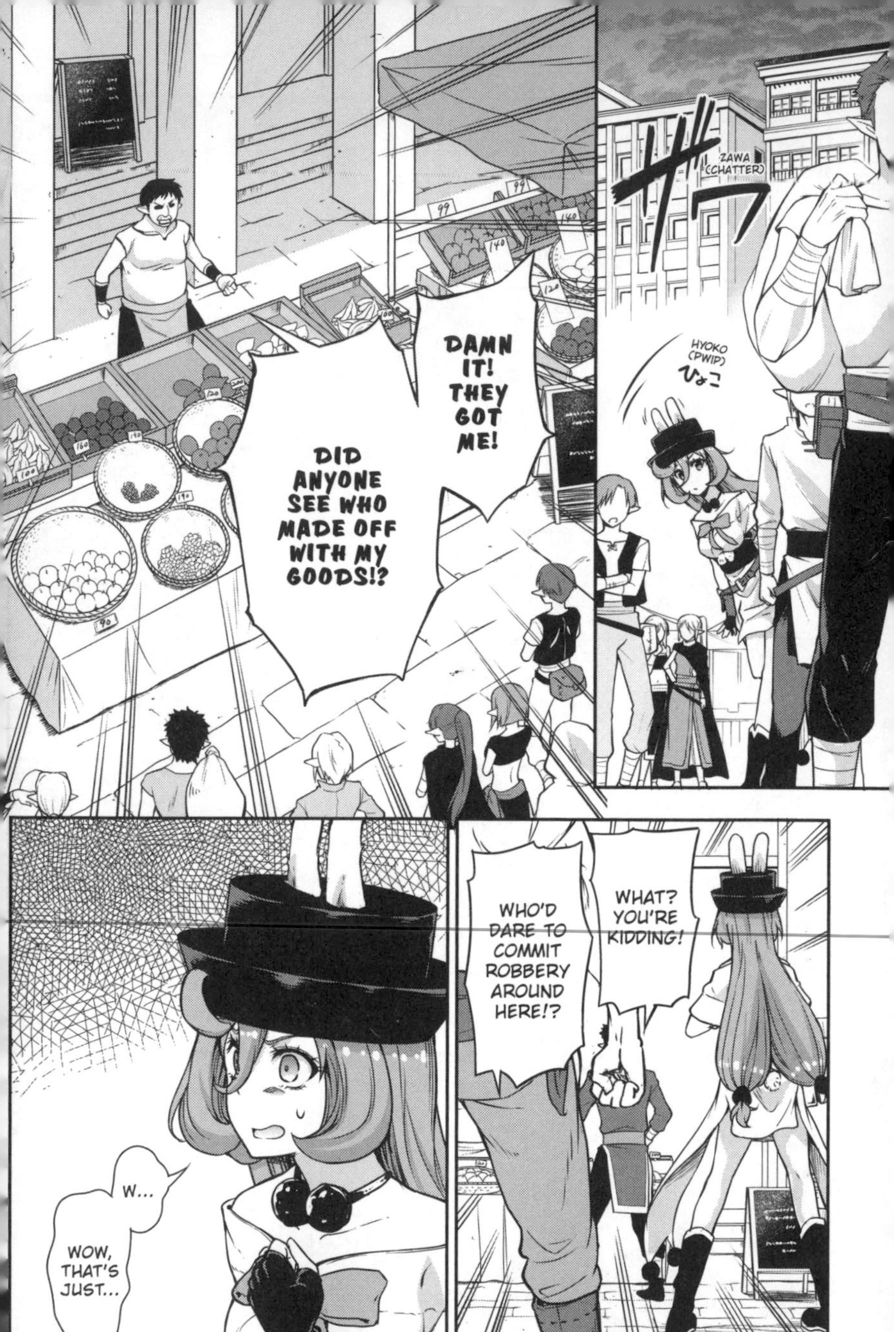
ザワ
ZAWA (CHATTER)
HYOKO (PWIP)
ぴょこ
DAMN IT! THEY GOT ME!
DID ANYONE SEE WHO MADE OFF WITH MY GOODS!?
WHAT? YOU'RE KIDDING!
WHO'D DARE TO COMMIT ROBBERY AROUND HERE!?
W...
WOW, THAT'S JUST...

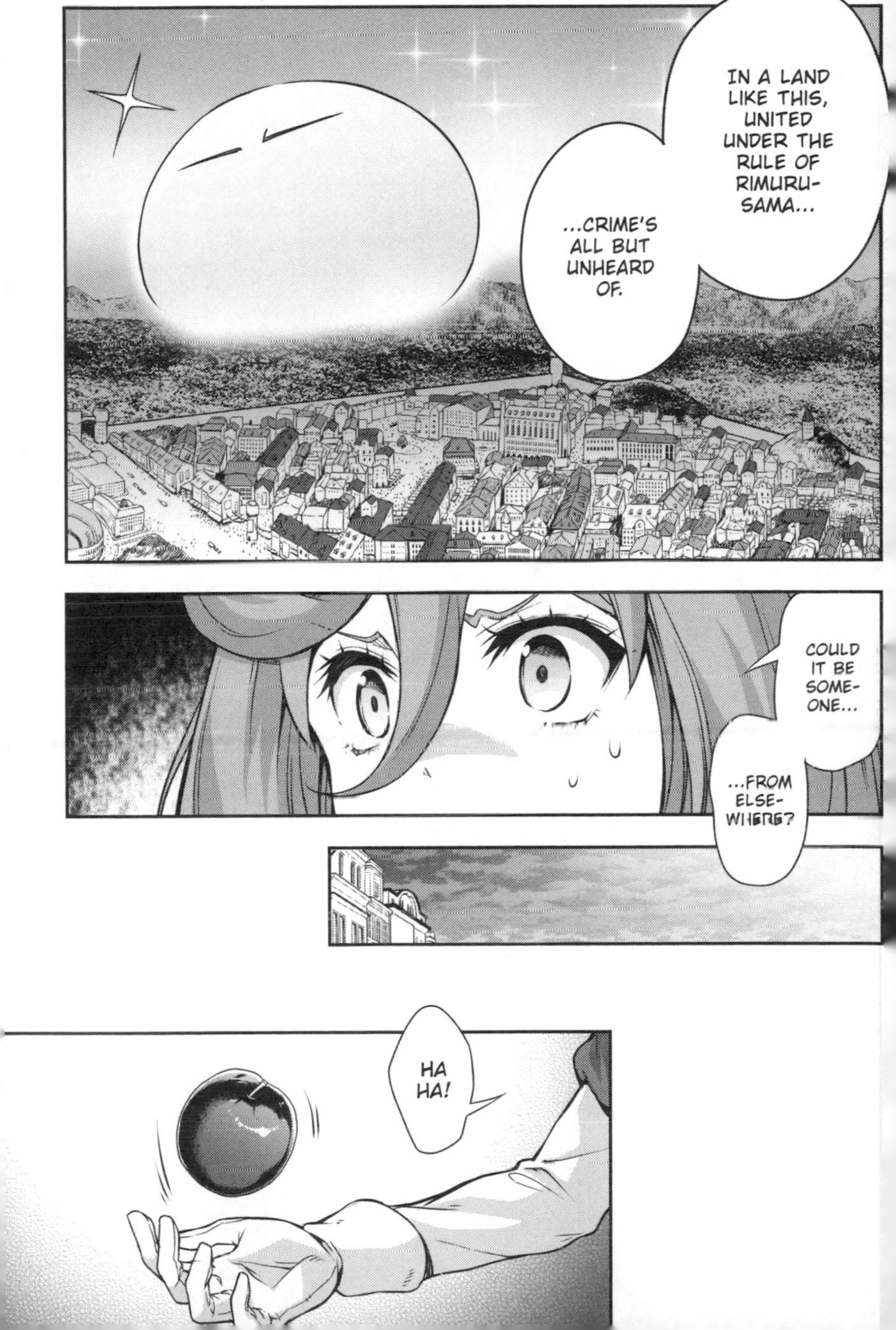
IN A LAND LIKE THIS, UNITED UNDER THE RULE OF RIMURU-SAMA...
...CRIME'S ALL BUT UNHEARD OF.
COULD IT BE SOME-ONE...
...FROM ELSE-WHERE?
HA HA!

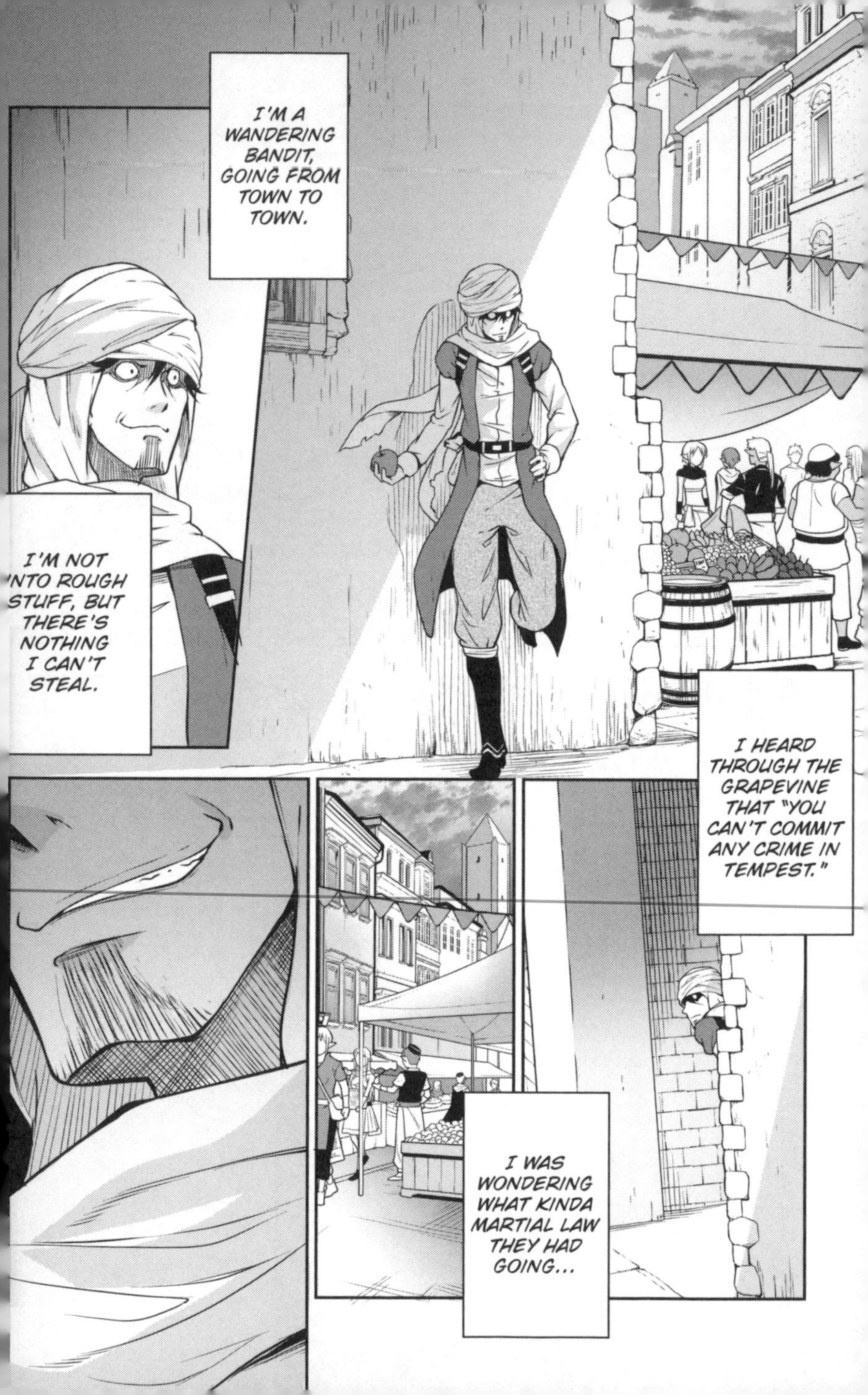
I'M A WANDERING BANDIT, GOING FROM TOWN TO TOWN.
I'M NOT INTO ROUGH STUFF, BUT THERE'S NOTHING I CAN'T STEAL.
I HEARD THROUGH THE GRAPEVINE THAT "YOU CAN'T COMMIT ANY CRIME IN TEMPEST."
I WAS WONDERING WHAT KINDA MARTIAL LAW THEY HAD GOING...

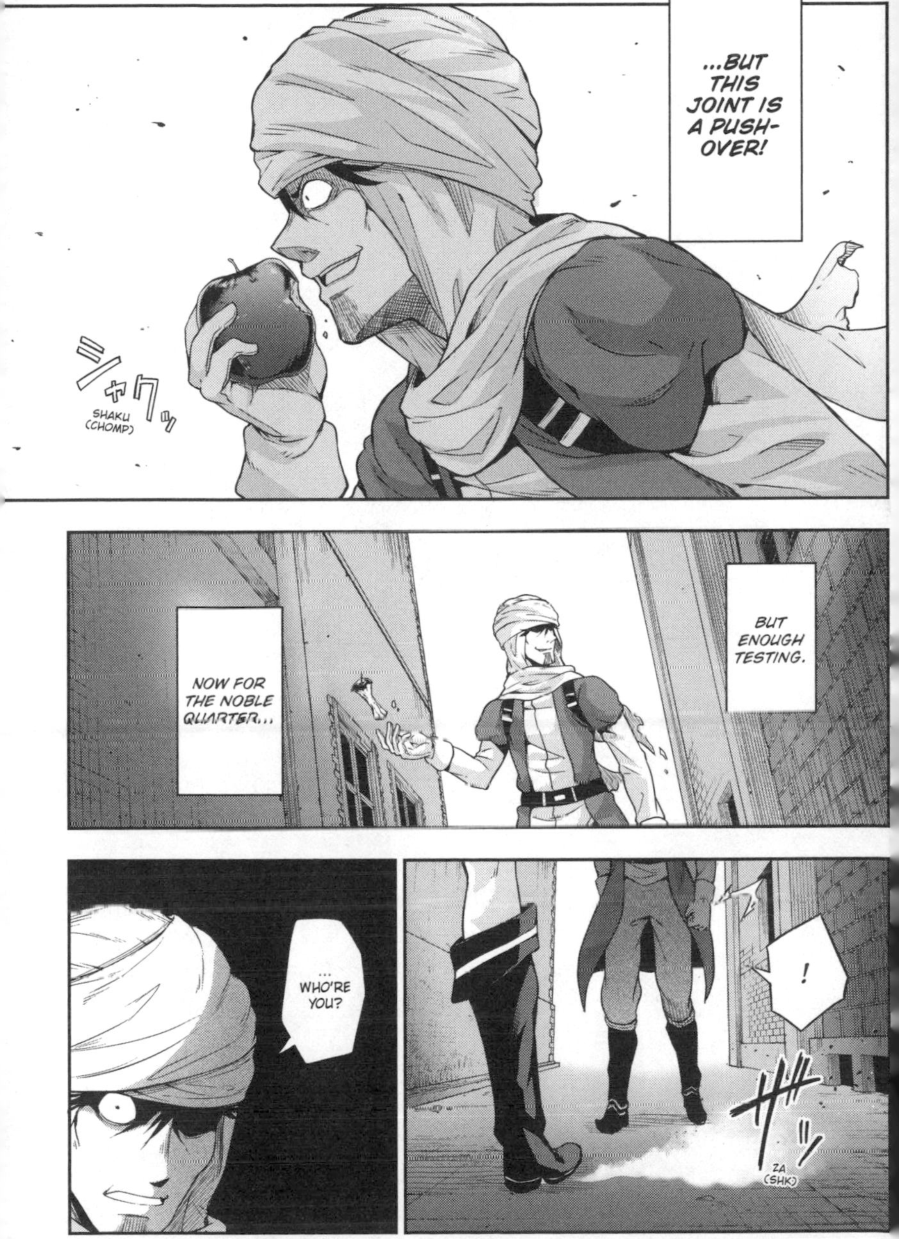
...BUT THIS JOINT IS A PUSH-OVER!
シャクッ
SHAKU (CHOMP)
BUT ENOUGH TESTING.
NOW FOR THE NOBLE QUARTER...
!
ザッ
ZA (SHK)
... WHO'RE YOU?

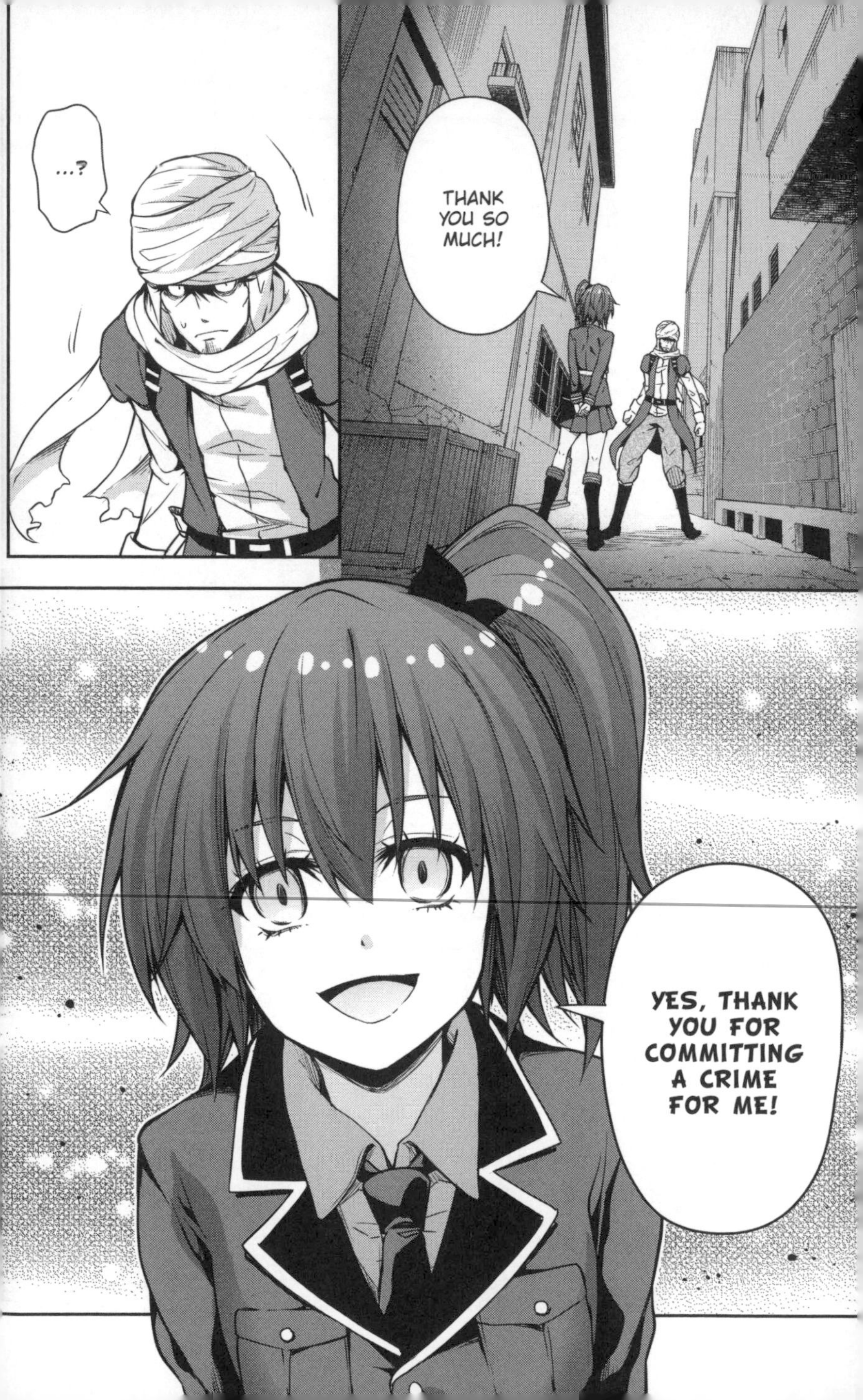
THANK YOU SO MUCH!
...?
YES, THANK YOU FOR COMMITTING A CRIME FOR ME!

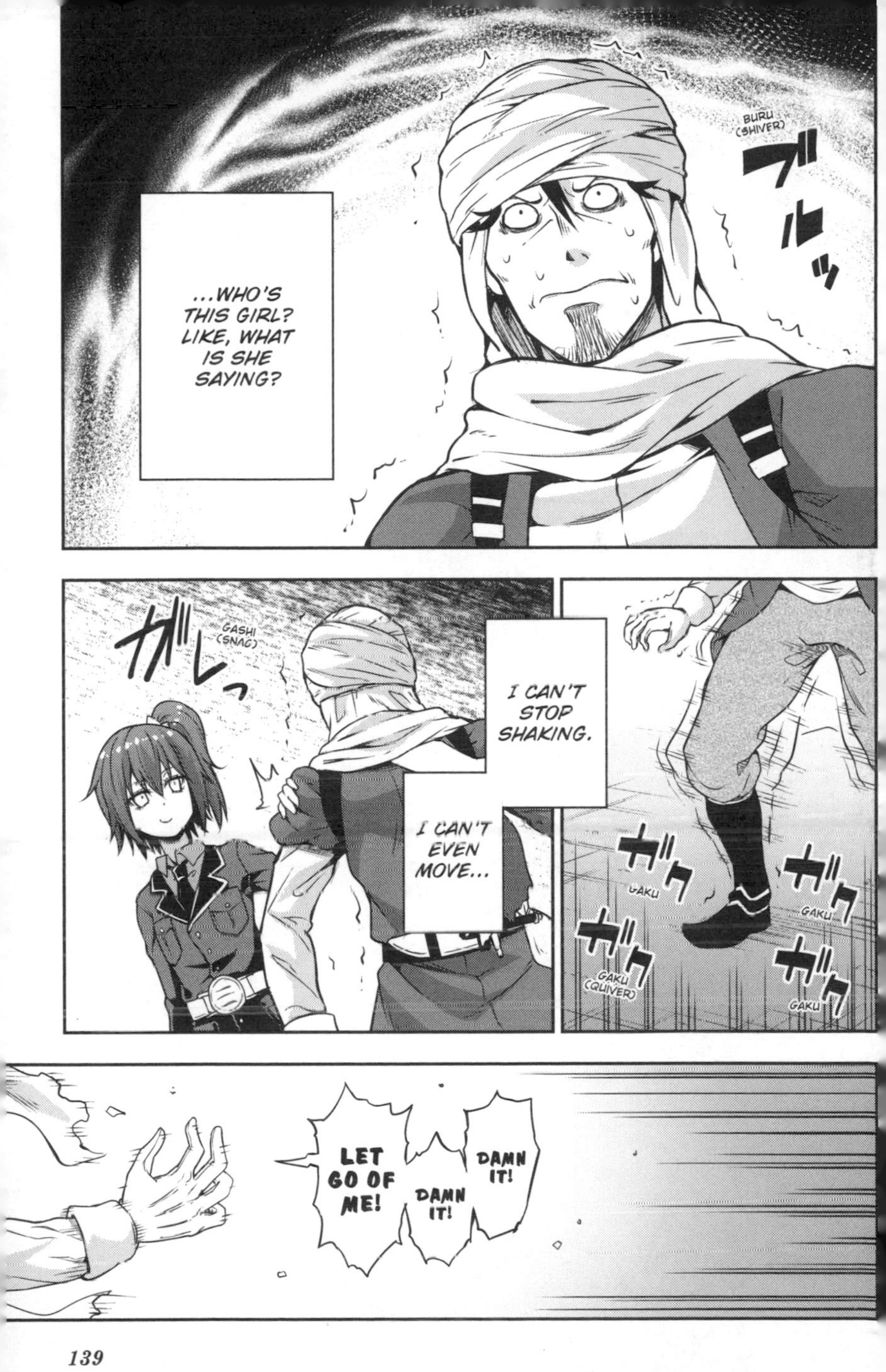
ブルッ
BURU (SHIVER)
...WHO'S THIS GIRL? LIKE, WHAT IS SHE SAYING?
I CAN'T STOP SHAKING.
ガク
GAKU
GAKU
GAKU (QUIVER)
GAKU
I CAN'T EVEN MOVE...
ガシッ
GASHI (SNAG)
DAMN IT!
DAMN IT!
LET GO OF ME!

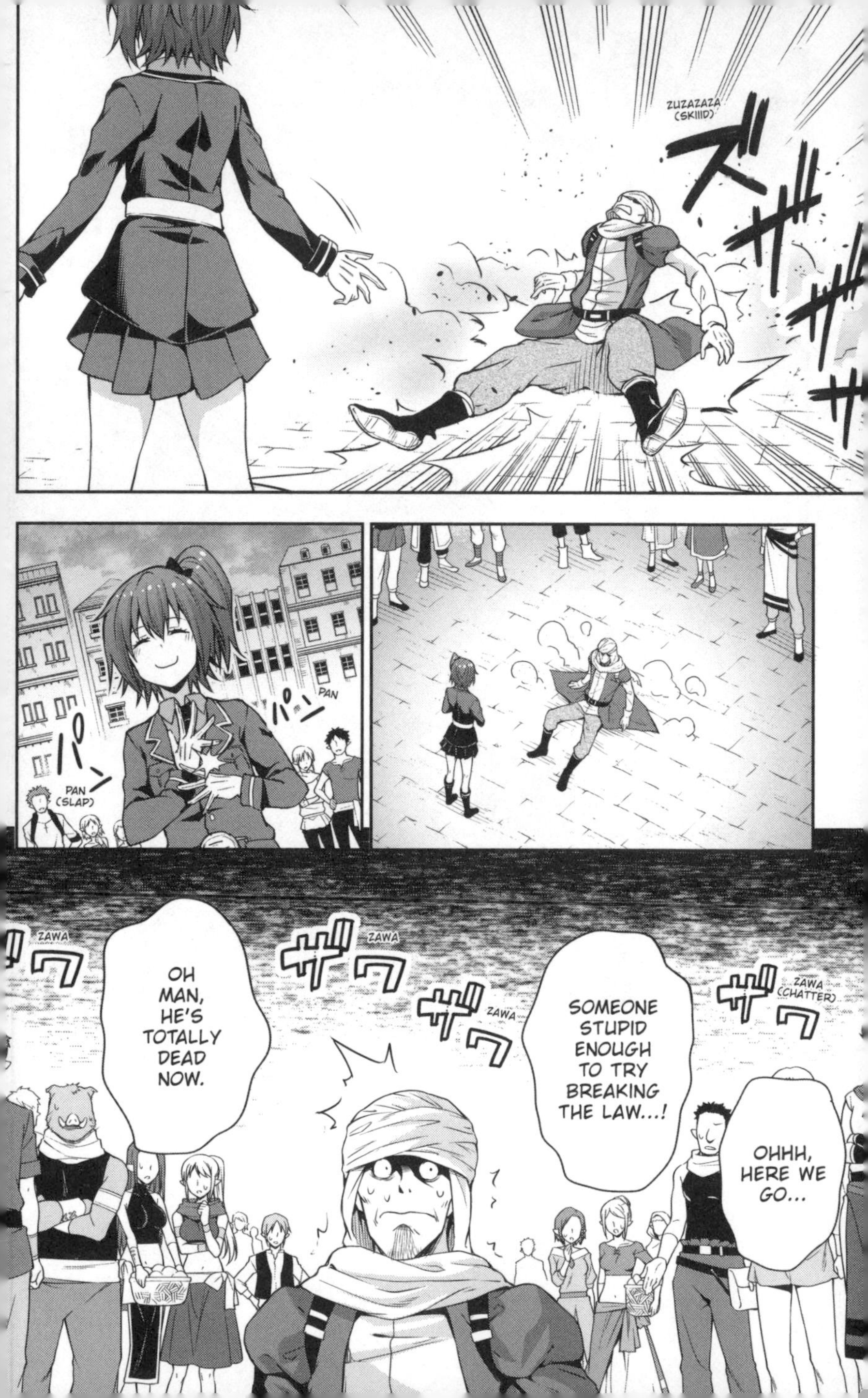
ZUZAZAZA (SKIIID)
PAN
PAN (SLAP)
ZAWA (CHATTER)
ZAWA
OHHH, HERE WE GO...
SOMEONE STUPID ENOUGH TO TRY BREAKING THE LAW...!
ZAWA
OH MAN, HE'S TOTALLY DEAD NOW.
ZAWA

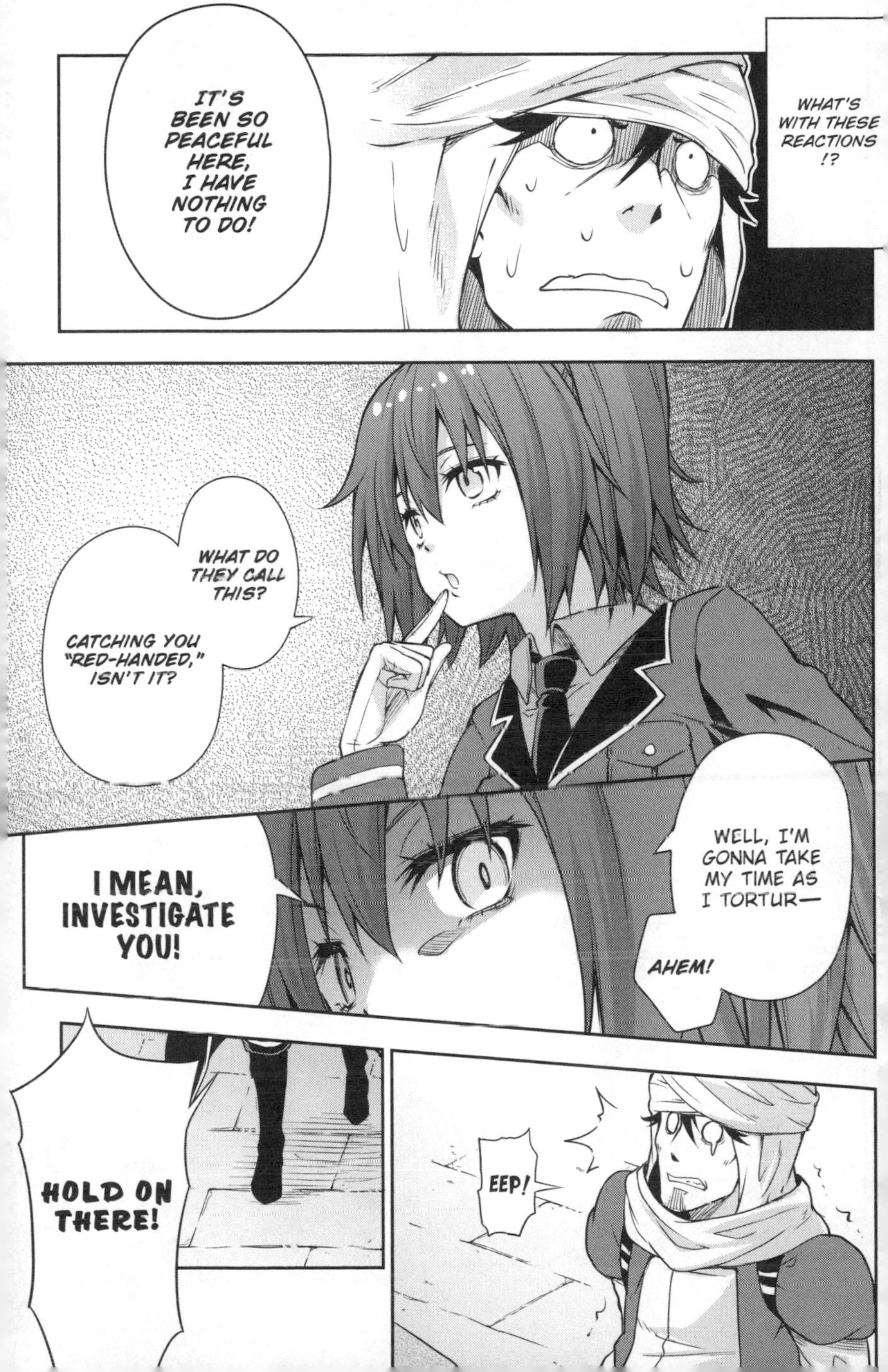
WHAT'S WITH THESE REACTIONS !?
IT'S BEEN SO PEACEFUL HERE, I HAVE NOTHING TO DO!
WHAT DO THEY CALL THIS?
CATCHING YOU "RED-HANDED," ISN'T IT?
WELL, I'M GONNA TAKE MY TIME AS I TORTUR—
AHEM!
I MEAN, INVESTIGATE YOU!
EEP!
HOLD ON THERE!

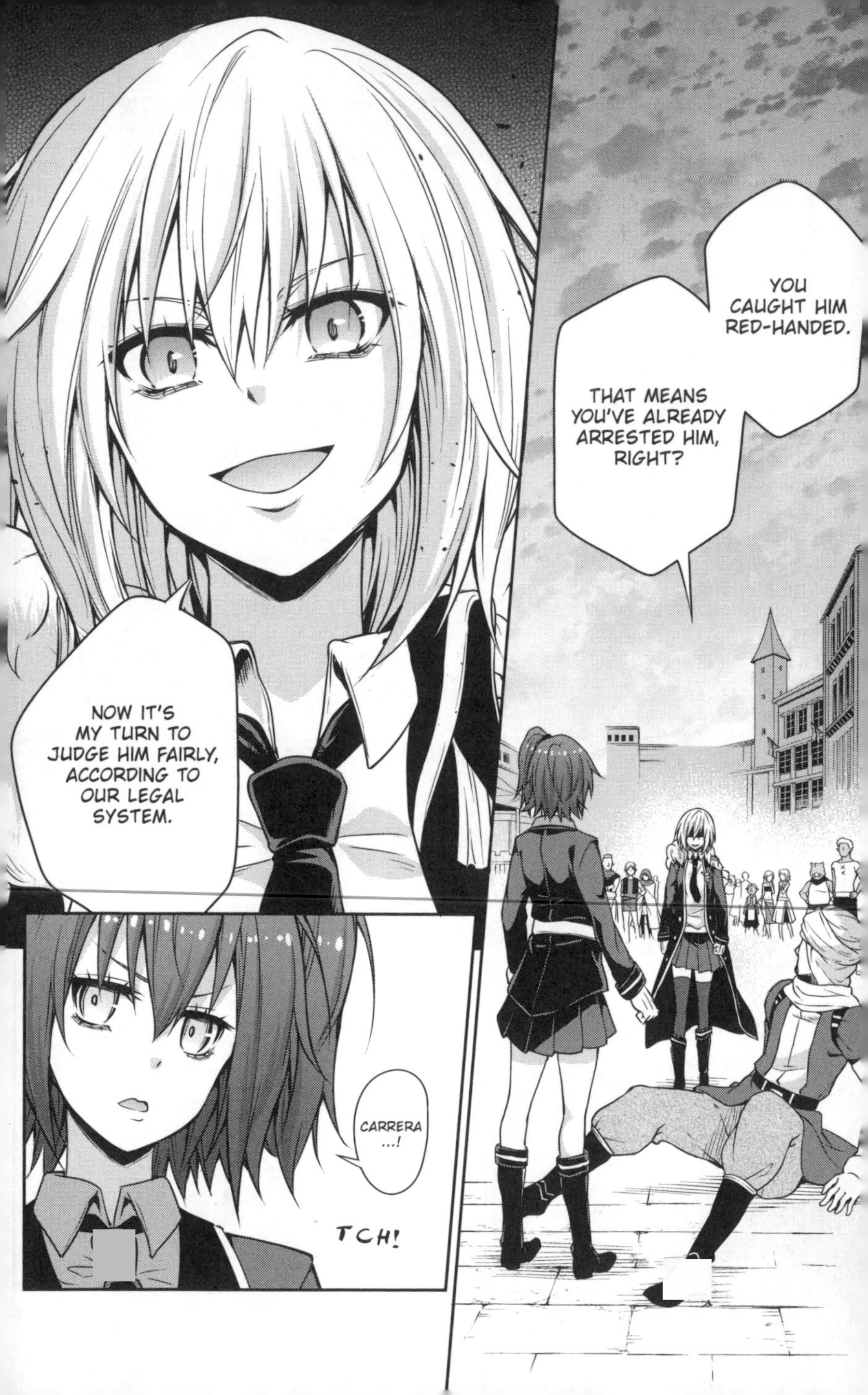
YOU CAUGHT HIM RED-HANDED.
THAT MEANS YOU'VE ALREADY ARRESTED HIM, RIGHT?
NOW IT'S MY TURN TO JUDGE HIM FAIRLY, ACCORDING TO OUR LEGAL SYSTEM.
CARRERA ...!
TCH!

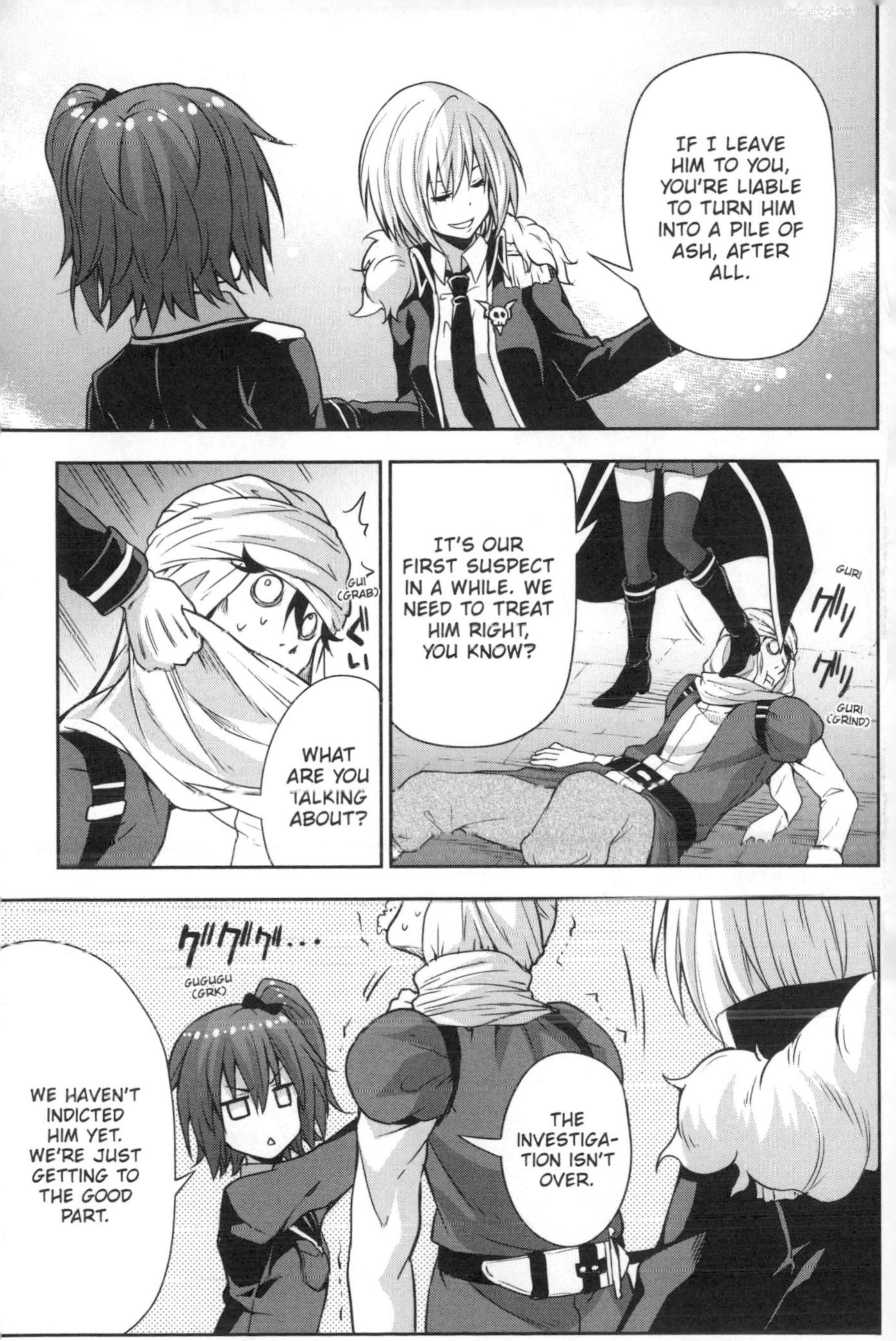
IF I LEAVE HIM TO YOU, YOU'RE LIABLE TO TURN HIM INTO A PILE OF ASH, AFTER ALL.
GURI
GURI (GRIND)
IT'S OUR FIRST SUSPECT IN A WHILE. WE NEED TO TREAT HIM RIGHT, YOU KNOW?
GUI (GRAB)
WHAT ARE YOU TALKING ABOUT?
THE INVESTIGATION ISN'T OVER.
GUGUGU (GRK)
WE HAVEN'T INDICTED HIM YET. WE'RE JUST GETTING TO THE GOOD PART.

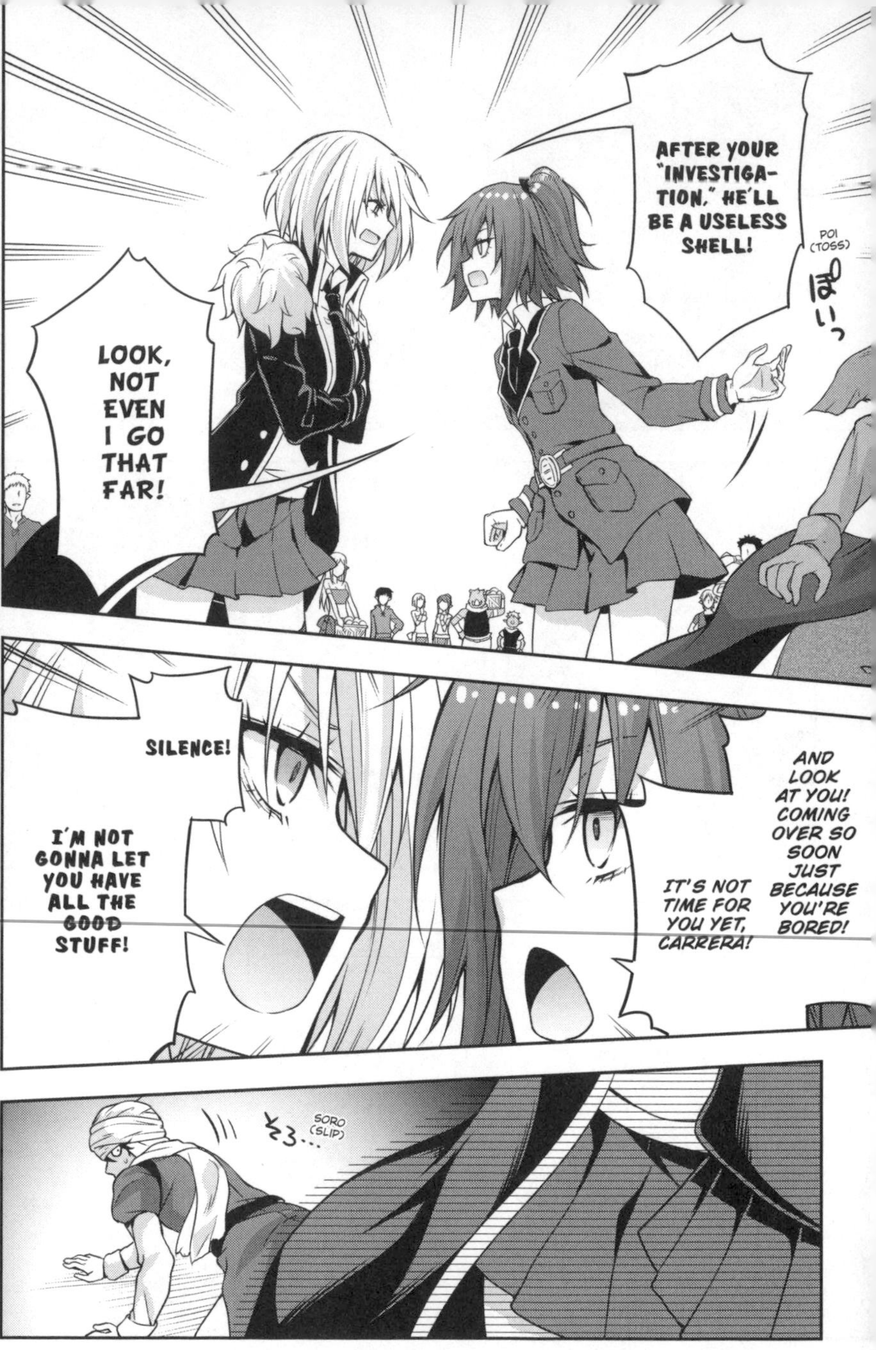

AFTER YOUR "INVESTIGATION," HE'LL BE A USELESS SHELL!
POI (TOSS)
ぽいっ
LOOK, NOT EVEN I GO THAT FAR!
AND LOOK AT YOU! COMING OVER SO SOON JUST BECAUSE YOU'RE BORED!
IT'S NOT TIME FOR YOU YET, CARRERA!
SILENCE!
I'M NOT GONNA LET YOU HAVE ALL THE GOOD STUFF!
SORO (SLIP)
そろ…

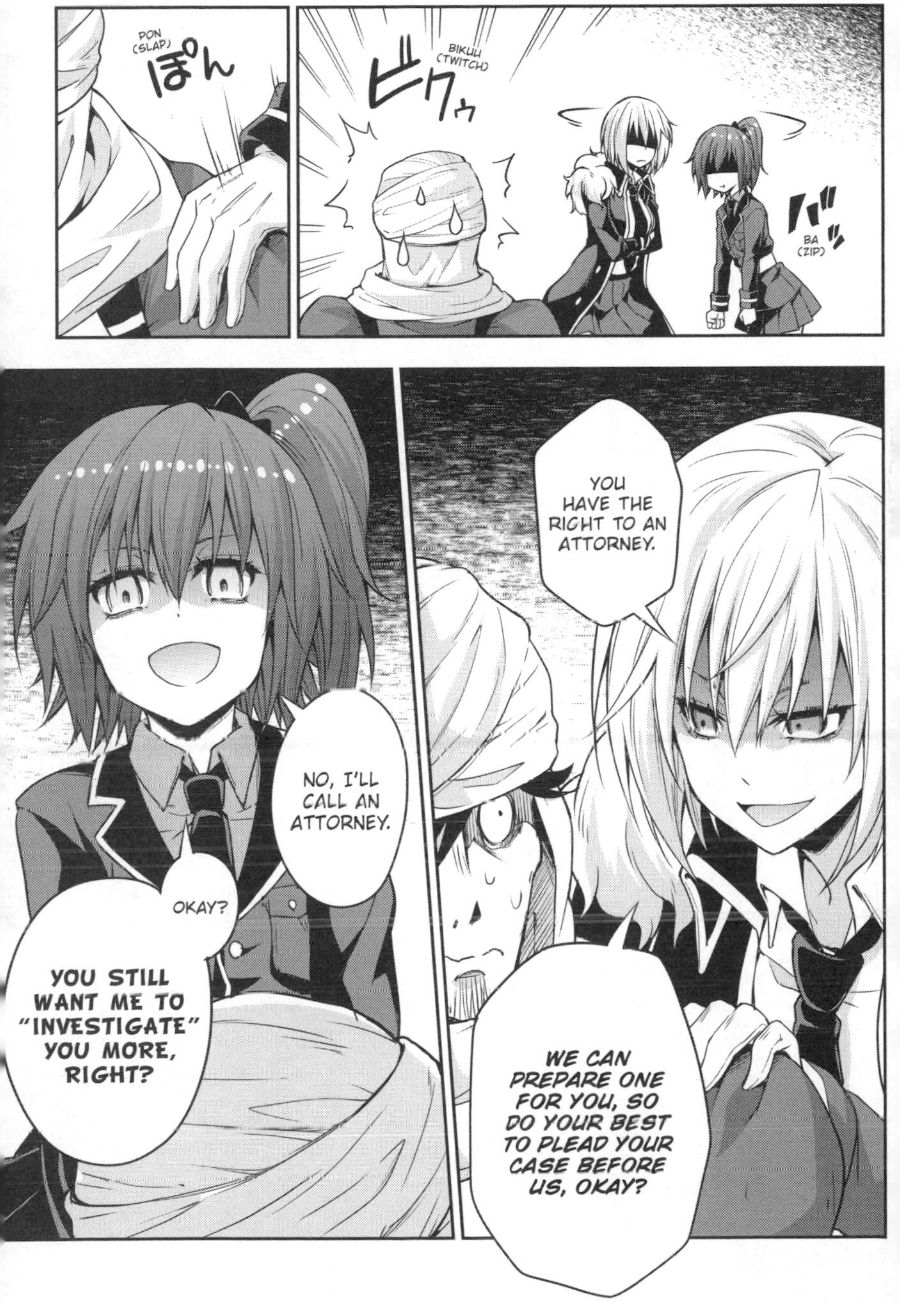
ビクゥ
BIKUU (TWITCH)
バッ
BA (ZIP)
ぽん
PON (SLAP)
YOU HAVE THE RIGHT TO AN ATTORNEY.
WE CAN PREPARE ONE FOR YOU, SO DO YOUR BEST TO PLEAD YOUR CASE BEFORE US, OKAY?
NO, I'LL CALL AN ATTORNEY.
OKAY?
YOU STILL WANT ME TO "INVESTIGATE" YOU MORE, RIGHT?

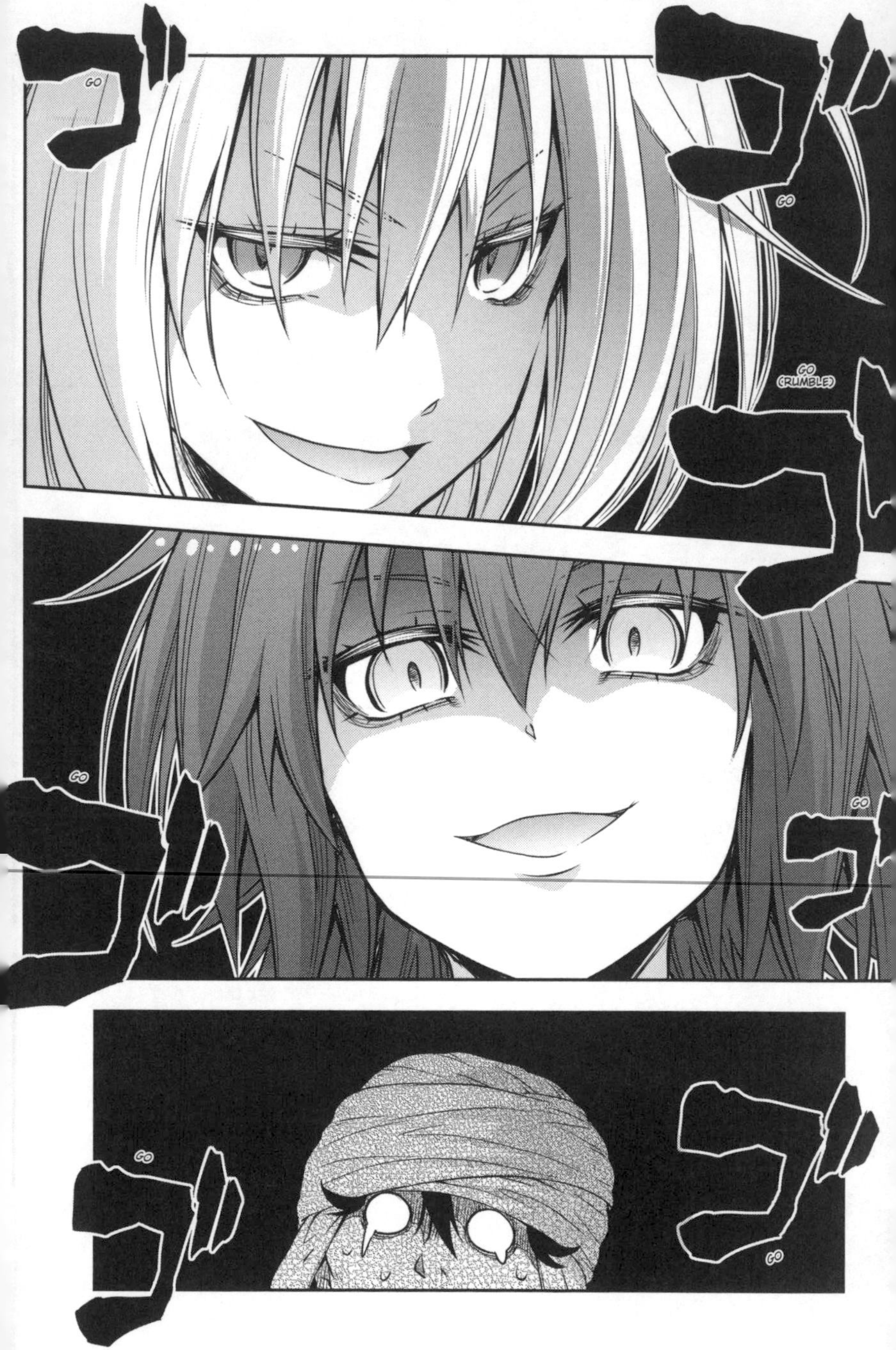
GO
GO
(RUMBLE)
GO
GO
GO
GO
GO

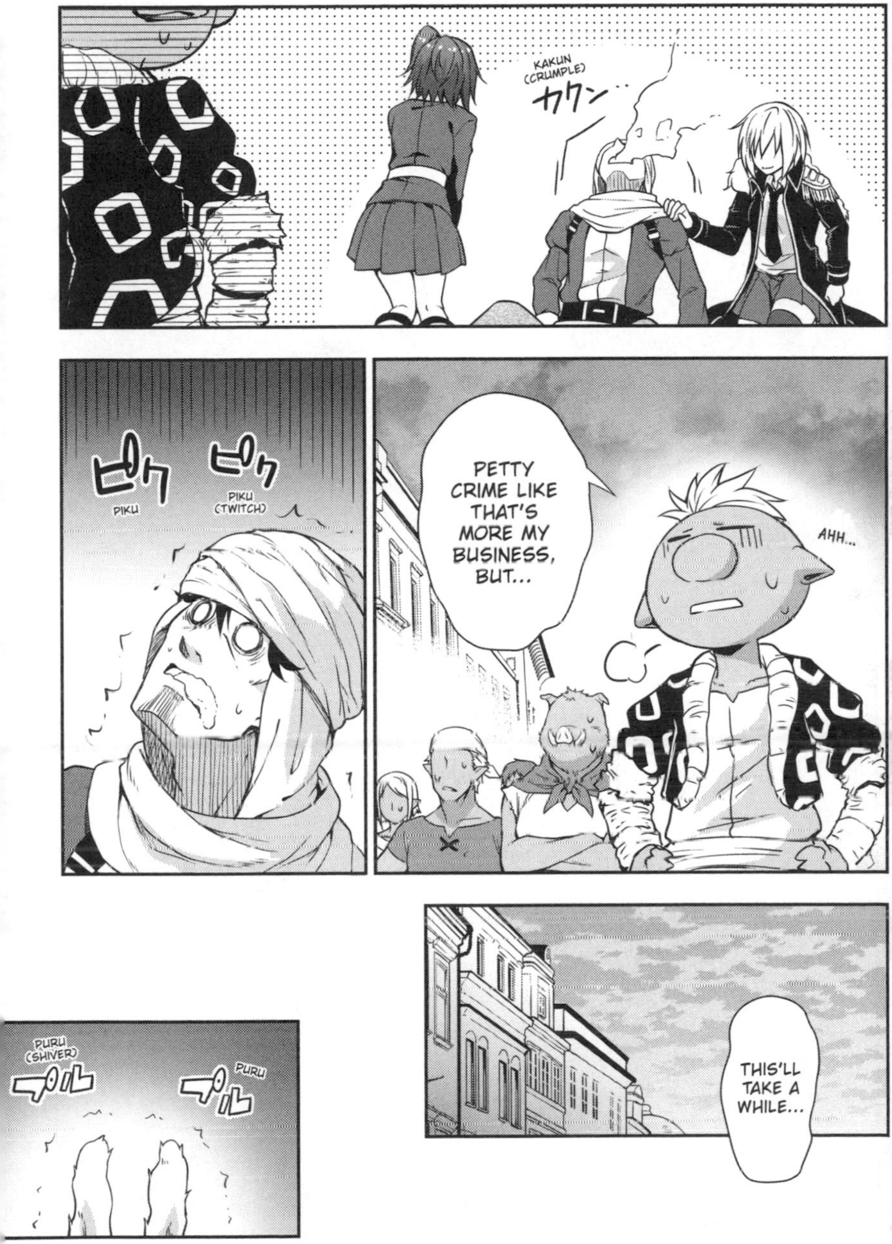
KAKUN (CRUMPLE)
カクン…
AHH...
PETTY CRIME LIKE THAT'S MORE MY BUSINESS, BUT...
ピク
PIKU (TWITCH)
ピク
PIKU
THIS'LL TAKE A WHILE...
プル
PURU
プル
PURU (SHIVER)

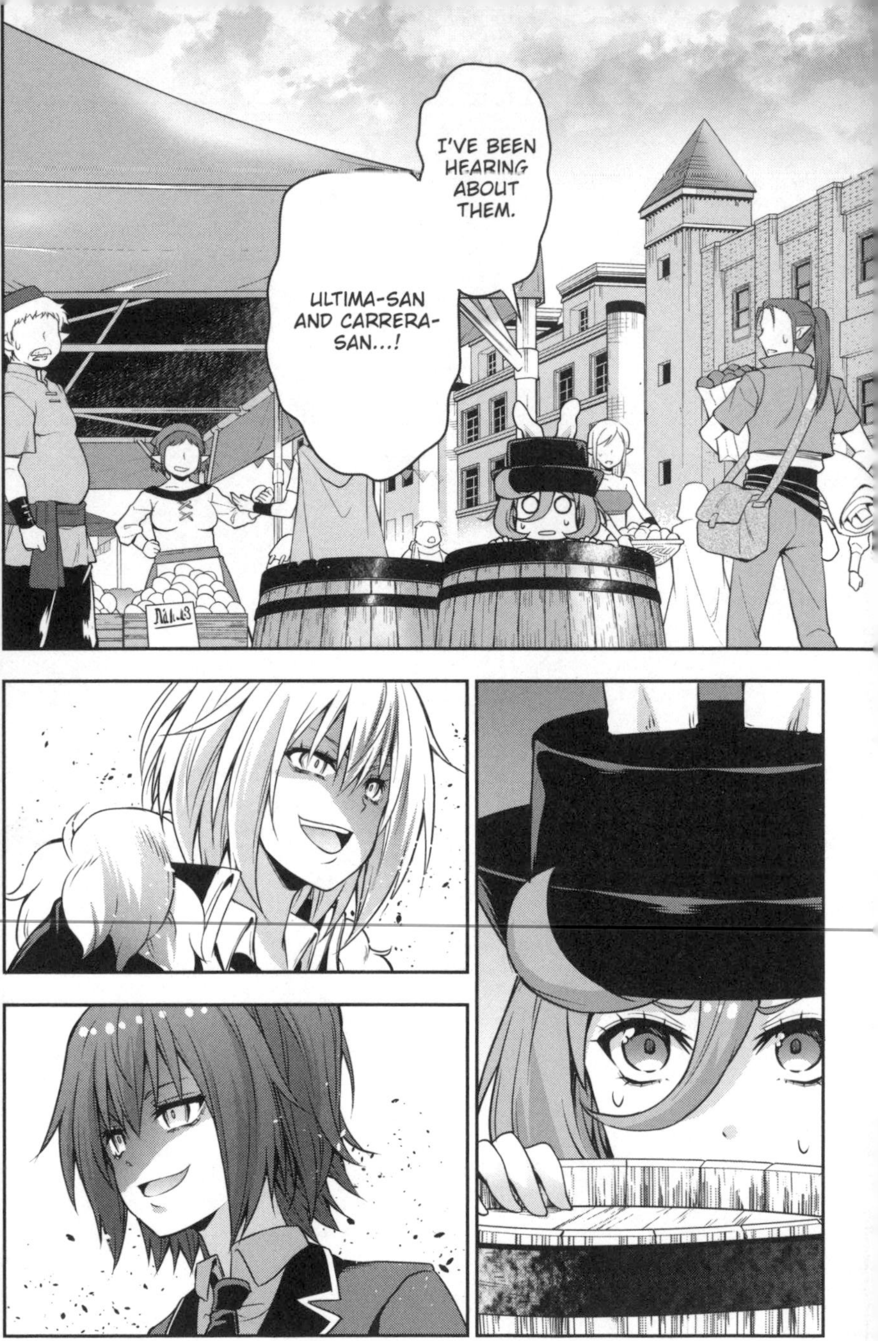
I'VE BEEN HEARING ABOUT THEM.
ULTIMA-SAN AND CARRERA-SAN...!

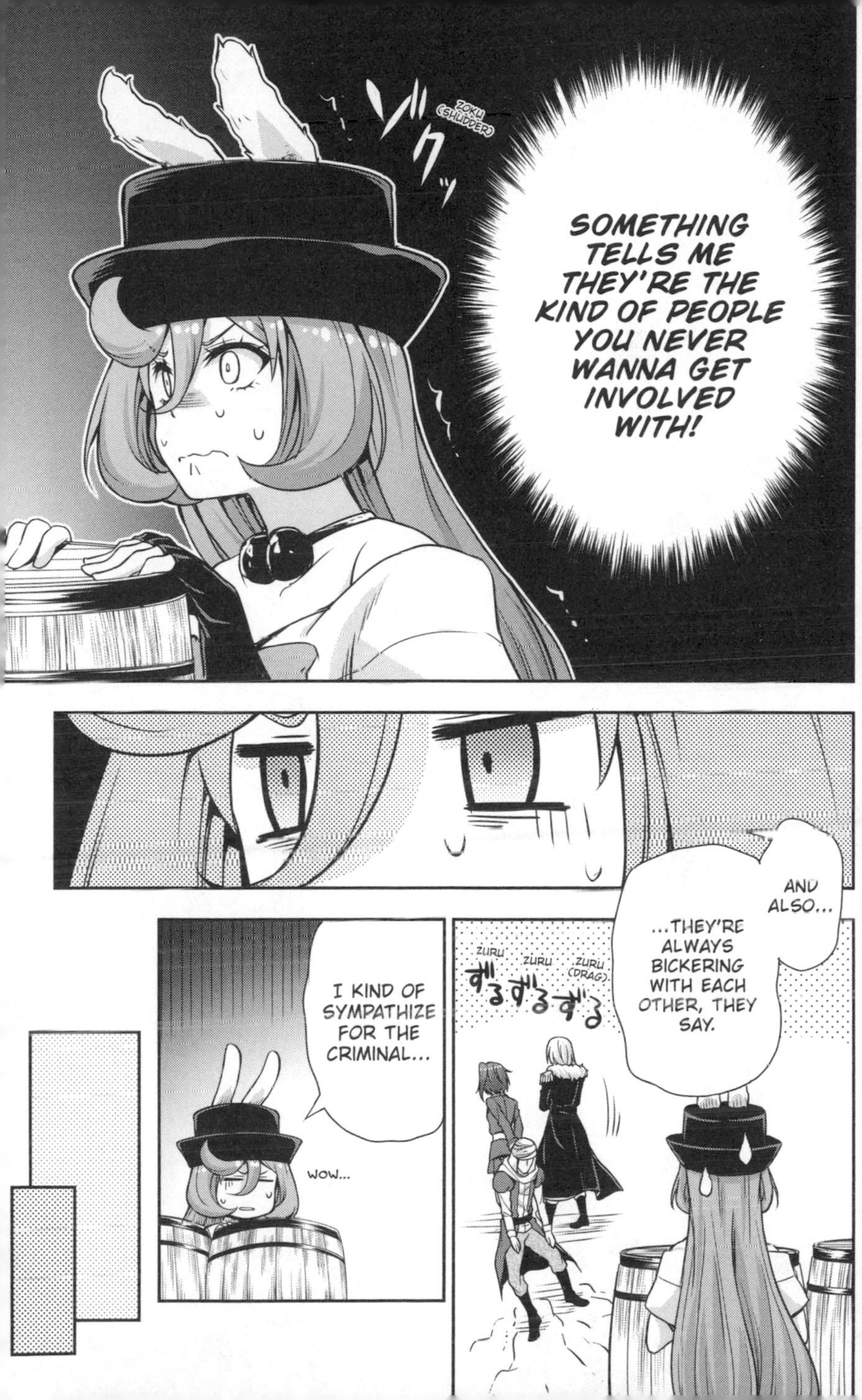
ゾクッ
ZOKU (SHUDDER)
SOMETHING TELLS ME THEY'RE THE KIND OF PEOPLE YOU NEVER WANNA GET INVOLVED WITH!
AND ALSO...
...THEY'RE ALWAYS BICKERING WITH EACH OTHER, THEY SAY.
ずるずるずる
ZURU ZURU ZURU (DRAG)
I KIND OF SYMPATHIZE FOR THE CRIMINAL...
WOW...

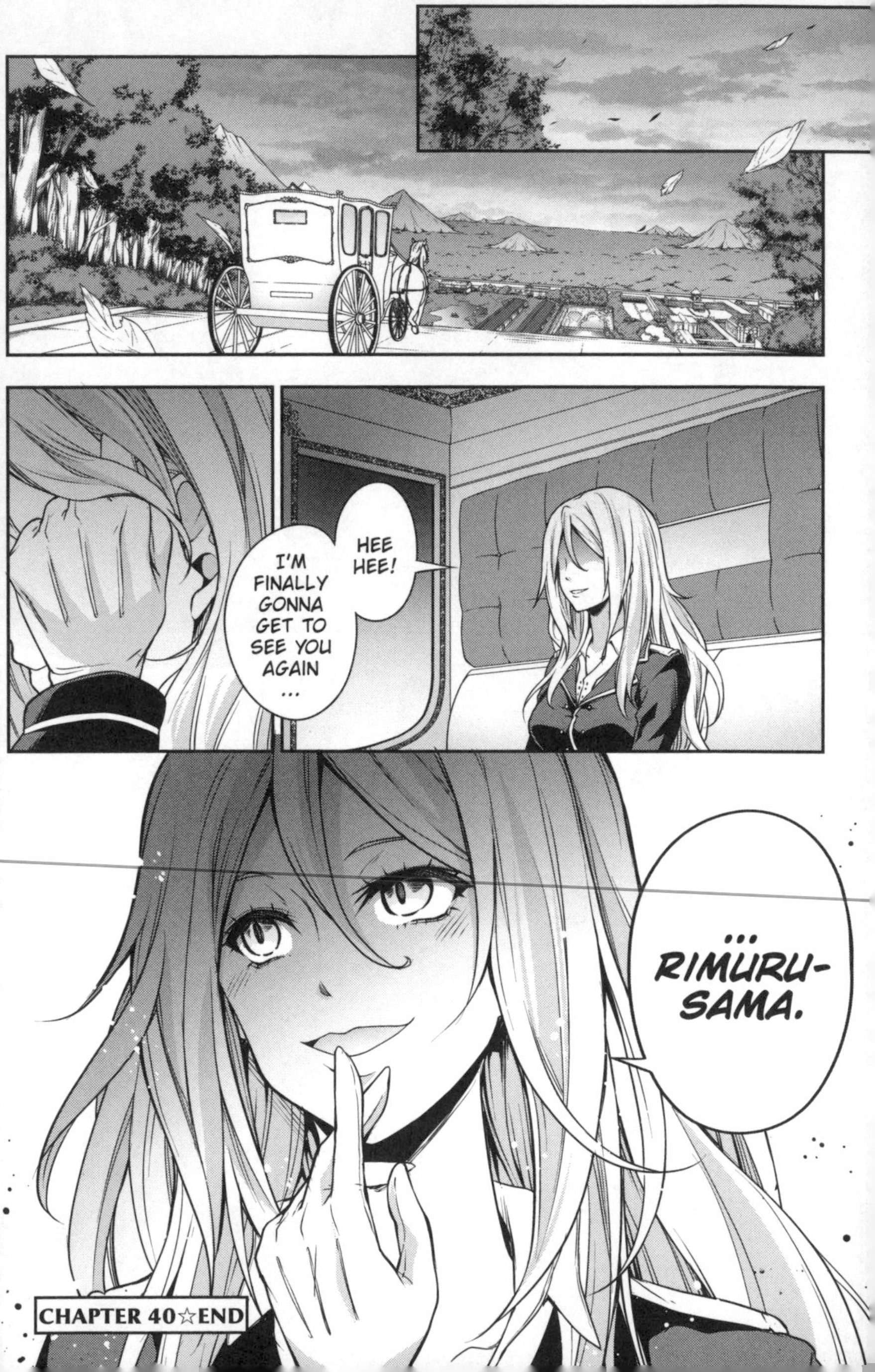
HEE HEE!
I'M FINALLY GONNA GET TO SEE YOU AGAIN ...
... RIMURU-SAMA.
CHAPTER 40☆END

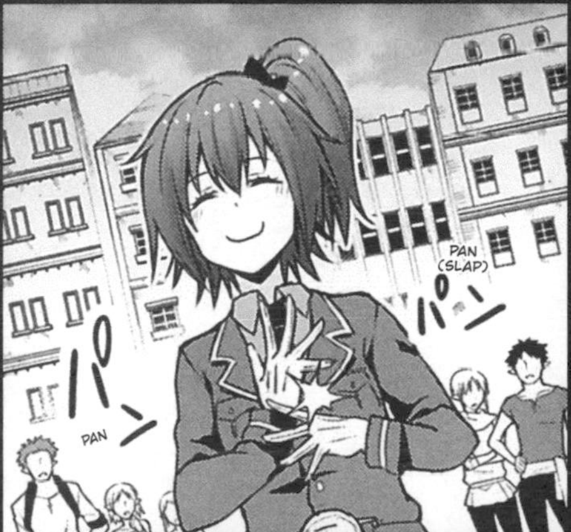PAN
(SLAP)
パン
パン
PAN

special thanks

CREATOR: FUSE-SENSEI
CHARACTER DESIGN: MITZ VAH-SENSEI

TAIKI KAWAKAMI-SENSEI
SHIBA-SENSEI
CHACHA-SENSEI
TAE TONO-SENSEI

ARAMASA-SAMA
MIZUMURA-SAMA
EZAKI-SAMA

FU YAMAGUCHI-SAMA
IBUKI ICHINOSE-SAMA
ALL THE EDITORS
SHUICHI KAWAKAMI-SENSEI

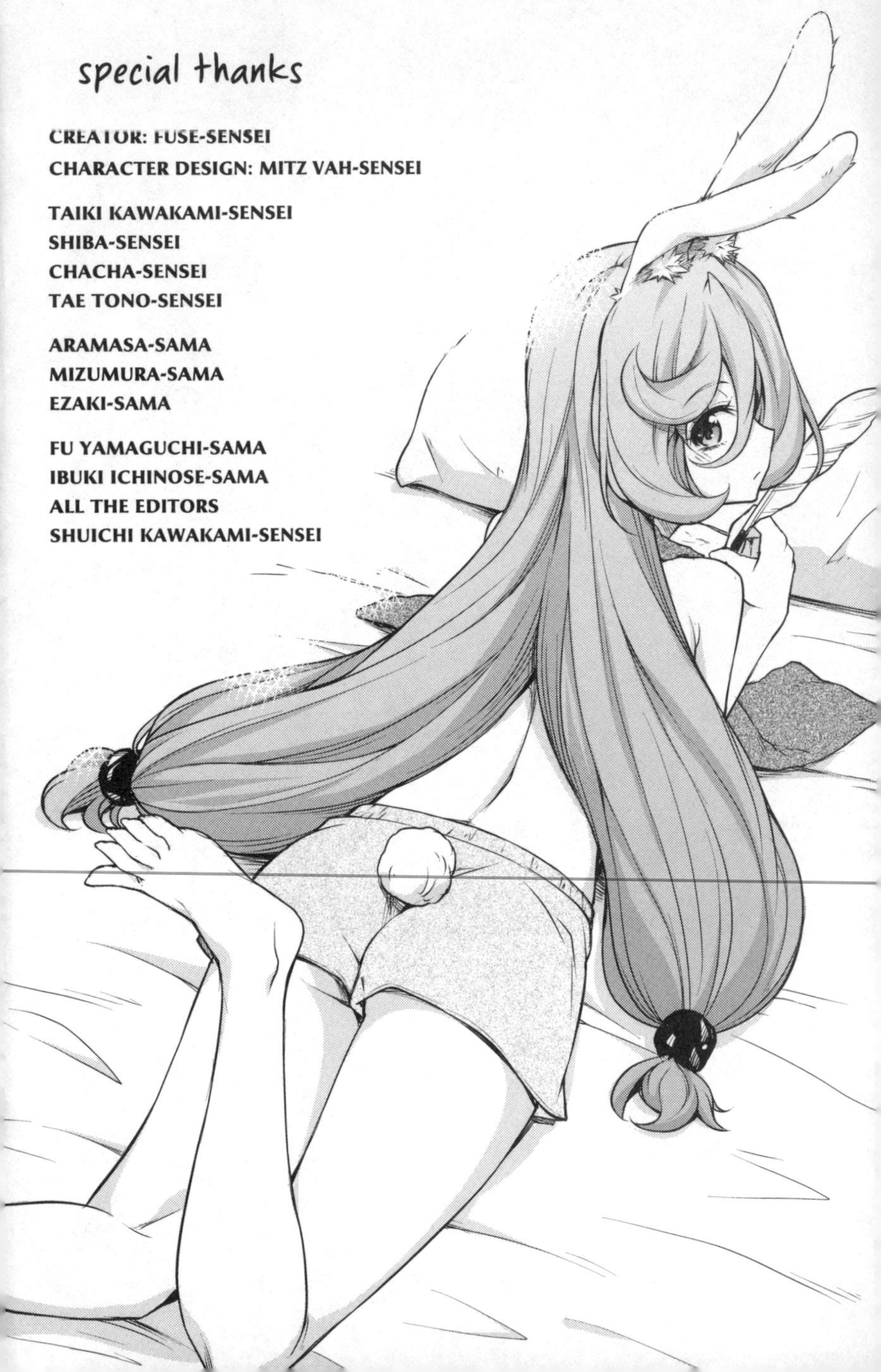

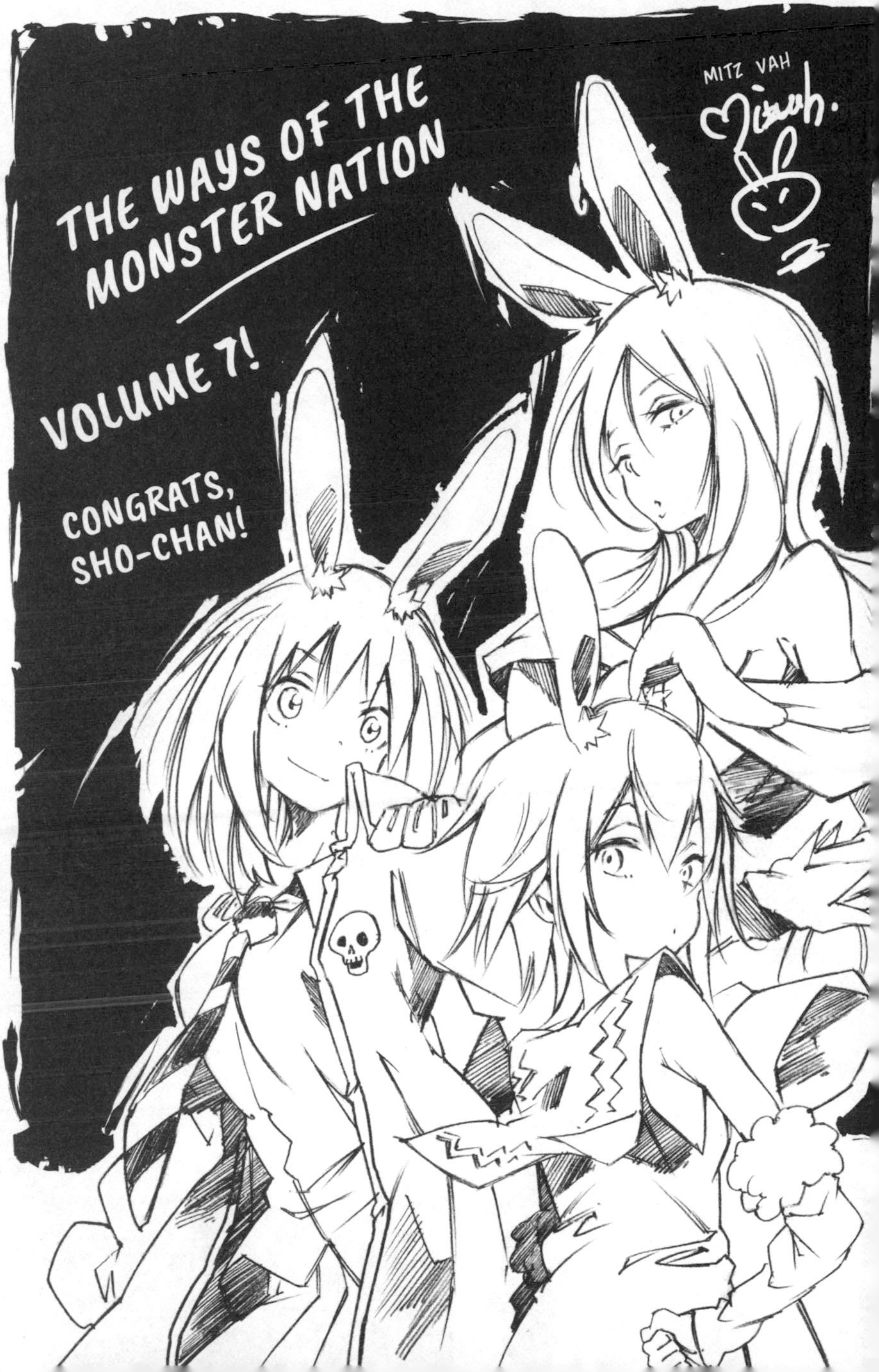
THE WAYS OF THE MONSTER NATION
VOLUME 7!
CONGRATS, SHO-CHAN!
MITZ VAH

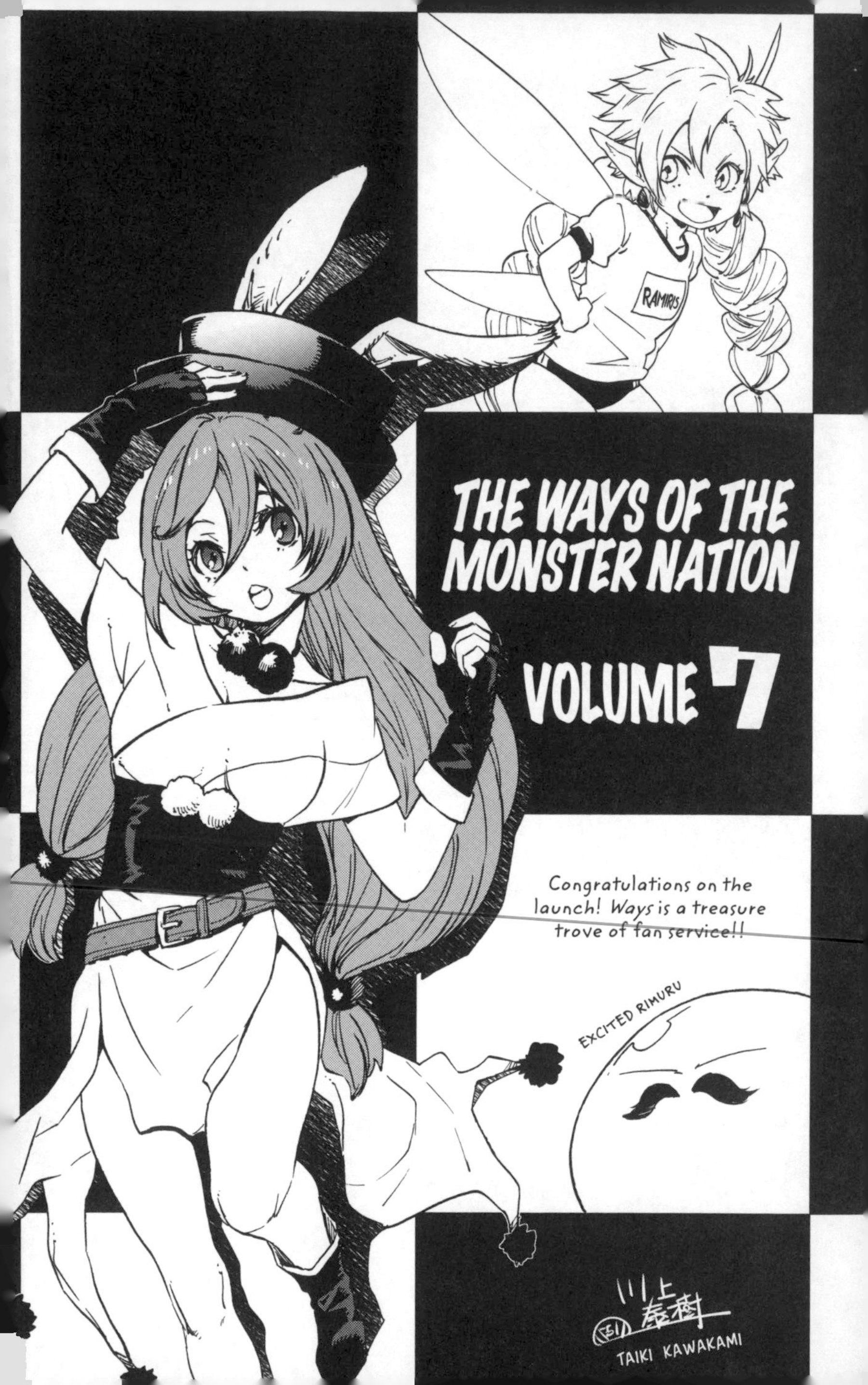
RAMIRIS
THE WAYS OF THE MONSTER NATION
VOLUME 7
Congratulations on the launch! Ways is a treasure trove of fan service!!
EXCITED RIMURU
TAIKI KAWAKAMI

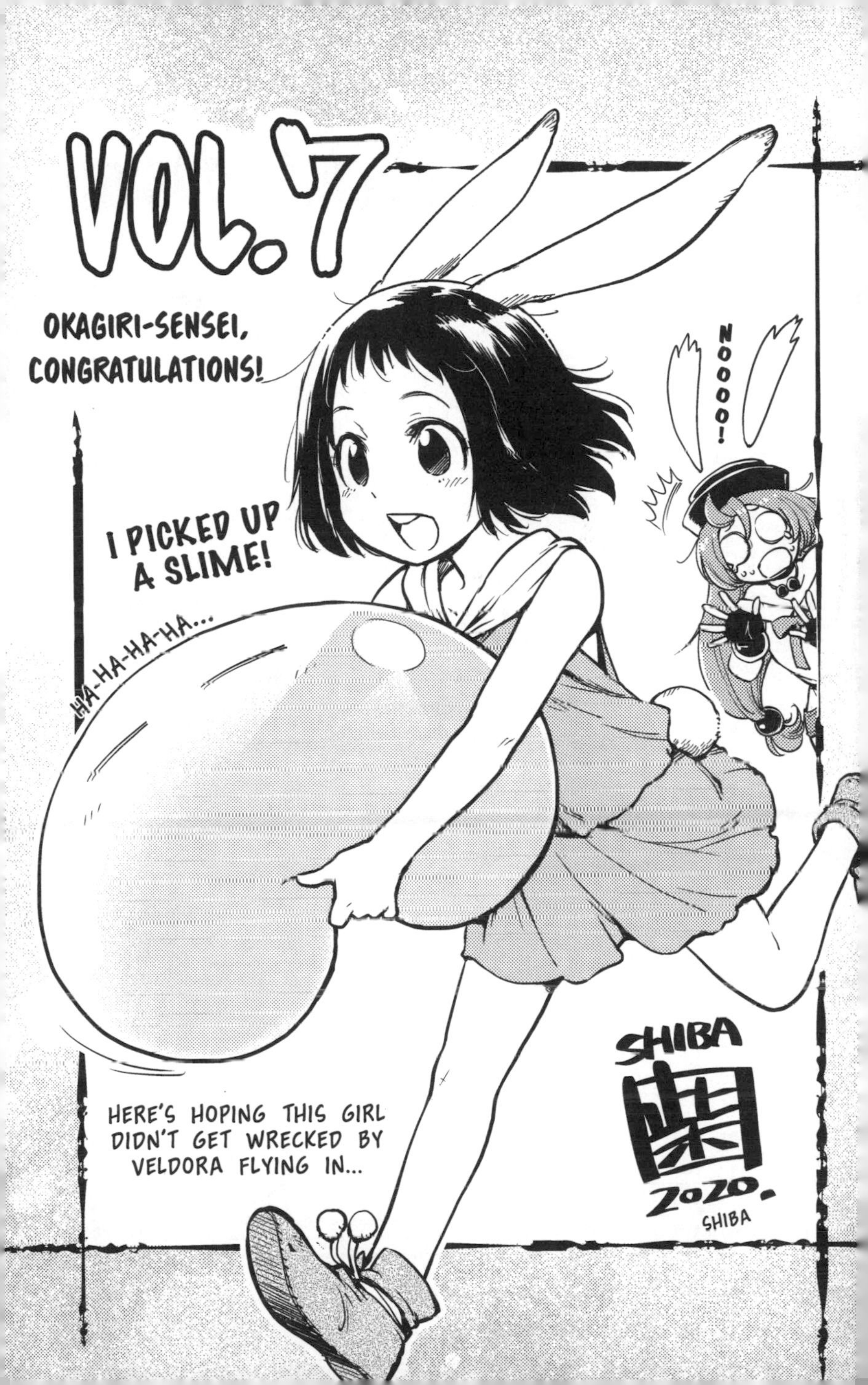
VOL. 7
OKAGIRI-SENSEI, CONGRATULATIONS!
I PICKED UP A SLIME!
HA-HA-HA-HA...
NOOOOO!
HERE'S HOPING THIS GIRL DIDN'T GET WRECKED BY VELDORA FLYING IN...
SHIBA
2020.
SHIBA

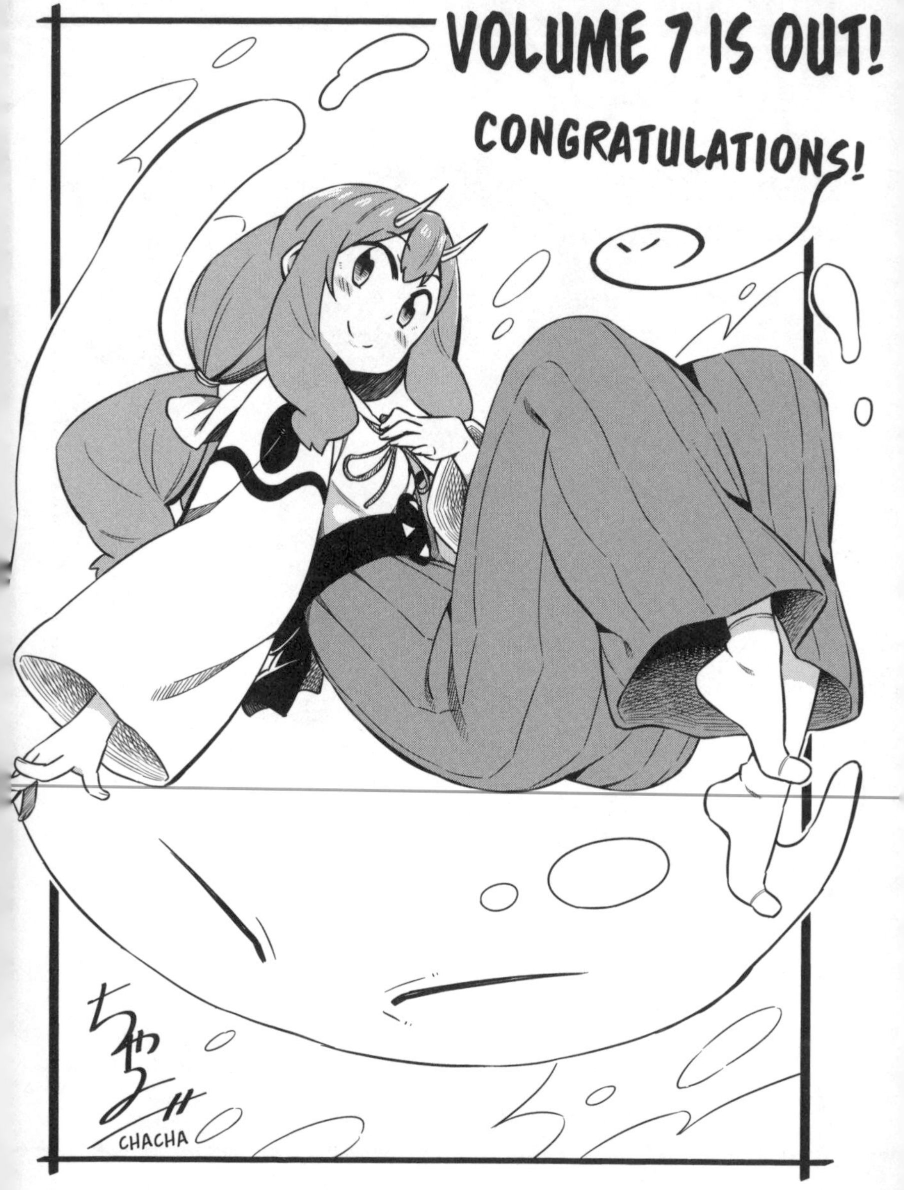

VOLUME 7 IS OUT!
CONGRATULATIONS!
ちゃちゃ
CHACHA

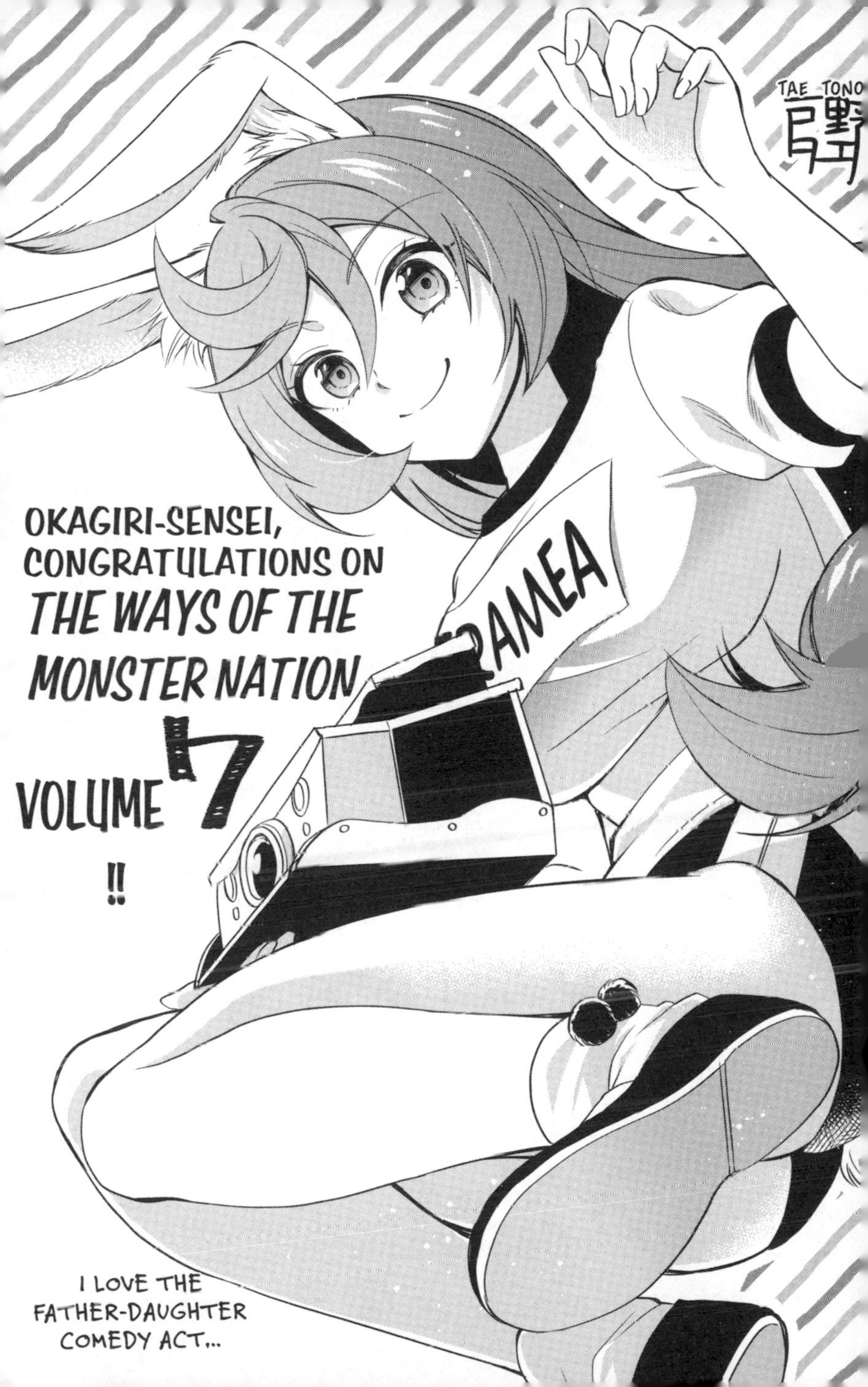
TAE TONO
OKAGIRI-SENSEI, CONGRATULATIONS ON *THE WAYS OF THE MONSTER NATION* VOLUME 7 !!
I LOVE THE FATHER-DAUGHTER COMEDY ACT...

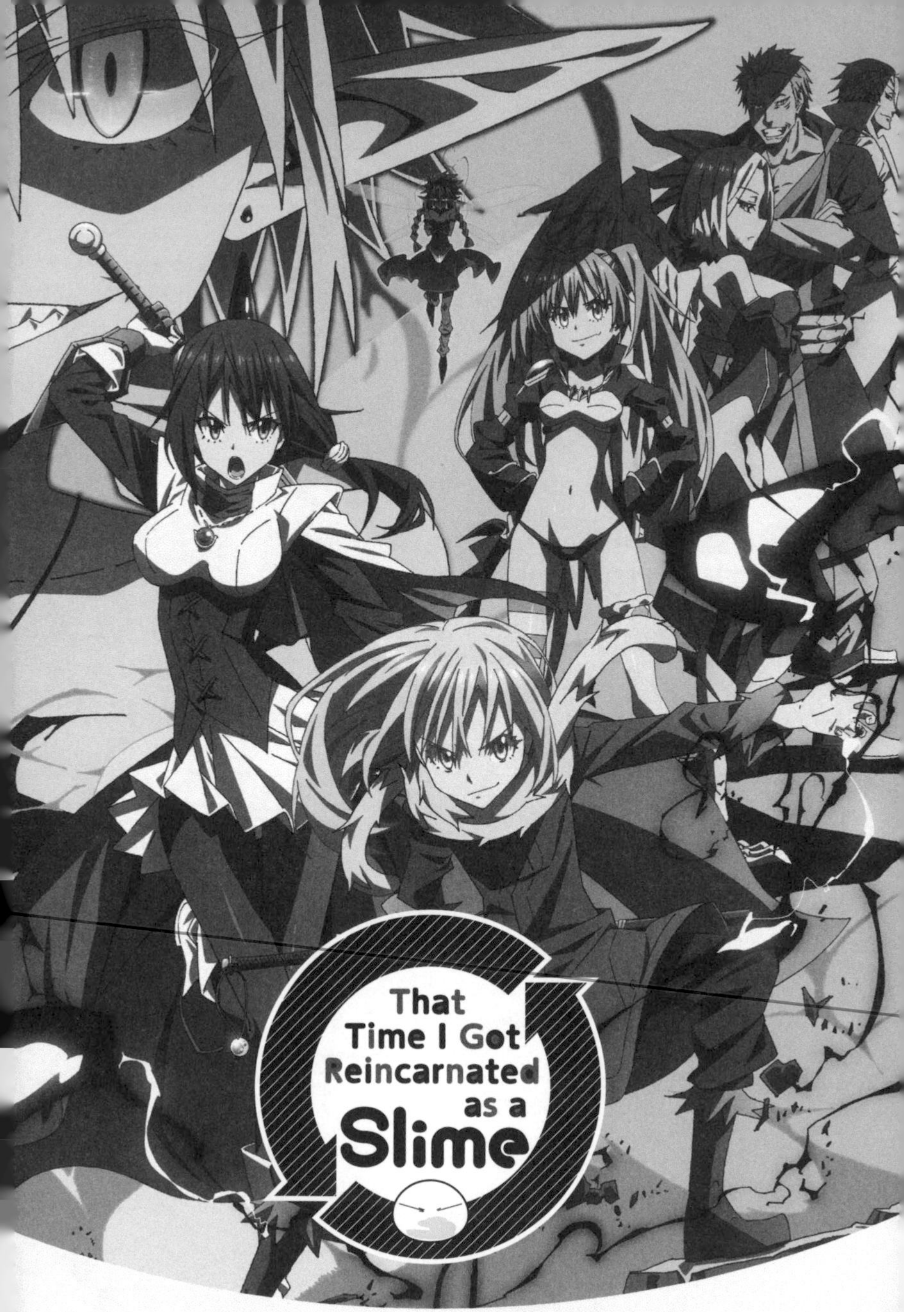
That Time I Got Reincarnated as a Slime

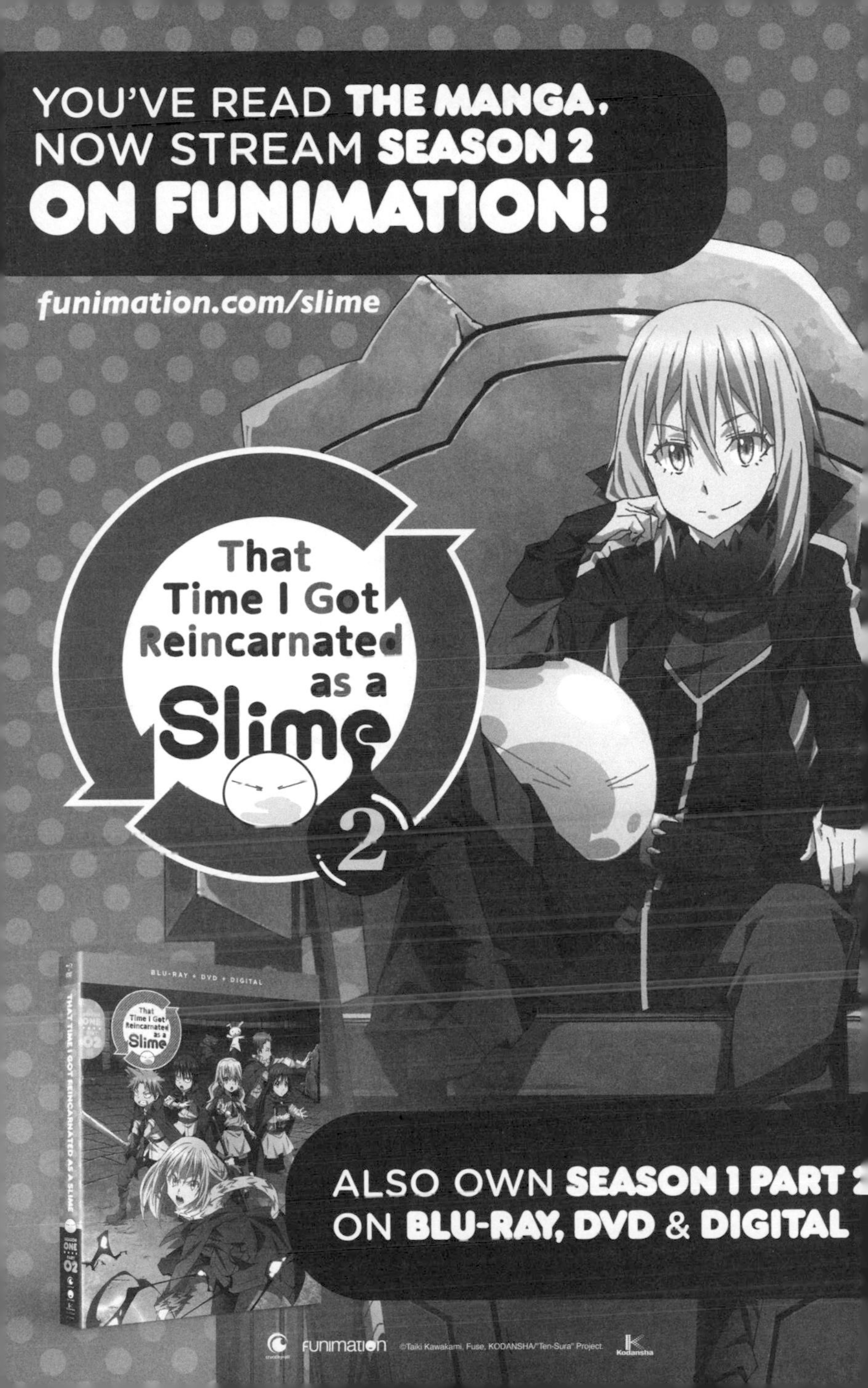
YOU'VE READ THE MANGA,
NOW STREAM SEASON 2
ON FUNIMATION!
funimation.com/slime
That Time I Got Reincarnated as a Slime 2
BLU-RAY + DVD + DIGITAL
THAT TIME I GOT REINCARNATED AS A SLIME
SEASON ONE PART 02
ALSO OWN SEASON 1 PART 2
ON BLU-RAY, DVD & DIGITAL
funimation
©Taiki Kawakami, Fuse, KODANSHA/"Ten-Sura" Project.
Kodansha

That **Time I Got Reincarnated** as a **SLIME**
The Ways of the Monster Nation

Translation: Kevin Gifford • Lettering: Barri Shrager

This book is a work of fiction. Names, characters, places, and
incidents are the product of the author's imagination or are used fictitiously.
Any resemblance to actual events, locales, or persons, living or dead, is coincidental.

TENSEI SHITARA SURAIMU DATTA KEN ~MAMONO NO KUNI NO ARUKIKATA~ Vol. 7
©Fuse 2020
©Sho Okagiri, Mitz Vah 2020
First published in Japan in 2020 by MICRO MAGAZINE, INC.
English translation rights arranged with MICRO MAGAZINE, INC.
through Tuttle-Mori Agency, Inc., Tokyo.

English translation © 2022 by Yen Press, LLC

Yen Press
150 West 30th Street, 19th Floor
New York, NY 10001

Visit us at yenpress.com
facebook.com/yenpress
twitter.com/yenpress
yenpress.tumblr.com
instagram.com/yenpress

First Yen Press Edition: April 2022

Yen Press is an imprint of Yen Press, LLC.
The Yen Press name and logo are trademarks of Yen Press, LLC.

The publisher is not responsible for websites (or their content) that are
not owned by the publisher.

Library of Congress Control Number: 2020936422

ISBNs: 978-1-9753-4243-2 (paperback)
978-1-9753-4244-9 (ebook)

10 9 8 7 6 5 4 3 2 1

LSC-C

Printed in the United States of America